Mastering Primary Languages

Mastering Primary Teaching series

Edited by Judith Roden and James Archer

The *Mastering Primary Teaching* series provides an insight into the core principles underpinning each of the subjects of the Primary National Curriculum, thereby helping student teachers to 'master' the subjects. This in turn will enable new teachers to share this mastery in their teaching. Each book follows the same sequence of chapters, which has been specifically designed to assist trainee teachers to capitalise on opportunities to develop pedagogical excellence. These comprehensive guides introduce the subject and help trainees know how to plan and teach effective and inspiring lessons that make learning irresistible. Examples of children's work and case studies are included to help exemplify what is considered to be best and most innovative practice in primary education. The series is written by leading professionals, who draw on their years of experience to provide authoritative guides to the primary curriculum subject areas.

Also available in the series

Mastering Primary English, Wendy Jolliffe and David Waugh

Mastering Primary Music, Ruth Atkinson

Mastering Primary Physical Education, Kristy Howells with Alison Carney, Neil Castle and Rich Little

Mastering Primary Science, Amanda McCrory and Kenna Worthington

Forthcoming in the series

Mastering Primary Art and Design, Peter Gregory, Claire March and Suzy Tutchell

Mastering Primary Computing, Graham Parton and Christine Kemp-Hall

Mastering Primary Design and Technology, Gill Hope

Mastering Primary Geography, Anthony Barlow and Sarah Whitehouse

Mastering Primary History, Karin Doull, Christopher Russell and Alison Hales

Mastering Primary Mathematics, Andrew Lamb, Rebecca Heaton and Helen Taylor

Mastering Primary Religious Education, Maria James and Julian Stern

Also available from Bloomsbury

Developing Teacher Expertise, edited by Margaret Sangster

Readings for Reflective Teaching in Schools, edited by Andrew Pollard

Reflective Teaching in Schools, Andrew Pollard

Mastering Primary Languages

Paula Ambrossi and Darnelle Constant-Shepherd

BLOOMSBURY ACADEMIC
LONDON • NEW YORK • OXFORD • NEW DELHI • SYDNEY

BLOOMSBURY ACADEMIC
Bloomsbury Publishing Plc
50 Bedford Square, London, WC1B 3DP, UK

BLOOMSBURY, BLOOMSBURY ACADEMIC and the Diana logo are trademarks of Bloomsbury Publishing Plc

First published in Great Britain 2018

© Paula Ambrossi and Darnelle Constant-Shepherd, 2018

Paula Ambrossi and Darnelle Constant-Shepherd have asserted their right under the Copyright, Designs and Patents Act, 1988, to be identified as Authors of this work.

For legal purposes the Acknowledgements on p. xv constitute an extension of this copyright page.

Cover design by Anna Berzovan
Cover image © iStock (miakievy/molotovcoketail)

All rights reserved. No part of this publication may be reproduced or transmitted in any form or by any means, electronic or mechanical, including photocopying, recording, or any information storage or retrieval system, without prior permission in writing from the publishers.

Bloomsbury Publishing Plc does not have any control over, or responsibility for, any third-party websites referred to or in this book. All internet addresses given in this book were correct at the time of going to press. The author and publisher regret any inconvenience caused if addresses have changed or sites have ceased to exist, but can accept no responsibility for any such changes.

A catalogue record for this book is available from the British Library.

A catalog record for this book is available from the Library of Congress.

ISBN: HB: 978-1-4742-9664-9
PB: 978-1-4742-9663-2
ePDF: 978-1-4742-9662-5
ePub: 978-1-4742-9665-6

Series: Mastering Primary Teaching

Typeset by Deanta Global Publishing Services, Chennai, India
Printed and bound in Great Britain

To find out more about our authors and books visit www.bloomsbury.com and sign up for our newsletters.

Contents

List of Figures	vi
Series Editors' Foreword	x
How to Use This Book	xiii
Acknowledgements	xv
List of Abbreviations	xvi
Introduction	**1**
1 **An Introduction to Primary Languages**	**7**
2 **Current Developments in Primary Languages**	**27**
3 **Languages as an Irresistible Activity**	**49**
4 **Languages as a Practical Activity**	**69**
5 **Skills to Develop in Languages**	**93**
6 **Children's Ideas – Promoting Curiosity**	**115**
7 **Assessing Children in Languages**	**139**
8 **Practical Issues**	**163**
Appendices	193
Bibliography	205
Index	213

List of Figures

1.1	Playing with words. A child from Nadine Chadier's class	9
1.2	San Juan and San Fermin festivals in Spain	11
1.3	Calligraphy lesson (photo by Axel Rouvin)	14
1.4	Types of knowledge	16
1.5	Matching task sample	17
1.6	Child's writing in Nadine Chadier's class	19
1.7	(a) Learning through exploration (b) Sitting at desks	23
1.8	Representation of Byram's 5 savoirs	25
2.1	On a gate on the Clordir Road side of Pontlliw Primary School	28
2.2	Different ways of delivering FLs in primary schools	30
2.3	The best moment is now	34
2.4	Choosing the right language for your school	35
2.5	Challenges faced by primary schools	36
2.6	YouTube clip on Chomsky's take on Universal Grammar	40
2.7	Representation of the five strands within the Languages Framework	42
2.8	First contact with other cultures has left a lot to be desired	44
3.1	Working towards a primary languages community of practice	50
3.2	Motivating teachers to meet the challenge	53
3.3	Activity around intercultural understanding (Moorish influence)	54
3.4	Motivation acting on teaching and learning	55
3.5	Building an effective and sustainable community of practice for FL teaching and learning	57
3.6	Search engines can be used as a quick access to FL audio files	61
3.7	Availability of information does not imply usage	62
3.8	Games get children excited about the game	63
4.1	Representation of the five strands within the Languages Framework	70

4.2	Reconceptualization of the Languages Framework	70
4.3	Primary classroom in Spain	73
4.4	A five-year-old wanting to engage with IU	75
4.5	Written symbols	76
4.6	Different written languages	77
4.7	Using knowledge about language to structure a sentence	78
4.8	How words change their grammatical function (Eng/Sp)	80
4.9	Broad features of Oracy	81
4.10	Graded questions	83
4.11	Spanish letters with very different sounds to the English equivalent	84
4.12	Vowel sounds in Spanish	84
4.13	(Let's go!) Spanish speakers use b/v sound indiscriminately	87
4.14	Playing with mnemonics (the keyword method)	89
5.1	Nadine Chadier's pupils' work on landmarks of London, and PGCE students' cross-curricular web planning on mini-beasts for Y3	95
5.2	Linking FLs with other subjects	97
5.3	Realia items for FLs	100
5.4	Representation of Hood and Tobutt (2009) levels of integrated learning	101
5.5	Seven 2D shapes in Spanish	103
5.6	Ancient French map showing Jericho	106
5.7	French/English checklist of what friendship should mean	107
5.8	Key interactive language around colour and technique	111
5.9	Forms of the imperative mode for the classroom	111
5.10	Mixing colours in French	113
5.11	Wordle of cross-curricular planning in languages	113
6.1	*The Guardian* newspaper excerpt on boredom	116
6.2	Representation of Sternberg's convergence of characteristics in creativity	119
6.3	A child's drawing of a dream containing a significant object	123
6.4	'I want to be a sailor'	128
6.5	Drawings of feminine nouns and masculine nouns	129
6.6	Paula Ambrossi's homework on masculine and feminine nouns	130
6.7	Representing the concept of regularity/irregularity in verbs	132

6.8	Representation of Spanish irregular verb To Be	133
6.9	Spanish nouns dictate gender for article and adjective	133
6.10	Greek Gods and their Roman denomination	134
6.11	Solar system in Latin	136
6.12	Children's work from Nadine Chadier's class	137
7.1	10–11-year-olds' spontaneous writing from memory	141
7.2	Dan Alliot, languages adviser	145
7.3	Language content from beginner to intermediate level	151
7.4	The eternal beginner: a vocabulary-based approach	151
7.5	Language progression through a sentence-based approach	152
7.6	Diagram charting the different aspects of language progression	153
7.7	Year 3 child's work around nouns and gender in Spanish	155
7.8	Accents in Spanish make a big difference	156
7.9	The European Language Portfolio	158
7.10	'Can do' Statements from the language portfolio	160
7.11	The language ladder (have one up on your wall)	161
8.1	Different uses of resources	164
8.2	Looking at languages resources in context	165
8.3	The wheel of primary languages resources	166
8.4	School children shopping at a French street, and making a radio show, at the Europa Center. Top right, film about a French girl's adventures	168
8.5	Sample of different types of resources	169
8.6	Sample list of authentic resources	170
8.7	Year 4 pupil's opening sentence of a story. Courtesy of Nadine Chadier	172
8.8	Twenty-seven different translations of *The Gruffalo*	174
8.9	Using the FL classical literature to inspire and as context	175
8.10	Using video (iMovie) as a vehicle for engagement and learning	176
8.11	French calligraphy (Seyès grid paper)	177
8.12	Stamps depicting Marianne (liberty), the face of the French Republic and India's yoga's sun salutation position	177
8.13	French Resources.org Learning classroom instructions	179
8.14	Using Makaton to enhance language learning	180
8.15	*The Guardian*'s education section for languages	180
8.16	French poem, 'Page d'écritures' by Jacques Prévert	182

8.17	Children line up for a game involving role play	183
8.18	Example of an anagram jigsaw in French	184
8.19	Wall display by Spanish children celebrating the international Day of Peace	185
8.20	The world in other languages	186
8.21	The Sun King, Louis IV	186
8.22	Possible statements from the Sun King himself	187
8.23	Nadine Chadier's alphabet pronunciation website	189

Series Editors' Foreword

A long and varied experience of working with beginner and experienced teachers in primary schools has informed this series since its conception. Over the last thirty years there have been many changes in practice in terms of teaching and learning in primary and early years education. Significantly, since the implementation of the first National Curriculum in 1989 the aim has been to bring best practice in primary education to all state schools in England and Wales. As time has passed, numerous policy decisions have altered the detail and emphasis of the delivery of the primary curriculum. However, there has been little change in the belief that pupils in the primary and early years phases of education should receive a broad, balanced curriculum based on traditional subjects.

Recent OFSTED subject reports and notably the Cambridge Primary Review indicate that, rather than the ideal being attained, in many schools the emphasis on English and mathematics has not only depressed the other subjects of the primary curriculum, but also narrowed the range of strategies used for the delivery of the curriculum. The amount of time allocated to subject sessions in Initial Teacher Education (ITE) courses has dramatically reduced which may also account for this narrow diet in pedagogy.

The vision for this series of books arose out of our many years of experience with student teachers. As a result, we believe that the series is well designed to equip trainee and beginner teachers to master the art of teaching in the primary phase. This series of books aims to introduce current and contemporary practices associated with the whole range of subjects within the Primary National Curriculum and religious education. It also goes beyond this by providing beginner teachers with the knowledge and understanding required to achieve mastery of each subject. In doing so, each book in the series highlights contemporary issues such as assessment and inclusion which are the key areas that even the most seasoned practitioner is still grappling with in light of the introduction of the new primary curriculum.

Readers will find great support within each one of these books. Each book in the series will inform and provide the opportunity for basic mastery of each of the subjects, namely English, mathematics, science, physical education, music, history, geography, design and technology, computing, art and design, languages and religious education. They will discover the essence of each subject in terms of its philosophy, knowledge and skills. Readers will also be inspired by the enthusiasm for each subject revealed by the subject authors who are experts in their field. They will discover many and varied strategies for making each subject 'come alive' for their pupils and they should become more confident about teaching across the whole range of subjects represented in the primary and early years curriculum.

Primary teaching in the state sector is characterized by a long history of pupils being taught the whole range of the primary curriculum by one teacher. Although some schools may employ specialists to deliver some subjects of the curriculum, notably physical education, music or science, for example, it is more usual for the whole curriculum to be delivered to a class by their class teacher. This places a potentially enormous burden on beginner teachers no matter which route they have taken to enter teaching. The burden is especially high on those entering through employment-based routes and for those who aim to become inspiring primary teachers. There is much to learn!

The term 'mastery' relates to knowledge and understanding of a subject which incorporates the 'how' of teaching as well as the 'what'. Although most entrants to primary teaching will have some experience of the primary curriculum as a pupil, very few will have experienced the breadth of the curriculum or may have any understanding of the curriculum which reflects recent trends in teaching and learning within the subject. The primary curriculum encompasses a very broad range of subjects each of which has its own knowledge base, skills and ways of working. Unsurprisingly, very few new entrants into the teaching profession hold mastery of all the interrelated subjects. Indeed for the beginner teacher it may well be many years before full mastery of all aspects of the primary curriculum is achieved. The content of the primary curriculum has changed significantly, notably in some foundation subjects, such as history and music. So although beginner teachers might hold fond memories of these subjects from their own experience of primary education, the content of these subjects may well have changed significantly over time and may incorporate different emphases.

This series, Mastering Primary Teaching, aims to meet the needs of those who, reflecting the desire for mastery over each subject, want to know more. This is a tall order. Nevertheless, we believe that the pursuit of development should always be rewarded, which is why we are delighted to have so many experts sharing their well-developed knowledge and passion for the subjects featured in each book. The vision for this series is to provide support for those who are beginning their teaching career, who may not feel fully secure in their subject knowledge, understanding or skill. In addition, the series also aims to provide a reference point for beginner teachers to consult repeatedly over time to support them in the important art of teaching.

Intending primary teachers, in our experience, have a thirst for knowledge about the subject that they will be teaching. They want to 'master' new material and ideas in a range of subjects. Teaching the primary curriculum can be one of the most rewarding experiences. We believe that this series will help beginner teachers to unlock the primary curriculum in a way that ensures they establish themselves as confident primary practitioners.

Judith Roden
James Archer
June 2017

How to Use This Book

This book is one of twelve books that together help form a truly innovative series that is aimed to support your development. Each book follows the same format and chapter sequence. There is an emphasis throughout the book on providing information about the teaching and learning of primary languages. You will find a wealth of information within each chapter that will help you to understand the issues, problems and opportunities that teaching the subject can provide you as a developing practitioner in the subject. Crucially, each chapter provides opportunities for you to reflect upon important points linked to your development of the in order that you may master the teaching of primary languages. As a result, you will develop your confidence in the teaching of primary languages. There really is something for everyone within each chapter.

Each chapter has been carefully designed to help you to develop your knowledge of the subject systematically and as a result contains key features. Chapter objectives clearly signpost the content of each chapter and these will help you to familiarize yourself with important aspects of the subject and will orientate you in preparation for reading the chapter. The regular 'pause for thought' points offer questions and activities for you to reflect on important aspects of the subject. Each 'pause for thought' provides you with an opportunity to enhance your learning beyond merely reading the chapter. These will sometimes ask you to consider your own experience and what you already know about the teaching of the subject. Others will require you to critique aspects of good practice presented as case studies or research. To benefit fully from reading this text, you need to be an active participant. Sometimes you are asked to make notes on your response to questions and ideas and then to revisit these later on in your reading. While it would be possible for you to skip through the opportunities for reflection or to give only cursory attention to the questions and activities which aim to facilitate deeper reflection than might otherwise be the case, we strongly urge you to engage with the 'pause for thought' activities. It is our belief that it is through these moments that most of your transformational learning that will occur as a result of engaging with this book. At the end of each chapter, you will find a summary of main points from the chapter along with suggestions for further reading are made.

We passionately believe that learners of all ages learn best when they work with others, so we would encourage you, if possible to work with another person, sharing your ideas and perspectives. The book also would be ideal for groups study within a university or school setting.

This book has been authored by Paula Ambrossi and Darnelle Constant-Shepherd, who are experienced and highly regarded as professionals in their subject area. They are strong voices within the primary languages community. By reading this book you will be able to benefit from their rich knowledge, understanding and experience. When using this ensure that you are ready to learn from some of the greats in primary languages.

Acknowledgements

We would like to thank certain key persons and groups of people for their generosity of mind and time, who have been indispensable in our careers as student teacher (PGCE) educators in the area of second language learning. We would like to thank Dan Alliot for bringing practical inspiration to our students and allowing us to include some of his ideas and expertise in this book – he has been a constant friend and language allied in our course. Our gratitude also goes to Nadine Chadier for providing us with some wonderful images of children-at-work, engaging creatively with languages in her classroom as well as some of the resources she has created. She continues to be an inspiration to our MFL PGCE students who visit her classroom every year and are inspired by her teaching and her passion for languages. Most of all, we would like to thank all the PGCE language specialist students who have come through our course since 2007. They have indeed been one of our greatest sources of inspiration, and as Bart Smith says in our introduction, being a language specialist was, 'an invigorating change' for them, but for us as well. Our students' own diverse backgrounds have provided us in turn with different ways of considering our approach and forced us to be as creative in our pedagogy as possible, for teaching is a two-way street, called, 'teaching and learning'. Finally and following this last note, we would like to thank Dr Karen Turner for being in a way, the bow that launched the arrow. She was Paula's PGCE languages tutor at the Institute of Education and she met Darnelle through the French language specialists' exchange programme with Paris. We were both mentored by Karen in our roles as the Primary PGCE foreign language specialist tutors, and we learnt much from her. Like all good teachers, she allowed us to find and follow our own paths.

We thank all our MFL colleagues, Primary or Secondary whose ideas have inspired us and have been a starting point for our discussion and ideas for generating resources. We would also like to thank the future readers of this book; having you as our sense of audience was extremely important, and we hope you find here encouragement for what you are doing as well as some light to help you. We wrote this book for you.

Paula Ambrossi and Darnelle Constant-Shepherd

List of Abbreviations

AFL	Assessment for Learning
CLIL	Content Language Integrated Learning
CPD	Continuous Professional Development
EAL	English as an Additional Language
EYFS	Early Years & Foundation Stage
FL	Foreign Language
FLL	Foreign Language Learning
HLTA	Higher Level Teaching Assistant
ITE	Initial Teacher Education
ITT	Initial Teacher Training
IU	Intercultural Understanding
IWB	Interactive Whiteboard
KAL	Knowledge about Language
KS1	Key Stage 1
KS2	Key Stage 2
L1	First language
L2	Second language
LLS	Language Learning Strategies
MFL	Modern Foreign Languages
NC	National Curriculum
Ofsted	Office for Standards in Education
PGCE	Post Graduate Certificate in Education
PPA	Planning, Preparation and Assessment
PSHCE	Personal, Social, Health and Citizenship Education
SEL	Social Emotional Learning
SEN	Special Education Needs
SLA	Second Language Acquisition
TL	Target Language
The Framework	Key Stage 2 Framework for Languages

Introduction

The real voyage of discovery consists not in seeking new landscapes, but in having new eyes.

Marcel Proust

I remember my time as a student teacher; focusing on languages was a very welcome and invigorating change to the endless 'literacy and numeracy' as well as being a chance to put a bit of your own personality into the subject. Having lived somewhere and being able to use the experience and the language as an 'expert' was also heartening. As a class teacher, I would highlight the advantage of doing a 'whole school' approach to keep up a sense of excitement and continuity. For example, during assemblies we would teach certain phrases that had to be used by everyone that week. Also, whole school events such as carousels, are easy to set up. We did a 'Hispanic' day where each teacher in a key stage prepared a 30 minute session on a Spanish speaking country and the classes moved around over the course of an afternoon. Such short, sharp, broad interventions seemed to be fun and memorable.

Bart Smith (ex PGCE student)

Having now taught Spanish for four years, from nursery to year 6, I can say with confidence that it is the subject I enjoy teaching most. Primary aged children love to learn new languages, and are constantly asking when the next Spanish lesson is.

Something that I have found really exciting has been the power of MFL to inspire those children who may struggle in core subjects. My Spanish classroom is a very inclusive space, in which the normal spectrum of attainment becomes less relevant. I have often noted the engagement of children who in other subjects find concentration and motivation difficult.

As an MFL coordinator, I have been able to develop a culture of language learning at the school, running Spanish days and events as well as a trip to Madrid (the highlight of my teaching career so far). Becoming a Spanish specialist has opened so many doors and helped me develop my leadership skills in a number of ways. Since languages have become a statutory requirement from KS2 up, I have noticed a real increase in the attention paid to them by senior leaders. It seems like a good time to be getting involved in the provision of MFL; I cannot recommend it enough!

Nicky Pear (ex PGCE student)

Bart and Nicky above were two of our students some years ago. We have kept in touch with some of our students in the course of the last ten years, and it is encouraging to see how each has found their own way of engaging children with languages, or continuing on their own linguistic or cultural development. Each story is different, but the one common denominator for me is the idea of flexibility and resourcefulness around language teaching and learning. There is no one way. As the Spanish poet Antonio Machado said, 'Caminante, no hay camino. Se hace camino al andar.' (Wayfarer, there is no path. You make the path as you go.) What we need as wayfarers or explorers in the world of language learning are the skills and understandings that allow us to make our own path. In other words, we need to engage with the art of being, pulling resources from every aspect of our lives, and lead children by example. We need to constantly reinvent and envision the path we want to see ourselves in, for this path will change with every new experience we have.

If you had asked me in my early twenties, 'Paula, would you like to become a teacher?', my reply would have been a resounding no. I remember explicitly not wanting to be a teacher. Overall, the role models I have had in my native country, in both primary and secondary education did not excite my curiosity for the profession. Having been brought up in a culture where the textbook was (and still is) king, day in and day out, did not do much to give me alternative viewpoints. It had never occurred to me that teaching – let alone school learning – could be a creative endeavour in the first place. However, there were other aspects that made those school years stand out very positively. Children in classes were never grouped according to their academic ability. We were all given access to the same content, and followed it according to our individual capabilities and dispositions. Travelling has allowed me to understand that different educational systems offer different experiences that shape us for life, but this, however, does not mean that we don't have the power to look back, reflect and change if necessary, however old we are.

As my original aim had been to become an educational psychologist I was advised to train as a teacher first. But what could I teach? Well, I could offer Spanish with some French. This I did, rather reluctantly at first, but after some invaluable academic and pedagogical input at the Institute of Education, I remember the first day I set foot in an English classroom and found – to my delight – no textbooks. The system was expecting the children to learn from me, through me. I had to create a lesson; think of a plan of action; find the right content for these particular students in this particular context; I had to inspire them and catch their imagination – for they were certainly not a captive audience. I had to learn to let go of the way I had been school-taught myself – my mother having been a far better model of creative thinking – for she taught me by example how to captivate children – 'how to hold a wave upon the sand'. So there I was in my early thirties, with twenty-eight waves all at once, each one of a slightly different frequency and amplitude, each one as important as the next.

It is the children that really matter. To honour them we must thoroughly prepare as teachers, which requires critical thinking. Learning 'only-on-the-job' leaves far too many important thoughts and considerations unexplored, unchallenged. Mastery implies critical reflection, and this, in turn, needs a proper forum.

It was the challenge that really inspired me. Being critically reflective made me question beliefs I held about things. I saw my Latin American culture through English eyes, and found new nuances, contradictions and appreciations. I shared all this with the children because dialogue is extremely important to me and to them. I wanted to know their views and opinions and maybe, just maybe, they would want to hear in turn what I had to teach them. I passed many an afternoon detention at the beginning of my NQT year, getting to know the children, which really paid off.

I was very glad to become a teacher. It offered an exciting amount of challenge and required an interesting mix of specific knowledge and pedagogical understanding. Most of all however, I valued the room it gave to creativity. I was lucky enough to have been brought up at home in an atmosphere where curiosity and wonder were cherished aspects of everyday life, therefore creativity had a fertile ground in my life. This really came to the fore for me as a teacher. Could I in any way replicate this in the classroom?

This type of teaching and learning is what this book is all about. Both my colleague Darnelle and I have 'foreign' backgrounds so to speak, and her journey has not been less life-changing than mine.

* * *

Although I have had a rich language journey from birth as Paula mentions above, and it has been life-changing at various moments in my life, I was not aware of just how rich and transforming it has been until I was in the middle of a higher language degree in the mid-1990s. Interestingly, it took a Master's degree to give me the space and opportunity to read and reflect critically on such matters. I arrived in England at the beginning of the second year of my secondary education, speaking very little English. While in all other areas of the curriculum it was a struggle to understand the academic language employed by teachers, in my French class however, my teacher single-handedly (in my eyes, then) and for the first time, focused his attention on my abilities rather than on my deficits. The whole class saw me in a different way as my linguistics skills became a source of confidence and new light. Suddenly my self-esteem was as high as can be and I realized I had some abilities which students all around me were trying to acquire. And if they were able to learn French while living in England, then I could certainly learn English, having the advantage of constantly being immersed in English life. I had no excuse whatsoever. I was right here where English is the culture, where everywhere you turn someone was speaking English, the radio, the television, on the bus, in the underground and in the classroom of course. This experience made me realize, even then, that language is power. Power for the individual to view the world he or she lives in and power which reaffirms this identity. It was this teacher, who spoke French with an English accent, who made all the difference to me. It was him and his passion for teaching languages that inspired me to understand language and its place in our personal life as well as in society. It was in his class that we listened to live French radios, such as Radio Luxembourg – he insisted that we listened to real French speakers at the normal speaking speed. He also ensured that the culture of French-speaking worlds such as La Réunion, Martinique or Guadeloupe featured regularly in his lessons (and this was before the internet). I never actually asked him about his travels to these French-speaking worlds, but by the end of the year in his language class, I knew more about these faraway lands than ever. You could say that I had the language bug. So it was not surprising that later on in my career as a French secondary teacher, I embarked on a Master's degree in applied linguistics while teaching primary refugee pupils how to find their way into the curriculum with the surface English skills they already had. The language bug never left me.

Our experiences as both language learners and teachers are integrated within the pages of this book together with research. Between us we have many years of language teaching experience, ranging from primary pupils, secondary and university students. We have both worked with primary school trainee teachers for quite a long time, and have developed an input that encapsulates all aspects of language learning, not just the pedagogy of new vocabulary. We have placed culture and intercultural understanding at the heart of our rationale for FLs. Teaching children how to be an explorer in a land of different words and visions is an art in itself, to be undertaken thoughtfully and conscious of the affective nature of the profession. The attitudes, values and beliefs around others that you bring to the classroom will make a marked difference to a child, and the very least any practitioner should do is to be well aware of their own beliefs and attitudes. In each chapter we will encourage you to examine and challenge your own views, if not at least to become aware of them.

Your motivation to teach FLs will be the key, as will be your understanding that far from hindering a child's English language development, FL learning is in fact an empowering and engaging process which directly fits into the cognitive repertoire of the child's higher thinking level. Learning a second language is a far more conscious activity than learning our first language – our mother tongue. While we agree that there are some similarities between these two processes, it is the conscious effort of SLA that gives teachers the opportunity to foster explicit knowledge about language in children, so that they can manipulate it and become as independent as possible in their language journeys.

We cover a range of areas in this book; we make suggestions and guide you around the four interconnected skills of language learning: listening, speaking, reading and writing, within the context of culture and experience. We use research and provide you with examples of how activities can support and motivate learners to engage with the target language. We recognize that readers of this book will be teachers of various languages and although our activities are either in French or in Spanish, the pedagogy and principles laid out can be applied to any language being taught in primary schools in England or elsewhere.

In Chapter 1, 'An introduction to primary languages', we pose, as we have implied, that mastery requires critical engagement. In terms of primary language learning, this will mean the theoretical framework that underpins many of the current practices around the pedagogy of FL teaching and learning. Our purpose is also to get you thinking about your own beliefs systems which support your attitudes and approach to languages and forms the foundation for your rationale.

In Chapter 2, 'Current developments in languages', we look at the state of primary provision of FLs in England. We explore aspects of the curriculum being taught, the contexts of teaching, as well as the professional development of teachers. We examine some of the implications of delivering languages in the primary context, as in the danger of schools seeking 'experts' to deliver the language together with the issue of who benefits the most from learning a FL, and the impact these decisions have on teachers and children.

In Chapter 3, 'Languages as an irresistible activity', we highlight the importance of motivating the teachers as much as the children themselves because teachers are at the forefront of children's motivation in the classroom. We examine some of the apprehensions teachers may have around delivering languages, particularly if they are monolingual themselves. We focus on how motivating children should tap into their right to explore new worlds and new visions in the safety of the classroom, and how languages can offer a platform for this exploration, particularly when delivered across the curriculum. Finally and following from this last point we warn against the dangers of viewing and reducing primary languages learning to 'fun and games', a superficial approach that may only serve the short-term engagement – or rather, 'entertainment' of children, with little impact on lasting, long-term motivation to learn languages.

In Chapter 4, 'Languages as a practical activity', we guide you through one of the most important documents published that have helped shape the delivery of primary languages. The Languages Framework (DfES 2005) organized and compartmentalized language learning in terms of content and age-appropriateness. Although this book is predicated on that framework, we nonetheless place a very different weight on the aspects it covers, bringing intercultural understanding at its heart, as the most significant strand in the framework, the one in which all others nest in terms of purpose and motivation, and as the most inclusive aspect of language learning.

In Chapter 5, 'Skills to develop in Languages', we look at languages across the curriculum. We guide you in the art of making links across different subject areas, which will enrich the daily learning experiences of the children in your classroom. There will be a space to reflect on how working cross-curricularly can work for you and how beneficial it is for your pupils. Whether you are a beginning speaker of the TL or a native speaker, we hope you are able to examine issues about language learning and teaching and reformulate your existing beliefs of what can be achieved when you start making links across different subject areas. Linking knowledge and understanding in children's learning experiences will enable them to participate as the 'apprentice citizens' that they are.

In Chapter 6, 'Children's ideas -promoting curiosity', we closely follow the previous chapter on motivation, as these three concepts are interlinked. We highlight the relevance of cultural, relational capital of teachers and children and its impact on our approach to teaching and learning, examining how these issues impact on children's curiosity and potential creativity. We discuss one of the most relevant theories on creativity in the context of education, ending with an exploration of how this can look like in the FLs classroom, giving you some practical ideas on how to encourage your own creative processes.

In Chapter 7, 'Assessing Children in Languages', an exploration is offered on the different ways in which the language classroom gives us opportunities to assess our learners. The chapter unpicks and attempts to demystify this process in which we all continually engage throughout our lives. We will see what assessment has looked like in the primary language classroom, resources used and its future directions. We interview an expert languages adviser, Dan Alliot, who will hopefully dispel some of the anxiety teachers have around assessment in languages.

In Chapter 8, 'Practical Issues', we consider the type of resources that best support the delivery of primary languages within the five strands of the Languages Framework. We believe that having access to the right resources is one of the key ingredients to the successful implementation of FLs, and that this aspect should not necessarily be an onerous one, but on the contrary, it can be an opportunity for creative thinking. The resources mentioned are those commonly used in either schools, university training (PGCE course) or by outsourced teachers employed by schools or education authorities.

Chapter 1
An Introduction to Primary Languages

Just take that morning's newspaper and start running through it with the students, and ... You can't miss it. Story after story, you can see the hidden presuppositions, bias, subordination of power, things that are excluded, the way it's put, and so on. It's ubiquitous. You can do it with the school textbooks: it is the same thing. That's intellectual self-defense. Defend yourself against what you're submerged in, and ask why.

Noam Chomsky interviewed by Arianne Robichaud, in *Radical Pedagogy*, 26 March 2013

Chapter objectives

- To allow you to begin the process of developing your own rationale for teaching and learning languages; the motivation behind the purpose;
- to consider issues around our beliefs and ways of approaching certain aspects of foreign cultures;
- to acquaint you with the theory that underpins many of the current practices around FL teaching and learning;
- to explore aspects of the social constructivist theory and its role in language pedagogy;
- to present the authors' own rationale for the delivery of languages in the primary classroom.

In this chapter we address the question of why we should 'bother' with languages in the primary classroom. Our aim is to highlight the point that no practice (be it to engage or not to engage with languages) happens without some vision or rationale behind it, whether we are aware of it or not. We also pose that in order to achieve mastery of any sort, we need to be aware of what drives our practice, values and attitudes towards a particular subject.

This is a question of attitudes towards languages rather than a forum for answers. Pragmatically speaking, we could present the views of the Confederation for British Industry which sees languages as a necessity in order to develop a global marketing potential, ensuring a degree of financial competitiveness. However, this kind of reasoning ignores a more useful and revealing dimension to our connection with language. Language is a personal construct; it is one of the aspects that define who we are in a social space and time (Hall 2002). Different languages have different status. Strangers will form opinions about us based on our language, and then, they may refine this opinion based on our particular accent. They will give us a place and a complete social context which may or may not be true, but will be meaningful to them in that particular moment. Although this is more evident when it comes to our first language – our mother tongue – it can also apply when we hear someone else speak in a second language. We may be indifferent, impressed or put off by a colleague or acquaintance who suddenly speaks in a second language. Again, how we feel about this will tell us much about ourselves and our attitudes to learning a FL. We must not let these moments pass us by; moments when we become acutely aware that we hold a particular opinion on something which produces an emotional response in us. These moments can be the precursor of awareness, change and growth. If we wish to develop our practice we need to be self-aware. If we are going to be in charge of shaping other people's attitudes – our children's attitudes – we first must try to unpick our own.

Tell me where is fancy bred.
Or in the heart or in the head?
How begot, how nourishèd?

Although we do not refer to 'desires' as Shakespeare does in the extract above, we do need to consider where the attitudes that drive our desire to engage with something – or not – comes from, and how this affects our responsibility as active agents in the attitude formation of others.

Our understanding of 'mastering' or 'expertise' will be underpinned by the values and attitudes we hold on knowledge and learning (Birdwel, Scott and Reynolds 2015). We may not always be aware of the theories we have come to internalize, but we have them nonetheless, 'We are individuals and also members of social and cultural groups. We have our own experiences, beliefs, knowledge, attitudes and preferences. All of these contribute to our theories which we bring to the job of teaching the children or students in our care' (Conteh 2003).

> **Case scenario**
>
> **Figure 1.1** Playing with words. A child from Nadine Chadier's class
>
> A twelve-year-old boy enters the French classroom in his secondary school for the first time. He had learned some French in primary school and remembers a few things. As he steps into the classroom, he smiles genuinely at his new teacher and says, in his best French, 'Bonjo Miss Marchant!'
>
> Discussion point
>
> - How do you think his teacher will respond? Why?

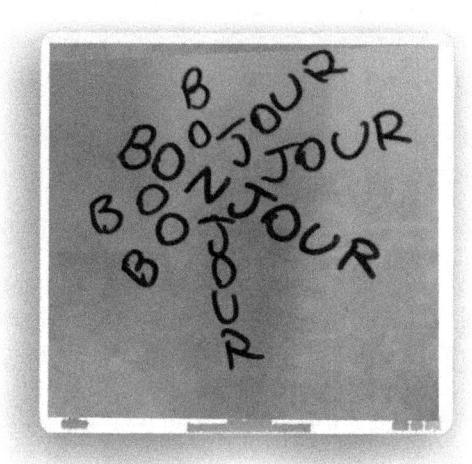

The teacher in this case has some clear options. What she says in response to 'bonjo' will set the tone of their teaching and learning relationship.

Whatever the teacher's response, you can be certain of one thing; it will be a reflection on her attitude to language learning – a knee-jerk reaction if not careful – and they will pass it on. I would hope that Miss Marchant smiles back, returns his greeting with a correctly pronounced, 'bonjour' (and we may debate what 'correctly' means) and continues repeating the greeting to each child that comes in. The boy will soon pick up the 'desired' pronunciation, and Miss can be thankful that his attitude to language needs no such correction; he entered her lesson with a smile and a willingness to have a go. Had it been the other way around, it would have taken her the best part of a year, if at all, to change his attitude, that is, 'I will only have a go if I am certain of not making a fool of myself', making the learning a stressful situation for the pupil (Ketabi and Simm 2009; Hashemi 2011).

In an ideal world we would have children that have been exposed to the right pronunciation and the right attitude. However, this is not always possible and, faced with the choice of one over the other, in the case of an eleven-year-old child, which one would you choose? Which one is the easiest to correct?

In the primary context, we would not want children to be afraid of having a go; to fear that getting the sounds wrong is a bad thing; that only 'some people' are good at languages; that it is not worth trying unless you do it perfectly well. In short, that only 'experts' can engage with languages.

> ### Case scenario
>
> A class of eight-year-olds is about to have their first French language lesson. An expert has been sourced in (we will discuss 'expert' in due course), a French teacher from a secondary school. The French teacher is confident and outgoing, and asks the class teacher to join in with the lesson. The class teacher smiles nervously and says, 'Oh no. I'm terrible at languages. I'm just going to go to the staffroom to do some marking. Enjoy the lesson', and she leaves the classroom.
>
> Discussion points
>
> - What is the message the children receive from the teacher's words?
> - What do the children learn from the teacher's actions?
> - If you had been the class teacher, what would you have said or done? Why?
> - What if this had been a mathematics lesson? Would you feel differently about things? Why/why not?

The issue raised above is a very important aspect in education. The main question for us is, what is more powerful, words or actions? Do children acquire attitudes from words or from the adults' role modelling? This is why literature around teaching and learning is so very important for anyone involved in education. There is always more to teaching and learning than mere content and method. One could argue perhaps, that teaching is one of those professions where, being an expert in a subject is simply not enough. Maybe even having the right pedagogy is not enough either. The affective nature of the profession is just as important; the attitudes and values that you bring to the classroom can make a very important difference to a child, and may mark them for life. The very least any practitioner should do is to be self-aware.

The class teacher as the 'expert'

The Independent Review of the Primary Curriculum (DCSF 2009) points out that 'enhancing the role of primary class teachers is a consistent preference of schools and head teachers'. Some research (Jones and Coffey 2006; Driscoll, Jones and Macrory 2004) argues that the primary class teacher *is* the best person to teach FLs and to provide continuity and long-term sustainable provision. Driscoll (1999) had

Figure 1.2 San Juan and San Fermin festivals in Spain

already put forward the idea that children achieved better results when taught by primary generalist teachers than when taught by secondary specialists. Although there is still the chance that we might come across some primary schools which, out of choice or necessity, have a visiting teacher to deliver the FLs, it is accepted within the profession that while 'experts' are unlikely to provide long-term language learning continuity and consolidate on what learners do and expand them to achieve their potential, they are nevertheless filling the gap in the workforce.

Case scenario

A class of nine-year-olds is having a Spanish native teacher sourced in from the local secondary school. The idea is to give children an immersive experience, where only Spanish is heard and spoken for the duration of each of the weekly lessons, spanning six months. Children engage with Oracy and Literacy through games and activities that encourage listening, speaking, reading and some writing. During one of the lessons the teacher shows a map of Spain where three locations have been marked. Each location points to an image of what appears to be a street party with the following heading for each:

- Fiesta de San Fermín: Pamplona
- Carnaval: Alhama de Granada
- Hogueras de San Juan: Alicante

> There follows a brief video clip for each, with no subtitles. The teacher says, 'Estas son fiestas en España. Repetid: fiestas'. The children repeat the word, 'fiestas'. Many hands go up. The teacher chooses one of them, and a girl asks, 'What are they celebrating?'. The teacher knows she must stick to Spanish only and says, 'Cada una celebra algo distinto, diferente. Otro dia os explico.' After all, her objective was to show the map of Spain with some typical activities that took place, and go through the months of the year with a song from the festival of Pamplona.
>
> Discussion points
>
> 1 What would you say are the strengths and weaknesses of this 'immersive' approach?
> 2 Who might be best suited to deliver an immersive approach?
> 3 If you were the native speaker teacher, would you have responded differently (staying in the target language)? How so?

In the example above, one of the disadvantages of the immersive approach is that it does not give a platform for the child's curiosity, so how could it possibly foster it in significant ways? It does perhaps *spark* their curiosity but it cannot address it, and this may lead to the child's eventual realization that this is not the place to show curiosity or specific interest. As long as the lessons are engaging enough the child will participate willingly, making him or her dependent on the teacher's power to motivate in the moment.

Curiosity is the precursor of creativity, and although most teachers praise children's sense of curiosity and want to foster creativity, this rarely happens in schools where so many demands are made in terms of meeting targets and record-keeping. There is a well-known adage by American author Ursula le Guin that reads, 'The creative adult is the child who survived,' and it is an interesting quote to discuss with colleagues, for it will mean different things to different people, but it does tap into a common thread in us all. Are we survivors?

Curiosity and creativity are weighty topics and we will discuss them in Chapter 6 in terms relevant to language teaching. All we would tentatively say at this point is that, although creativity is easily perceived in the world of Arts (music, painting and literature), you should have a broad understanding of it, for there is not a single area of human endeavour where curiosity and creativity have not played a part. You need only look around you. Thus, in this book, creativity and the ability to foster curiosity are not seen in the extent of a teacher's subject knowledge (otherwise all native speaker would be classified as highly creative individuals) but rather, we will discuss these through the lens of pedagogic approaches and attitudes. Therefore, we may have a teacher with an intermediate level of French who is, nevertheless, very creative and resourceful in their approach to teaching as well as in their knowledge of primary pedagogy. He or she may model curiosity as well as strategies for learning and communicating beyond verbal remits. As Nunan and Choi point out, 'Effective communication requires much more than mastering the phonological, lexical, and grammatical subsystems of the language' (Nunan and Choi 2010 , p. 11).

Personal motivation as well as the power to motivate others plays an important part in any learning situation (Masgoret and Gardner 2003). Sources of motivation are varied and complex and will be discussed in subsequent chapters, but at this point, how a teacher motivates a pupil is another significant marker on their attitude to language learning. Does the teacher use an element of competition or collaboration? Do they use an element of surprise and/or carefully chosen resources or physical activity? Some children are highly motivated by the grade they might get in a test, while others might be put off by the stress of it. In the case scenario above, an important element of motivation was missed; personal interest and curiosity. The motivation used was, instead, that of engaging children with games and songs which, valuable in terms of vocabulary and pronunciation, are temporary in nature; they can only engage in the moment, whatever the content. One of the questions for educators is how to motivate learners through specific content, and for life, thus turning children into independent learners, able to motivate themselves. This kind of long-term motivation, in our view, can only come from a personal connection between the child and the subject at hand, not with translated words or actions but with the meaning within the situations or ideas that those words can express, as conveyed by the teacher. Independent learning cannot easily be encouraged when there is a constant emphasis on memorization (Cable et al. 2012); it will rather create students who can only skim the surface of every item, engaging merely with its reflection rather than be moved by the import of its content (Airey 2004). What impact might the teacher's knowledge of his or her class have on the power to motivate those children? The question is worth considering. Children do not construct their worlds in isolation, but frame their understanding by observing and, 'trying on' the behaviours and ways of thinking of the adults around them (Rogers 2008). What is the relevance of St John's night (San Juan) in Spain? Do we have anything similar in England? Why/why not? What has it got to do with religion? Why are Spain and England different in this respect? Or, as a ten-year-old child once asked one of my student teachers, is it true that all Spanish speakers are Catholics? All these questions could be explored by someone who may or may not speak any Spanish, but who is interested in Spanish culture. The answer to whether we should provide children with a space to engage with these issues during their FL lessons will be dependent on your view of the relationship between Language and Culture. In this book, as in most of the literature on the topic, we suggest that they are inextricably connected.

Case scenario

You are embarking on a one-year Mandarin course, and you have a choice of joining one of two classes. The first class is run by a Chinese teacher who speaks very little English, and the second class is run by an English person who studied Mandarin and lived in China for two years. The Chinese teacher will model the perfect Mandarin pronunciation, delivering the lessons mostly in the target

Figure 1.3 Calligraphy lesson (photo by Axel Rouvin)

language through a textbook. The English Mandarin teacher does not have a native-like pronunciation, but, they have something the Chinese teacher can never have; the experience of knowing what it is like for an English speaker to learn Mandarin as a second language.

Discussion points

1 Look at the five Languages Framework strands explored in chapter two. Which teacher can address best which strand?
2 Which class would you join and why?
3 What does your choice say about you? (What factors can affect your choice?)
4 What would your reaction be if your primary school decided to teach Mandarin?

It can be easy to believe that the act of being a native speaker may turn someone into an 'instant' expert, or that a languages teacher from a secondary school must be an expert too, even if they have had no training in primary pedagogy. Some primary teachers who are themselves a FL beginner, can have such an acute understanding of primary pedagogy that they become 'experts' in terms of grammar and learning skills. They may have very good general knowledge and an understanding of French culture through getting acquainted with French literature (translated form) and other French art forms. The fact of not being French themselves could make them able to reflect on the nuances of different customs and ways of thinking between the two cultures, including how grammatical structures differ or are similar in general terms.

This last point – becoming aware of nuances and the reflection that we can have and can provoke in children following an acquaintance with a new culture – is one of the most vibrant reasons why we should bother learning a new language. We argue in this book that it is the intercultural elements of learning a new language that are both the motivation and final destination of learning languages.

As teachers however, we also need to be aware of the bigger picture in terms of our FL pedagogy. This takes us to examine the theoretical underpinning of our practice, for, if we equate languages to the tip of the iceberg, and culture to what lies beneath the surface, then the ocean itself becomes the theoretical underpinning, where everything hangs together.

Why bother with theory?

Mastery of any subject will include an element of theory. The link between theory and practice must be explicit for anyone interested in developing a good understanding of a given field.

Engaging with the theory behind the practice is what will help you become an independent practitioner, capable of creating and manipulating methodologies, activities and resources in an informed manner. Understanding the relationship between theory and practice will support and enhance your teaching, allowing you to express and implement your ideas and objectives in the simplest and most effective terms.

When we speak of theory we refer to the academic literature on the field. This is known as codified knowledge; what you may find in textbooks, academic educational journals and books, which explicitly deal with an academic subject. For instance, there are well over a hundred journals dedicated to research on SLA published in English. If we include research published in other languages this number would increase significantly. This codified knowledge around SLA is what we would understand by theory, which is, unfortunately, not as accessible as other types of literature.

We need to be aware of the attitudes and values that, as teachers, we bring to our practice. This is known as 'cultural knowledge', and many of the discussion points we presented were aimed at unpicking this type of knowledge; becoming aware of what constitutes our values and attitudes, thus challenging our preconceived beliefs and assumptions about languages and their place in society and in the curriculum.

Teachers (and any profession) also have a third kind of knowledge, what is often called 'the craft' or the 'knowledge of the trade'; ways of doing things that are effective in their particular contexts and which are, therefore, difficult to distribute in written form or other formal ways. This knowledge comes from professional practice, often through careful observation, imitation and trial and error (in the details). It is, however, limited in its scope unless developed further through reflection and shaped or informed by theory. Many books are based on craft knowledge or practice alone (without engaging explicitly with theory). These books are often found in the, 'How to...' section, and offer ways of doing things; tips and ideas, games and activities,

Figure 1.4 Types of knowledge

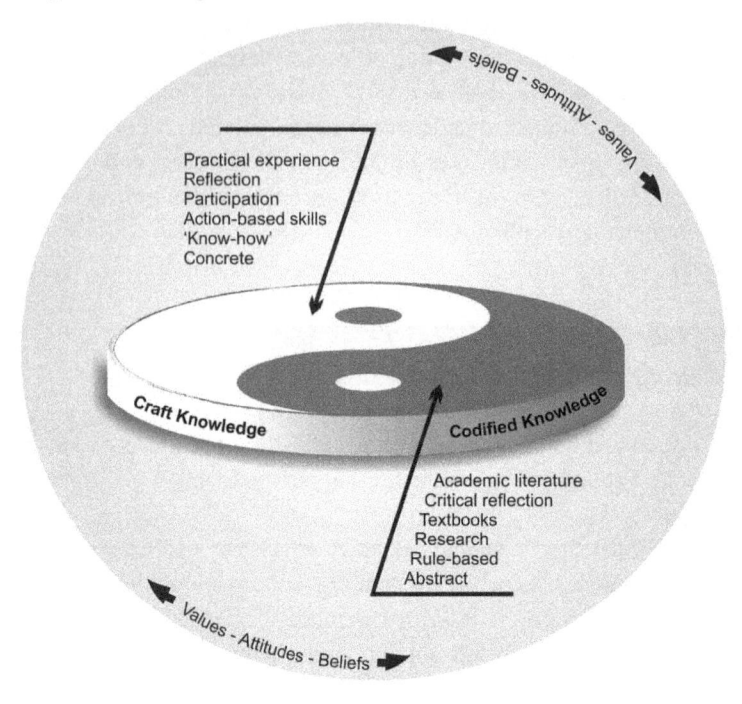

Practical experience
Reflection
Participation
Action-based skills
'Know-how'
Concrete

Craft Knowledge

Codified Knowledge

Academic literature
Critical reflection
Textbooks
Research
Rule-based
Abstract

Values - Attitudes - Beliefs

sequences and patterns of 'best' results. Although useful in terms of trying out different strategies, what they lack is a discussion on why or how these things work (or might not work) exactly; ignoring underlying theories and development histories which may be implicit in them, and which, more importantly, may have allowed you to create your own strategies by understanding your pedagogy inside out.

Unlike cultural knowledge which we pick up on our everyday interactions, codified knowledge does not come to you; you need to seek it out explicitly, through study. It is easier not to do it, as it requires concentration, time and intellectual effort. It requires dialogue with colleagues and often reiteration as our understandings shift, but this is the very merit of it. It takes a determined, open-minded person with an enquiring mind to engage with it. However, one might also say that 'fear' of practice may keep many 'academics' somewhat chained to their desks, unable to understand the 'craft' knowledge inside out. It is easier to sit behind a desk and to teach adults who are there by choice, than to stand in front of a class of thirty children that have no choice. As you can see, there is merit in both types of knowledge.

While discussing issues related to the gap between codified and 'craft' knowledge, Elaine Wilson refers to the way in which Donald McIntire approaches the challenge, which, in his view, has lacked adequate attention. Referring to research and to classroom teaching, these two types of knowledge are, in his view, complementary, 'on the premise that research can be helpful in improving the quality of classroom teaching, but equally on a second premise that research cannot be helpful except through quite complex processes culminating in classroom teachers engaging in dialogue with research-based proposals' (McIntire 2005, p. 362–3 in Wilson 2013, p. 3).

What does this look like in the context of FL learning? In this book you will be delving into all three types of knowledge – for we firmly believe in the interaction that McIntire proposes above, a yin-yang of knowledge continuum, as well as in the inevitable fact that our own values and beliefs will affect what we propose, as much as yours will affect the interpretation of what you read.

Case scenario

You are observing a class of seven-year-olds learning ten colours in Spanish. The teacher has flash cards painted in the particular colour with the accompanying Spanish word underneath. He shows the card to the pupils, says the word a few times using different voices and intonations, and then the pupils repeat. Once he feels confident that the children can read and say all ten colours without his help, he proceeds to assess their recall with a matching game.

Figure 1.5 Matching task sample

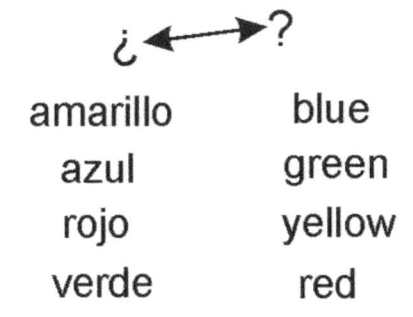

¿ ⟷ ?

amarillo	blue
azul	green
rojo	yellow
verde	red

As the teacher walks around the classroom, he is pleased with the good recall the children seem to demonstrate on paper. However, as he assesses their pronunciation recall, he notices that not all is well. Two words are consistently being mispronounced.

Discussion points

- Which graphemes are the children finding difficult to decode in Spanish?
- What is happening?
- How might you have enhanced the children's phoneme pronunciation recall?
- What is the role of pedagogy in this?
- Are you able to answer all these questions?
- Are you missing a particular kind of knowledge?
- Do you feel intrigued or indifferent?

What you observe in a particular teaching and learning situation can, to some extent, give you an indication of where in the knowledge continuum a teacher may be. Activities in themselves can be innocuous, but how they are used and responded to can tell you much. Answering the points above will require some codified knowledge and some 'craft' knowledge. You will need, for instance, codified knowledge belonging to the field of Phonetics in order to know what, 'to decode a grapheme' means. Being a native speaker will be of little help here, unless you have that knowledge and understand its application. We will revisit similar scenarios and address the four first questions in Chapter 4, but at this point it is important to highlight the last two questions, as they are the ones that will have the greatest impact on your career: Are you aware that your understanding may need further developing, and are you proactive in seeking out opportunities and challenges that move you forward? If yes, do read on.

Thinking outside the box; thinking outside the textbook

You may find that you have already been using some effective pedagogy in your practice, but are unaware of the theory that underpins it. The word 'effective' needs to be treated with caution; effective practices can serve very different aims. If the teacher's objective is to get children to obtain the highest possible grade in a test set by an authority outside their classroom, that is, textbook tests, national exams, entry exams, then the effective practice may well be to train the children's powers of memorization and give them as much experience of tests and test technique as possible, what is often termed, 'teaching to the test'. If, on the other hand, the objective is for the children to obtain some depth of understanding on a topic, enabling them to apply new ideas and information in experimental, creative ways and on different contexts, the teacher will then need to engage children in activities that encourage dialogue (with others and with self) that connect their current understanding to the new information, so that they may 'build' their knowledge on a scaffold constructed by the teacher's pedagogy and the child's past and present experiences. If formal assessment is required, the children may produce a poster, a video, prepare a presentation, etc. This is known as the social constructivist approach, and one of its foundations is Lev Vygotsky's social development theory which states that it is the social interactions we experience and engage in from infancy, that shape our linguistic, cognitive and behavioural development. This may seem obvious to us right now, but it was not so at the time it was written in 1930.

Figure 1.6 Child's writing in Nadine Chadier's class

> ## Case scenario
>
> You have decided to read Lev Vygotsky's *Mind in Society* book – freely available online – and as you reach Chapter 8 you encounter the following lines:
>
> *Writing should be meaningful for children, that an intrinsic need should be aroused in them, and that writing should be incorporated into a task that is necessary and relevant for life.*
>
> Discussion points
>
> - What evidence of this do you see in your school?
> - How might we bring meaning and relevance to writing in a seven or a ten-year-old child?
> - What might this look like in the context of a FL scheme of work?
> - Is this just about Literacy (reading and writing)?

Vygotsky poses that play is essential to children's social and cognitive development, so this perhaps may help in your discussion points above. However, we must be careful not to be simplistic in our interpretation of 'play'. Play is a significant and essential aspect of children's lives, and they will spontaneously construct play with very specific rules and objectives. Play serves a number of sociocultural roles as children's identities and understandings develop, and as adults it is very difficult to recreate the purpose of play for a child. At best, it is possible to engage them in strategies that bring some sort of reward or challenge, as in games, which is a very behaviourist track. The challenge is how we may motivate children to see writing as a meaningful activity in itself, and meaningful in terms of the child, not us.

Another important aspect of engaging with codified knowledge is becoming acquainted with theory, for this is what gives us a framework in which to expose our argument. What this means is that our ideas about teaching and learning FLs, in this book, are seen through a particular lens, what is termed, a theoretical framework, which in our case is social constructivism as we briefly touched on above. These frameworks are subject independent, and you can see in this book how we present our argument on learning a FL in the primary context, through this lens. Had we framed our argument purely through behaviourism, the content of the book would be quite different, more akin to a manual on how to use particular teaching behaviours in order to cause a particular pupil behaviour. Behaviourism does play a role in teaching and learning, for instance, much of the pedagogy used in vocabulary acquisition, as in any activity that leads to a desired event (teacher's praise, rewards, a good grade or any 'well done' token) could be classified as a behaviourist approach. Radical behaviourism, a term coined by B.F. Skinner, looks at 'instructional and reinforcing practices of our language community' (Owen 2002), seeing verbal behaviour as ecobehaviour or contextual behaviours, and we engage with this approach when explore strategies used for the teaching of Oracy and Literacy.

As way of example, we will look at an abstract from a relevant journal article, *Reading in a FL*, and explore how it may relate to your practice. The abstract looks at the impact that commercial publishers of FL textbooks can have on how teachers approach their practice, particularly relating to multilingual learners.

> Commercial publishers have shaped reading and writing instruction in American schools through their interpretations of state-developed reading and writing standards and standards-aligned materials, which teachers then implement in English classes, including those serving multilingual learners. This paper uses microethnographic discourse analysis to examine how reliance on published texts for reading activities led a teacher to focus on correct answers and formulaic writing tasks, whereas teacher-created activities fostered greater engagement among multilingual learners. Focused on a ninth grade English class at a California public high school, this study's findings suggest that reading was used primarily in service of preparation for high stakes writing assessments, but teachers can adapt their instruction to better build on multilingual students' existing knowledge and curiosity.
>
> Gilliland 2015, p. 272

> **Pause for thought**
> - Does your school use textbooks to teach FLs?
> - How do the ideas expressed in the abstract above support or challenge your own practice?
> - What questions are you left with after reading the abstract? How would reading the whole article enhance your understanding?

The last point above touches on your ability to critically analyse a text. At master's level, you would be expected to go beyond an abstract in order to ascertain if its claims are valid and reliable, as well as judge if they are relevant to your particular teaching and learning context. There may well be aspects of the study's methods, choice of participants or analysis that you might either challenge or find not pertinent to your context. For instance, does the paper present a balanced argument? Caution must also be employed when comparing studies that look at the ways English is learnt as a FL as opposed to the ways other languages are taught and learnt as FLs to English native speakers. English around the world is part of a narrative belonging to a wealth of political complexities of a local social, cultural and economic nature (Pennycook 2013), and it is, therefore, likely to act upon students' motivation in very different ways.

In terms of the use of textbooks, caution and understanding needs to be employed. Textbooks can quickly be turned, from a resource carefully employed by the teacher, into a mindless tool of 'easy teaching' and monotonous learning; an object incapable of adjusting its content and strategy to a classroom's unique variety of learners and situations. Textbooks deal only with content and general strategy. They do not 'know' the children like the class teacher does. Once commissioned at a large scale by curriculum agencies, their principal aim is to be sold. Most countries around the world use textbooks to deliver FLs and it has become an imbedded aspect of learning – expected by parents, schools and children. The market is therefore a multimillion-dollar industry. Textbooks are not cheap, and many parents struggle to afford all the textbooks their child's school demands – usually one per subject. The following entry in a Spanish parents' forum captures some of the issues that arise:

> The choice of school textbooks is done by the school management. As far as I know, Editorial companies get in touch with the school giving them information and prices ... some schools choose editorial companies that are expensive simply because these have given them some present for the school in exchange. Other schools just look at the content and do not consider the price at all.
>
> (Foro enfemenino 2010)

It is one of England's greatest assets that its teachers are trained to create and consider their own lessons and their children's learning, from start to finish, without the aid of textbooks, other than as an occasional resource or just part of a repertoire. The exception being private schools, in which competition tends to favour memory and technique over application and creativity in order to pass entry exams. Success in private schools can more readily be accredited to the small number of pupils per class and the cultural capital children bring from home rather than to the pedagogy employed. Once again, it becomes an issue of values and attitudes to learning as well as the social contexts we come from that influence our stance on this matter.

An abstract thus can only go so far in showing you the whole picture of its study – and the study is only a fragment of a larger theme – but what it can do is to give you enough information in terms of whether the subject and findings are relevant to your particular interest.

In this book you will notice that many of the points made have references in brackets, that is to say, what we argue is guided, supported or inspired by the works and findings of others (codified knowledge). These will also allow you to find the original papers and see for yourself what those authors' arguments were in greater detail. This is a very important aspect in the academic approach which allows you to ascertain an author's awareness of the academic literature in the field, as well as giving you the opportunity to follow up particular threads in an argument.

Are you a social constructivist practitioner or is your practice entirely based on memorization, games, rewards and sanctions?

The question above is entirely rhetorical. You could indeed be both things – and most of us are. The question is rather, are you aware of which theories underpin any of your arguments or particular practices? What might you owe to authors such as Vygotsky, Piaget, Bruner, Bandurra, and in the case of SLA, Krashen or Byram?

We will outline the contribution some of these authors have made, through the lens of FL pedagogy. We recommend that for a broader understanding of their theories you engage in further reading.

We will start by examining the two pictures below. We will do what is called a, 'text analysis' of these two photographs or types of text. A text is any printed material that can be examined and discussed because it is imbued with social meaning; it can be interpreted. We will narrow the field of analysis to 'second language learning', and we will ask if there is room for a social constructivist approach in your primary classroom.

Pause for thought

Look at the two pictures below.

- What do you see? What is happening?
- What might be the nature of their motivation in each case?

- What are you able to infer about their learning, or would you need to wait for the test results to find out?
- If this were a language lesson, what might they be doing?

Figure 1.7 (a) Learning through exploration (b) Sitting at desks

The extract below may help your discussion.

The best methods are therefore those that supply 'comprehensible input' in low anxiety situations, containing messages that students really want to hear. These methods do not force early production in the second language, but allow students to produce when they are 'ready', recognizing that improvement comes from supplying communicative and comprehensible input, and not from forcing and correcting production.

I will also conclude, that the best methods might also be the most pleasant, and that, strange as it seems, language acquisition occurs when language is used for what it was designed for, communication.

Krashen 1982, p. 7

What does the social constructivist FL classroom look like? Social constructivism, as mentioned earlier, poses that children learn through solving problems in the context of social interactions – past and present. When we solve problems we have to think about possible courses of actions and predict possible outcomes. By careful consideration and the use of trial and error we can find the most effective solution for that particular moment. However, what can the problem possibly be in an FL lesson? It might be easy to think of Science as the perfect candidate subject in which to see a problem needing a solution (how can we stretch a shadow, etc.), however, this may be part of the answer, as many schools now are opting to deliver FL cross-curricularly, though another subject, what is called CLIL (content and language integrated learning). Children are thus faced with a 'reason' to communicate with each other.

Piaget considered different stages of development which children have to experience in order to go on to the next stage. For instance, the question, 'What is heavier, a tonne of bricks or a tonne of feathers?' will be hard for very young children, as they have not developed the cognitive ability to take the sentence apart and see relationships or key words between certain objects. We learn thus that activities need to be 'age appropriate'. For Piaget, language acquisition is an outcome; it occurs when the child has reached the right developmental stage. In this way, we are unlikely to discuss the use of subordinate clauses with five-year-olds, nor the subjunctive mood with nine-year-olds. Or maybe we could. Bruner suggests that, rather than a fixed sequence of developmental stages, children's cognitive capabilities also depend to a certain extent, on the adults around them as they scaffold the child's learning. For Bruner, language acquisition is what causes (not an outcome of) a child's cognitive development. This reminds us of the cultural capital children bring from home, homes where, for instance, play, dialogue and reading may be everyday events, or households where more than one language is spoken, where children may develop an early awareness of language and ways of communicating. This is not to say that they are able to articulate such awareness, but it may make a difference to the kinds of discussions and activities a social constructivist teacher can bring to the classroom. Vygotsky developed the concept of the zone or proximal development (ZPD) in children's learning, which relied on the child being exposed to another 'more knowledgeable other' in order to move their understanding forward. Bruner called this the i+1 effect, which means that any child, whatever their cognitive development, is able to move their understanding forward if they are exposed to the next step in their understanding, via the use of the appropriate scaffolding. We are thus beginning to see that there is more to learning than mere content.

When it comes to SLA, Stephen Krashen (1982) made the distinction between 'acquired' and 'learned' systems of FL learning. The first 'acquisition' system is akin to our first language acquisition, our mother tongue, full of meaningful interactions, driven by the need to communicate. The second, the 'learning' is through formal instruction. One of the five strands in the Languages Framework is precisely about this type of learning; 'Knowledge About Language' (i.e. grammar) which necessitates a conscious process on the learner's part. Interestingly, for Krashen it is the 'acquisition' system that is more important for second language learning, but this is not what we tend to observe in classrooms of formal instruction, where learning becomes more detached and compartmentalized.

Another of Krashen's contributions to the field is his affective filter hypothesis, which deals with the affective factors (motivation, self-confidence and anxiety) that can operate on the learner. This filter is particularly important when it comes to primary and secondary school children, as they are not learning a language by choice. Teachers will need to motivate appropriately, focusing on communication rather than on 'correction' of errors – which tend to raise children's anxiety levels. Unfortunately, one of the 'real life' problems children end up having to solve during FL lessons is how to 'survive' the moment, particularly in the secondary context. For primary children, not yet in the grips of adolescence, this can be less of an issue, depending of course on the teacher's approach. Traditional, performance and competition-driven styles of teaching tend to 'raise' the affective filter, encouraging children to find ways of escaping or tolerating the anxiety rather than engaging with the learning. What was your experience around this?

> **Pause for thought**
>
> Looking back at the pictures above, can you think about how each picture might or might not meet the socio-constructivist classroom characteristics outlined below?
>
> - Children construct knowledge through active enquiry and discovery
> - Children can reflect on their experiences and have a safe platform for expression of such
> - Children are challenged by new understandings
> - Emphasis on collaboration rather than competition
> - They use and test ideas, skills and understandings through relevant activities
> - Children deserve culturally varied experiences that encourage the acquisition of new perspectives
> - They need proximity to others' greater understanding, either from tutors or peers, as these play a vital role in learning

We would like to end this chapter by mentioning the work of Byram (1997), who gave shape to the notion of how intercultural competencies can have an impact on second language learning.

This time we would like to ask you to remember your own school days of language learning; the type of learner that you have been encouraged to become (and we do not refer to learning styles).

Examine Figure 1.8 and think about how your educational experiences have shaped your engagement with the two photographs shown earlier on. Conversely,

Figure 1.8 Representation of Byram's 5 savoirs

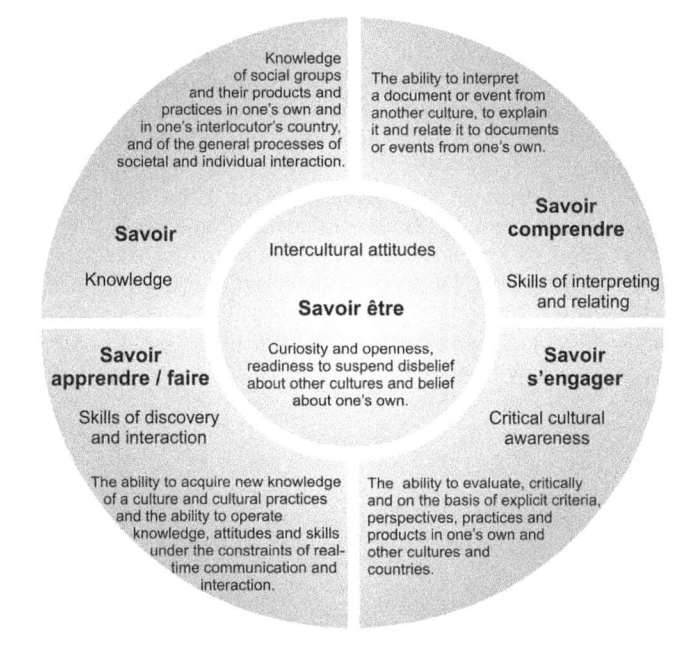

Savoir
Knowledge
Knowledge of social groups and their products and practices in one's own and in one's interlocutor's country, and of the general processes of societal and individual interaction.

Savoir comprendre
Skills of interpreting and relating
The ability to interpret a document or event from another culture, to explain it and relate it to documents or events from one's own.

Savoir être
Intercultural attitudes
Curiosity and openness, readiness to suspend disbelief about other cultures and belief about one's own.

Savoir apprendre / faire
Skills of discovery and interaction
The ability to acquire new knowledge of a culture and cultural practices and the ability to operate knowledge, attitudes and skills under the constraints of real-time communication and interaction.

Savoir s'engager
Critical cultural awareness
The ability to evaluate, critically and on the basis of explicit criteria, perspectives, practices and products in one's own and other cultures and countries.

think about which picture might more readily encourage the types of learning in the representation given in Figure 1.8?

All the *savoirs* mentioned in Figure 1.8 require some kind of interaction, dialogue and reflection on the part of the learner and between teacher and learner. This type of practice is based on a socio-constructivist approach to teaching and learning, and being aware of this can allow us to critically engage with it, whether we wish to encourage it, change it or improve it (or even ignore it).

We invite you to consider how your teaching and learning environment and practices give or deny opportunities for this type of approach, and why.

Summary

We have exposed in this chapter two important aspects that you must consider carefully if you intend to master the teaching and learning of FLs: your rationale for teaching and learning languages as well as the theoretical underpinnings of the pedagogy you employ. Both rest on particular beliefs, and explicit, craft and codified knowledge which you should be aware of. This understanding will give you independence and allow you to grow as a practitioner, be approachable and sensitive to those colleagues around you who may need guidance, and ultimately and most importantly, will help you give the children the best language experience that you are capable of giving, modelling a can-do attitude, from an informed position.

Recommended reading

Byram, M. and Gribkova, B. and Starkey, Hugh (2002). *Developing the Intercultural Dimension in Language Teaching: a practical introduction for teachers*. Language Policy Division, Directorate of School, Out-of-School and Higher Education, Council of Europe, Strasbourg.

Chomsky, N., (2013). On Education, interviewed by Arianne Robichaud, Forthcoming in Radical Pedagogy, interview 26 March 2013, https://chomsky.info/20130326/.

Powell, K. C., and Cody J. K., Cognitive and social constructivism: developing tools for an effective classroom. Education, 130(2), p. 241, 2009 on Academy OneFile, accessed on 2 August 2017.

Yang, L. and Wilson, K. (2006). Second language classroom reading: A social constructivist approach. *The reading matrix*, 6(3).

Chapter 2
Current Developments in Primary Languages

It has always seemed strange to me that in our endless discussions about education so little stress is ever laid on the pleasure of becoming an educated person, the enormous interest it adds to life. To be able to be caught up in the world of thought – that is to be educated.

Edith Hamilton (classical scholar)

Chapter objectives

- to give you an overall view of the state of primary languages at a national level;
- to explore some of the challenges as well as support and strategies, that schools have had so far implementing languages;
- to examine some of the implications in context, like the danger of schools seeking 'experts' to deliver the language;
- to consider some of the advantages around inclusive practice in primary languages, looking at the impact that decisions made by management can have on teachers and children.

This chapter traces the nature of primary languages provision in England, the curriculum being taught, the context of teaching and the professional development of teachers. It includes primary languages principally in KS2 but some attention is also given to primary schools that have extended language provision to KS1.

As we write this chapter, a new briefing paper has just emerged from Westminster called Language Teaching in Schools in England (Scotland has been far ahead in their implementation of primary languages). This is a significant improvement from the last five years, when schools were in the dark on how to implement the FLs curriculum, as there were little guidelines. Teachers knew they had to teach it, but how and where to find support they did not know.

However, this revolution in language learning in primary schools in England did not come from nowhere; it has been a subject of debate for many years until 2002 when the Department for Education (DfE) finally published its National Language

Figure 2.1 On a gate on the Clordir Road side of Pontlliw Primary School

Strategy: Languages for ALL: Languages for Life, which we referred to in the previous chapter. On the other hand, it was not until 2009, with the publication of the Independent Review of the Primary Curriculum when Sir Jim Rose placed FL learning on an equal par with Literacy and Numeracy that primary languages gained momentum. One of Rose's remit for the report was to introduce FL learning in the Primary Curriculum and to make it compulsory at KS2. In 2002, Lord Dearing's Language Review had left it as an entitlement only at KS2, leaving primary schools to decide whether they would deliver this FL learning entitlement and how they would do it. It is to be said, to the credit of many primary schools in England; by March 2007, 70 per cent of English primary schools were already teaching FLs or had plans to do so. By the autumn 2007, this figure had risen to 84 per cent according to the 2007 survey of language learning provision at KS2.

In July 2009, the National Foundation for Educational Research (NFER) published a long-awaited report which took three years to complete. It was a longitudinal survey of the implementation of the National Entitlement to Language Learning at KS2. The report found that in 2008 92 per cent of primary schools were offering languages to its pupils in KS2 within class time, a 22 per cent increase from 2006.

The report also stated that provision and uptake of languages training had increased between 2006 and 2008 and that for the majority of schools, the KS2 Framework for Languages provided the basis of their school languages programme. Respondents' main challenges were time allocation for delivering the FL lessons, teachers' expertise, an overcrowded curriculum and budget issues. Transition from KS2 to KS3 was still perceived as a challenge, and language progression of pupils remained a cause for concern. However, there were positive in how schools were managing assessment although those schools using assessment procedures remained in the minority.

Be that as it may be, the state of primary languages as we speak is still growing healthier than ever before. It has Westminster's attention and the paper aforementioned makes reference to an Ofsted survey report published in January 2011 which tells us that achievement in Primary schools was good or outstanding then, in just six out of ten of the primary schools visited and that teaching was good in two-thirds of the schools visited.

A quick browse around schools' and education local authority's websites indicates that there is indeed a great deal going on in many parts of England to implement the primary language curriculum. There are training and CPD (Continuous Professional Development) advertised like never before and the point to make here is that there is a feeling that primary languages is not only growing healthier, but also there are signs to indicate that it is being prioritized by many schools and indeed many local authorities.

What primary schools are doing?

Between 2014 and 2015, 99 per cent of primary schools who responded to the Language Survey were teaching languages. Twelve per cent of that percentage said they started teaching a language at the start of the academic year 2014–15. This evidence indicates that primary schools were either strengthening or formalizing the language provision in their schools. In 2016, all 556 responding schools reported that they now teach a modern or an ancient language, as part of their KS2 curriculum. However, it has to be said, that there are signs to indicate that some schools are struggling to meet the new national curriculum requirements.

> **Pause for thought**
>
> Think about the statement below and then attempt the following questions.
>
> > All Years 3–6 do French, but it is not very systematic – teachers use a number of schemes, and do not effectively build on previous learning: they each tend to do their own thing.
> >
> > Language Trends Survey 2016, Chapter 4, p. 43
>
> - Where would you situate your school in its language provision for pupils?
> - Is there a systematic and consistent language teaching in your school?
> - What resources does your school use?
> - How does your school build on previous learning?
> - Consider Figure 2.2. What is the state of primary languages in your school? What are the advantages and disadvantages in each case?

Figure 2.2 Different ways of delivering FLs in primary schools

outsourced FL expert

no FL delivery in evidence

class teacher delivering FL

team teaching/training: CT + FL expert

If you are reading this book, chances are that you are investing time to inform yourself about the current landscape of primary languages. This will focus your actions with regard to teaching the primary language that your school has decided to deliver to the pupils and it might also produce results that might pleasantly surprise you in terms of those resources hidden deep into the resource cupboards which have been forgotten, but still are very relevant to the implementation of primary languages currently.

Maynard (2012) draws our attention to the fact that for primary languages to thrive it needs to take its rightful place in the Primary Curriculum. She refers to the Independent Review of the Primary Curriculum which had put primary languages, appropriately, with understanding English, communication and languages. The implication therefore is that primary languages rather than being aligned with foundation subjects should be practised regularly and not be 'covered at the end of half-term to show it has been, "done" (Maynard (2012), p. 7). That is to say that it needs to be taught consistently if it is to flourish and provide children with a coherent language learning experience. As we already pointed out earlier, we need to offer children an enriched experience and a continuum of language learning which can be built on Muijs et al. (2005) and McLachlan (2009).

In 2010, an Ofsted survey report found the Primary Languages Curriculum to be good in under half of the ninety-two schools visited. It was outstanding in seven schools but inadequate in five schools. The report listed the characteristics of outstanding schools' curriculum provision for language learning:

- all Key Stage 2 pupils learning a language
- integration of languages with other subjects

- discrete language teaching once each week, with the time allocated to it often increasing as the pupils got older, and short daily integrated sessions of language learning
- one main language (or even two languages) but frequent, and planned, references to other languages, especially to those used by the school's pupils
- the Key Stage 2 Framework used as the main tool for planning
- careful tailoring of any external schemes of work or commercial materials to the needs of different classes
- progressive planning for skills development focused on listening and speaking, with reading and writing underpinning these skills
- opportunities for pupils who spoke other languages to demonstrate and/or teach these to other children.
- parents and adult speakers of other languages invited into school
- pupils' achievement in languages celebrated regularly through assemblies and languages days.

(Ofsted (2011) 'Modern Languages Achievement and Challenge 2007–2010')

> **Pause for thought**
>
> **Questions:**
>
> 1 Can you identify items from the list which might describe your own school?
> 2 How would you describe the language curriculum provision at your own school in terms of strengths and weaknesses?
> 3 What are your answers based on?

Taken as a whole, Ofsted's findings and report in 2011 remained the most positive survey results for primary languages so far, yet the curriculum provision was still found to be weak. It highlighted how schools, though attempting to develop the skills of classroom teachers, were nevertheless finding the task challenging in the short term. For example, in one particular school, a specialist teacher taught French in Year 4 to Year 6 and was employed on a part-time basis. This teacher was employed for the rest of the week by the local education authority as a language adviser. The school had decided to use this specialist teacher to ensure progression, but it must be noticed that this is not the class teacher delivering the primary language to her class. It is well recognized and argued that one of the conditions for success in embedding primary languages in the curriculum is to ensure that primary class teachers were able and willing to teach modern

FLs. Morin (2016) commented that there was a lack of clarity in policy and long-term educational aims for primary languages; she also argues that policy was being developed in a vacuum and that there was no adequate funding and support from central government to scaffold the integration of primary languages in the curriculum.

Turning to another kind of provision, another school has decided to move towards creating a sustainable condition where primary languages can thrive. The language coordinator had a postgraduate certificate in education with specialization in primary languages. Ofsted observed that the school was in a good place with this particular coordinator to develop the school's languages curriculum. It highlighted the head teacher's excellent support and how *the* specialist language teacher was working in team with other classroom teachers to develop their skills and knowledge of primary language pedagogy. The classroom teacher's time was designated in the classroom to work with, and eventually take over from the specialist teacher. In this instance, the Year 3 teacher who had learnt how to teach languages by observing and team-teaching with the specialist teacher/coordinator was able to take her own language lessons the following academic year. When observed by Ofsted, her language lesson was judged to be effective. This is the approach, judged sound by Ofsted, which the school plans to take on.

Forward into academic year 2015–16, the Languages Trends Survey found that 37 per cent of responding schools are fully implementing the National Curriculum requirements for KS2. Provision ranges from the employment of a language specialist teacher, to native speaker coordinator.

As provision for primary languages evolves, schools are creatively managing and implementing the National Curriculum in whatever ways are available to them.

> *We have appointed an HLTA to teach French across a range of age groups as part of PPA cover (including EYFS and Key Stage 1) – some provision is still provided by class teachers. Currently looking into a commercial scheme to ensure development and progression through Key Stage 2.*
>
> Languages Trends Survey 2015–16, p. 52

Evidently however, some schools are still some way off from creating conditions for a sustainable primary language provision. In the above example, we may be back to the problems encountered when languages are not delivered by the class teacher, in that the status of the subject is in question; pupils might perceive it as a low priority, progression could be an issue and so could transition and continuity in learning the language, unless the Higher level teaching assistant (HLTA) is specifically trained to deliver the Primary Languages Curriculum.

In Ofsted's own report on primary languages in 2016, Sir Michael Wilshaw highlighted some interesting issues. Primarily, he draws attention to the fact that schools' focus on the so-called '3Rs' has pushed other compulsory subjects, namely

Science and FLs, virtually off the Primary Curriculum in many schools, stating the government's concerns in that, if this trend continues, children who started school in September 2015 and are set to take the full suite of the English Baccalaureate (EBACC) subjects when they sit their exams in 2020 will be at a disadvantage. If schools' provision for primary languages is not fully implemented and if it is diluted and does not provide children with enough time and hours of tuition in FLs, it will be unlikely that progression will be sufficient to allow them to reach the required level for the English Baccalaureate once in secondary school.

So upon review of the quality and breath of provision of FLs in primary schools, Ofsted found that while the majority of primary-age pupils enjoy having the opportunity to learn a FL, there are serious weaknesses in the quality of provision due to:

- a lack of time allocated to the study of science and FLs
- a lack of teaching expertise, particularly in respect of FLs
- a poor working arrangements with partner secondary schools that failed to ensure effective transition and progression

Out of 106 primary schools visited, Her Majesty's Chief Inspector (HMCI) found that around two-thirds spend less than one hour per week learning a FL. The common remarks to visiting inspectors were related to time constraint and an already tight curriculum. Parents who responded to HMCI's questionnaires revealed that at best they felt the provision for FL in their school was sporadic and tokenistic and at worst children did not feel that they were making any progress.

Notably the generation of teachers entering the profession in recent years was not, in the main, required to study a FL to general certificate of secondary education (GCSE); consequently there is a shortage of a skilled workforce in view. A significant investment in professional development for primary school teachers is now a must in order to meet the challenge.

Sir Michael Wilshaw further argues that if the best primary schools are capable of providing effective teaching of FLs alongside other subjects without undermining pupils' progress, then all schools can.

> If children are 'switched off' by poor, unchallenging lessons, this is likely to have an impact on the future take-up of these subjects. We must therefore ensure that primary-age pupils are inspired by effective teaching of science and foreign languages, from properly trained and qualified staff, and that the pupils' enquiring minds and natural curiosity are nurtured.
> (Wilshaw, HMCI's monthly commentary: May 2016)

His report does acknowledge, however, that Ofsted as an organization needs to also take responsibility for this failing, as Ofsted inspections too, in recent years have tended to prioritize the quality of provision in English and Numeracy at the expense of other Primary Curriculum subjects.

Pause for thought

Figure 2.3 The best moment is now

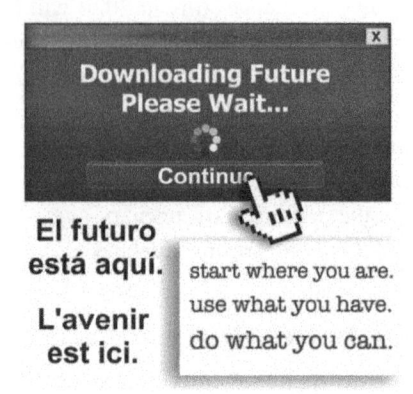

> Downloading Future
> Please Wait...
> Continue
>
> El futuro está aquí.
> L'avenir est ici.
>
> start where you are.
> use what you have.
> do what you can.

Question:

- Have you thought about the strengths you may already have and can use around languages? (curiosity, communication, determination, ideas generation, leadership skills, etc.)

What language?

Factors that may affect a primary school's choice can involve the language capital of its staff, or the languages taught at the local secondary school. Expectations of parents may be another factor when considering which language is taught, but we imagine that by now, two years after primary languages became statutory, this decision has already been made in most primary schools. However, perhaps the decision should not be informed exclusively on the language capital of the existing staff at the time nor on the languages taught at the local secondary school, but rather, it should be informed by a clear rationale based on the intention to encourage a 'can do' attitude and a love of languages in young learners. Local educational authorities or trusts can also form part of the decision-making process in order to ensure coherence and smooth transition. For example, some education trusts have a strategic language policy to provide one language across their primary as well as their secondary schools.

Since 2012 languages taught by primary schools have not changed. Most primary schools in England teach French, with Spanish becoming a popular choice year on year. Language Trends Survey 2015–16 found that just over three-quarters of their 556 schools who responded to their questionnaires teach French. Spanish has been on an upward trend since 2012, and in the 2015–16 survey 22 per cent of responding schools said they offer Spanish. German remains stable at 4 per cent, but the survey was unable to comment on Mandarin or Latin as the number involved for both these languages were statistically too small. Although Elizabeth Truss, as junior minister of education in 2012, made a point to encourage schools to consider Mandarin as another primary language because, she claims it to be vital for the economic future of our country. However, economic or market values at that scale fail to enthuse teachers and pupils. This, coupled with the need to include an element of Mandarin Literacy (reading and writing) in the provision forced some schools to abandon Mandarin due to lack of expertise.

Elsewhere, schools are implementing the national curriculum requirements but not following the traditional route of popular languages, instead offering their pupils a holistic approach to language learning and an awareness of languages around them. They teach a language in depth in all year groups in KS2. Additionally they also have a system where each term brings the learning of a language. The school's thinking skills sessions are spent exploring the term's designated language once a week, allowing children to understand the nature of languages loosely in their different geographical families, such as European, Afro-Asiatic, Slavic and Celtic.

Exceptionally, some schools teach Latin as well as a modern FL, and of these, a small number teach Latin as the only FL. These schools have a clear rationale for deciding to make this ancient language their language of choice. They report that Latin develops children's knowledge of English language and supports their learning of other languages.

There is evidence to suggest that primary schools are offering pupils in KS1, the opportunity to learn a language and prominently it is the same target language taught in KS2. That said, the survey draws the conclusion based on its previous

Figure 2.4 Choosing the right language for your school

year's results that as schools turn their attention to implementing the KS2 statutory primary language requirement, there is a decline in the number of schools teaching a language in KS1.

Revealingly, 10 per cent of academies compare to four per cent of other schools, reported that they do not teach primary languages at all. This comes as little surprise as academies are not required to adhere to the National Curriculum and therefore can choose not to take on board the compulsory status of primary languages at KS2.

What challenges are primary schools facing?

While there is a number of important studies which together draw a comprehensible map of primary languages and its provision pre-2010, these studies look at progress made while primary languages had an 'entitlement' status only. As the compulsory subject that it now is, new research and studies will undoubtedly emerge to inform our practice as well as our understanding of what is working and what needs further modification. Although we can only rely on a limited number of sources at the present time, we are able nevertheless to verify the present challenges against the key challenges highlighted by studies previous to September 2014. We will explore the time factor, progression and assessment, teachers' professional training, and finally we will look into transition and collaboration between primary and secondary colleagues.

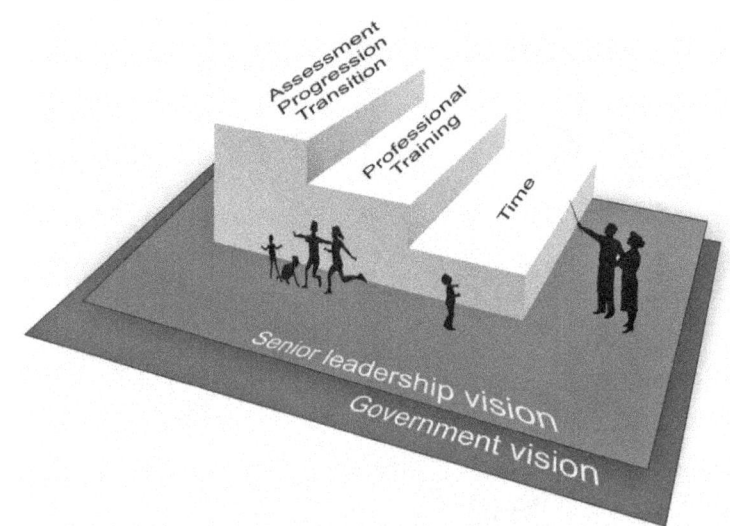

Figure 2.5 Challenges faced by primary schools

Time

The chief of Ofsted is not the first to highlight the time constraint of the Primary Curriculum, although he is right when he emphasized the fact that it is the intense focus on the 3Rs which has led to our current state of affairs where subjects like primary languages get less than an hour a week, if at all in some schools. And yet, the benefits of language learning are not all that unfamiliar to primary colleagues. In fact, they are very articulate of the reasons why primary children should learn languages, which range from helping pupils in literacy in their own language by seeing patterns of grammar and spelling to well-developed basic skills, such as organization, problem-solving and communication.

Nevertheless, finding sufficient time to teach a primary language is the principal cause for not meeting the National Curriculum requirement to do so at KS2. It is interesting to discover that those schools which have been teaching a primary language for a year or so, no longer list the time element as their main concern. Instead, their issues were around teaching expertise, confidence and access to professional development.

Referring to progression and assessment in KS2, Hunt (2009) found that teachers justified not engaging with assessment of the FL on the lack of time. Progression and assessment in primary languages is still an issue for a third of schools who responded to the 2015–16 survey. They reported not having a system in place to assess pupils' progress in language learning. Martin (2012) points out that even though assessment schemes were provided for in a scheme of work, children reported in interviews that their written work was being marked with general encouragement remarks rather than being specifically told how to move on.

Professional training

This can cause great concern for some teachers. Interestingly, some of the schools which had started teaching a language three to five years previously are the ones most likely to experience difficulties in accessing professional language training. The Language Trend Survey (2015–16) suggests that this is perhaps linked to the fact that centrally resourced training was being cut. Markedly, the Languages Company, set up to support the National Languages Strategy and to implement the Language Review of 2007, confirms the issue of funding on its website:

> In 2011 the Coalition Government decided not to continue with the Languages Strategy and to cut most central funding for languages. In common with most other bodies, The Languages Company received no further funding from the Government.
>
> (The Languages Company)

By 2011 two-thirds of the money which had been behind primary languages was re-allocated to the general school budget, causing many schools to suspend their very good attempt to develop primary language teaching and learning. Many saw the funding for local authority language advisers also cut (*The Guardian* Teacher Network, May 2015).

Inevitably, funding – or rather the lack of it – will impact on training and on the confidence of those teachers who are not language specialists. The Language Trends Survey 2015–16 found that there was a low level of engagement with CPD for languages. As many as 80 per cent of respondent schools never attend any national or regional language conferences or meeting with colleagues in other primary schools to discuss primary languages. They also noted that although teachers' confidence is less of a barrier to implementing primary languages now than before, the percentage is still noticeably high at 45 per cent.

This seems alarming to say the least, as in 2005 a two-year evaluation of the Primary Languages Pathfinder programme conducted by CEDAR (Centre for Education Development, Appraisal and Research) had already highlighted that collaboration between teachers, supports confidence and competence to work towards longer-term sustainability. It also pointed out that continuing professional development, appropriately differentiated and with a linguistic competence element as well as methodology, was found to be vital in addressing teachers' expertise, professional knowledge and understanding.

Finding qualified staff to teach primary languages is the most commonly cited measure that schools have taken to tackle the requirements of the new curriculum. They speak of employing a language coordinator who will redraft the language policy and create a scheme of work for KS2, buying new resources and organizing CPD internally. Some schools are ahead and enthusiastic about the kind of outcomes they want for their pupils:

> *We have employed a specialist language teacher to make sure that outstanding lessons and a love of languages is consistently taught through Key Stage 2.*
> (Language Trends Survey 2015–16, p 52)

On the other hand, some schools are facing challenges with regard to the sustainability of their provision on a weekly basis, facing clashes in the timetable when only one teacher is trained and equipped to teach FLs, and no contingency planning readily available for managing staff absences or long-term illness or leave.

Assessment, progression and transition

Since languages are compulsory in KS2, there is an expectation from central government that schools will ensure that pupils make significant progress in one language in order to lay the foundations for further study in KS3. In turn, KS2 'should lay the foundations for further FL teaching at key stage 3' (National Curriculum in England (2013) – KS2 languages programmes of study p. 2). There is an implication here that the transition from KS2 to KS3 needs to be rigorous and that collaboration between the two key phases will need to be set up and managed by both primary and secondary schools. However, findings from the Language Trends Survey 2015–16 are less positive than they had been in recent surveys. Twenty-nine per cent of secondary schools reported having no contact with their feeder primary schools. The most common type of contact for primary schools was in the form of informal exchanges of information, visits or joint participation in cluster or network meetings. This informal type of approach is difficult to unpick in terms of the impact it can have on children's progression. Nevertheless, there are also some positive models of transition between primary and secondary schools. Some secondary schools have employed a language teacher to work in local primary schools for half a day, to support language and team work with primary teachers in order to prepare Year 6 pupils to transition smoothly into secondary.

While 23 per cent of secondary schools say that most pupils arrive with no significant experience of language learning, 56 per cent report that most pupils arrive with a measurable level of language competence, while others arrive with at least some knowledge of vocabulary and linguistic concepts. Clearly, the goal that pupils will 'build on the foundations laid at Key Stage 2' still has some way to go, but there are some encouraging signs.

Hunt et al. (2008) found a diverse range of primary modern FL provision, information transfer and transition arrangements and pointed to the immense task ahead to maintain continuity and progression. This remains a key challenge, and to date there has been very little achieved towards a national, comprehensive and enabling primary-to-secondary transition process as far as language learning is concerned. Ofsted visits to secondary schools need to look for evidence of and appreciate the work some of them are doing to secure effective language learning continuity and progression within the primary years and between KS2 and KS3.

Delivering FLs and the danger of seeking experts

I can't teach French or Spanish because I can't speak either.

Should an expert linguist teach languages? People who ask this question often assume that a linguist is a polyglot (someone who speaks many languages) but while many linguists may speak many languages, linguists are people who are interested in the science of language; interested in the unconscious linguistic structures and behaviours humans carry within. For example, how do we acquire language as babies? One of the most prominent linguists of our time is Noam Chomsky, who tackled this very issue, helping develop the concept known as, Universal Grammar. You can listen to Chomsky's ideas on YouTube (Noam Chomsky on language acquisition).

Linguists can also be interested in how people use language to interact with others. They study how people acquire their knowledge about language (we will

Figure 2.6 YouTube clip on Chomsky's take on Universal Grammar

discuss this in details in Chapter 4 and apply it to how children learn languages). Linguists also explore in meticulous details how to represent the structure of sounds or meanings. They equally work with speakers of different language to discover patterns and to account for different linguistic patterns theoretically. So we begin to see that linguistics is a science and that, while a linguist may have at her command several languages, the core of her work is to do with learning *about* languages not *learning* languages. Someone who has a degree in linguistics may very well become an expert primary languages teacher if they have had also the required training and understanding of primary pedagogy.

Being monolingual (speaking only one language) is a commonly perceived barrier with the teaching of FLs in the primary context. The challenge is: How can we engage primary teachers – any teacher – in the delivery of languages? This very much depends on our understanding of 'FLs' in the context of a primary audience. A common perception is to equate FLs with a string of foreign words, sounds and phrases, alien structures and hidden meanings. This would indeed be a rather poor and misinformed version of what learning a FL constitutes. Although it may be part of the experience, it is by no means the whole story, nor the most important aspect at this early stage.

The current Purpose of Study offers a clear and enlightened rationale for the delivery of FLs, both for the primary and secondary context. This rationale will form part of the backbone of this book and, should you lose track of it at any point we urge you to refer back to it as you progress,

> *Learning a foreign language is a liberation from insularity and provides an opening to other cultures. A high-quality languages education should foster pupils' curiosity and deepen their understanding of the world.*
>
> (Department for Education 2013)

What is particularly relevant about this brief extract is the fact that indirectly, it emphasizes attitude over content. Content (foreign words, facts and structures) cannot foster curiosity in children by itself, it needs a human vehicle. Teachers, through their pedagogy and attitudes, can engage pupils in ways that may open their minds to other cultures and foster their curiosity. A teacher can go beyond a game with words and create activities that engage children with meaning rather than mere translations.

> A teacher's view of his or her role is critical. It is the specific mind frames that teachers have about their role – and most critically a mind frame within which they ask themselves about the effect that they are having on student learning.
>
> (Hattie 2012, p. 14)

One cannot foster curiosity for the world if children are only encouraged to repeat words through memory games. A dialogue is necessary, and class teachers are well placed to have constructive dialogue with their children. However, what does a dialogue within the remit of FLs look like? This is also an important question which will be determined by our understanding of 'FLs'. If the purpose of study is anything to go by, then this definition needs to be extensive and apt to meeting the rationale.

Engaging with this issue will help us highlight the qualities of a good or outstanding practitioner; the best person to deliver FLs in the primary classroom.

The Languages Framework which was introduced in 2005 and is, still, a valid and useful document, has also helped unpick what learning languages in the primary classroom can entail. In Chapter 4 we will look at the Languages Framework in greater detail (a complete version of the document is freely available online) but for now, it will suffice to give a brief description pertinent to this chapter. Primary schools began to deliver the entitlement of FL learning as they had been directed, building on foundations from current practice they judged to be good. Some schools managed to raise the profile of language learning very successfully. The usefulness of the Languages Framework when it was first introduced lay in the way it compartmentalized the teaching and learning of a FL both in content and age appropriateness, aimed at changing primary practice from a 'language awareness' approach to a 'performance approach'. The Framework considers not only language learning but also the relevant primary pedagogy to be used alongside it. It is a language-neutral guide which divides the teaching and learning of FLs into five sections, or *strands*. We have designed a table to give a brief example of each strand in Figure 2.7.

Figure 2.7 Representation of the five strands within the Languages Framework

5	FRAMEWORK FOR LANGUAGES
O	**ORACY** — Listening and Speaking
L	**LITERACY** — Reading and Writing
IU	**INTERCULTURAL UNDERSTANDING** — Learning about others' culture, examining our own.
KAL	**KNOWLEDGE ABOUT LANGUAGES** — Examining patterns and structures (grammar).
LLS	**LANGUAGES LEARNING STRATEGIES** — Acquiring skills that help us learn a new language.

The four language skills in the first two strands (listening, speaking, reading and writing) are only part of the big picture of language learning. We are encouraged to deliver them through – or within the context of – the other three strands. The framework guided us to plan for language skills progression within the last four years of KS2 for pupils (7–11-year-olds). It also invited us to create links with secondary schools in order to guarantee continuity in learners' language learning.

In this book, when we refer to FLs we hold a holistic view of what constitutes language teaching and learning, as the table above encapsulates. At points we may talk about Oracy or Literacy, which unfortunately seem to be, for many, the only aspect of language learning. This is like saying that an iceberg is entirely formed of what we are able to perceive on the surface of the ocean. It is true that Oracy and Literacy may be our first point of contact with another culture (although we come into contact with other cultures in translated form and imports much more than we are aware), and that these two features are very visible and audible, and therefore easily reduced to a measurable outcome; easily accountable to Heads, parents, politicians and policymakers which, altogether, increasingly pulls away from an education which should be 'attentive to the nuances of meaning' (Taubman 2009, p. 52). However, it is worthwhile remembering that language is a vehicle for expressing states, ideas and feelings; that words are not the end in themselves but merely a way of accessing new visions (Ambrossi 2015). How can we reflect this in the classroom?

What constitutes an 'expert' then will depend on the school's vision of languages; on what is viewed as 'expertise'. The attributes of a good primary languages teacher need to be carefully considered, and one of the strengths of the Languages Framework is that it can help us identify what those attributes can be, including knowledge on primary pedagogy. Paying attention to attitudes towards learning a FL in the primary context should also be included in the criteria. Attitudes form part of our character, and character formation is once more becoming a relevant issue in education (Birdwel, Scott and Reynolds 2015).

Who should learn a FL?

The UK government has made the learning of a FL compulsory for children between the ages of 7 and 11. This, therefore, is not a debatable issue in UK schools. In most other countries however, languages are delivered much earlier on, usually from the age of 5 if not earlier. Who should learn a FL is also a matter of opinion based, again, on our attitudes to second language learning. It was traditionally the case that all privately educated children as well as those perceived to have a particular intellectual ability should learn Latin and ancient Greek grammar, which is how our modern use of 'Grammar schools' acquired their name. This selection created an elite, a group of people who, not only were able to read Latin and/or ancient Greek, but more importantly, would have access to all the literature in those languages. In this way they would become acquainted with original works related to history, politics, philosophy, etc. They would be able to explore how other civilizations may have worked, prospered and fallen. This is important information which can have an impact on current social and political practices which affect us all now. Information is power through discourse, and discourse, genres and styles cannot be ignored when discussing power relations (Fairclough 2006), which is one of the reasons why learning English is important for non-English – speaking countries, just like Latin once was for Europeans a type of intellectual common currency. However, although a great deal of information uses English as its main 'spoken currency', English in no way possess all the information all of the time.

The British Academy confirms that 75 per cent of the world's population do not speak English as their first language:

> For example, it has been estimated that within 20 years most pages on the internet will be in Chinese. And the proportion of internet usage conducted in English is already on the decline, falling from 51 per cent to 29 per cent between 2000 and 2009.
>
> (British Academy: January 2011)

English-speaking countries have their own political agenda which they will pursue in their research and business interests, but we are increasingly realizing that our lack of understanding of other cultures can have dramatic consequences for all of us. How can we educate our young citizens so that they can appreciate the fact that negotiations are best done when we understand each other and have access to each other's way of thinking? First contact with another culture and hence, a different language, has often ended in conflict due to misunderstandings (Glenn 1981; Nelde 1987; Gao 2002; Spradley and McCurdy; 2012). There is a great deal to learn from ethnographic studies involving language.

Figure 2.8 First contact with other cultures has left a lot to be desired

> **Pause for thought**
>
> **Questions:**
>
> - What aspects of another country's culture would you be able to access just by acquiring their vocabulary?
> - How else might you acquire or enhance your understanding of other people's culture?
> - As a teacher, how might you pass on this understanding to your children?
> - Might there be children for whom this opportunity will be denied in your classroom? Who and why?

The last pause for thought above refers to a certain group of children who are sometimes denied the opportunity to engage with FL lessons. The reasons are often to do with the fact that these children speak English as a second or additional language (EAL) and, therefore, it is felt that the priority for them is to become as proficient as possible in English so that they may access the full curriculum. There is a caveat in the last statement; what is often meant by 'full curriculum' can turn out to be just maths and English Literacy, both of which are measured at national level, putting pressure on schools. These attitudes also reveal leftover notions of 'assimilation' into British culture, another topic which has once more acquired a high profile; the concept of 'upholding British values' now appears in the new Teachers Standards, with little understanding of what it really means.

Although we may understand what the needs of children are in order to judge what is best for them, we will often feel forced to follow a political or cultural agenda instead. The suggestion implied here is for teachers to be aware of hidden agendas, whether they rise against them or embrace them is a very personal choice. It is important to understand whatever system we find ourselves in. The Teacher Development Agency (TDA – no longer active) in 2007 developed an initiative that prepared primary student teachers in England – training to deliver a FL – by sending them to teach abroad for a month, where they could practise the target language in the foreign school (actually delivering the school's foreign language curriculum, when that language was English). One of the benefits of this exchange programme was that the student teacher got to see the English education system from the outside, gaining a different view of appreciation and criticality. Differentiation, for instance, means different things in different educational systems, and it is a valid experience to decentralize our current perspectives in order to acquire a more comprehensive understanding and awareness of variety, what Byram called, *savoir s'engager*. The primary classroom, like a secondary classroom, is composed of a varied audience. The language teacher needs to be prepared for diversity as they may have children who have never learnt a FL before, to children who may be native speakers of the target language. Therefore, for teachers, having spent time abroad, living a different educational system can be invaluable.

Case scenario

Below is the language profile of the pupils from a class of 30 eight-year-olds. The class will be learning French for the next four years.

Fifteen children have never learnt a FL before
Three pupils have recently arrived from Pakistan and speak little English
Seven pupils from Iraq have lived in England for the last two years
One pupil as special needs child (global development delay)
Two pupils are French bilinguals (French Guiana)
One pupil is a Spanish bilingual

Discussion points

- From the list above, which children would benefit the most (and who, the least) from being included in the French lessons? Why?
- What might be influencing your opinion?
- Look back at the five strands of the Languages Framework; are all strands relevant to all the children in the same way?
- Which strand can offer each group an opportunity to shine during the French lessons?

We would very much hope that all the pupils above are included in your FL lessons. Not only are languages compulsory at that age, but every child also has the right to participate. Every child has the right to receive an education that engages with the Purpose of Study, where teachers can 'foster pupils' curiosity and deepen their understanding of the world' (DfE 2013).

When asked about why language learning is important, it is common to have the response that learning a language enriches our lives. But perhaps what is not so common is to be told that Primary language learning is complementary to the skills development which includes learning about and through language that is going on elsewhere in the curriculum. It supports generic literacy skills and facilitates the revisiting and consolidation of concepts and skills learnt in the first language. It provides excitement, enjoyment and challenge for children and teachers, helping to create enthusiastic learners and to develop positive attitudes to language learning throughout life. The natural links between languages and other areas of the curriculum can enhance the overall teaching and learning experience.

As teachers of languages we find opportunities to fly the flag for languages. On 26 September each year across this country and other European countries, we celebrate European Day of Languages in schools. In 2015 the submission to its annual competition in England produced an overwhelming expression of concerns and wishes for world peace. Experiences like this in primary schools are becoming more common, where teachers run with their creativity and enthusiasm for languages and inevitably this creates a positive ripple effect on children's enthusiasm, their love of languages and their understanding of how interconnected they are to the rest of the world. However, less widely known or appreciated is the knowledge and understanding of how language learning continues to enrich our lives past Primary Curriculum and education. It comes from a report commissioned by the European Commission (SCILT Report 2009) summarizing the potential benefits as follows:

- Enhanced mental flexibility
- Enhanced problem-solving ability (including organizational skills)
- Expanded metalinguistic ability (intercultural skills)
- Enhanced learning capacity
- Enhanced interpersonal ability (team-working/communication and presentation skills/perception of the perspective of others)
- Reduced age-related mental diminishment (dementia, Alzheimer's).

Unlike the secondary context, having the easy opportunity of learning languages across the curriculum is one of the greatest assets in the primary setting – when delivered by the class teacher – and we will discuss this in detail in Chapter 5. This feature is what can make languages such an inclusive practice in a school, particularly among its staff, as different teachers have different strengths. For instance, for a teacher who is monolingual but has a keen interest in Art, teaching Spanish *through* Art may be less daunting than a 'Spanish lesson' as such. The language capital of the school staff can also inform what language is taught, so that a culture of support is more readily available, making monolingual teachers feel less isolated and more encouraged.

Summary

So what is the state of primary languages? It is not blooming yet, although compulsory status has had an immediate impact. Nonetheless, it could be flourishing in a few years from here, when schools' senior leaders recognize language learning as another valuable skill to develop in our children, when a reversal takes place in the reduction of training opportunities for practising teachers and when the challenges facing primary languages provision are confronted effectively. We will explore some of these in greater detail in subsequent chapters.

Who delivers the FL in the primary classroom is crucial. We need to look beyond mere language expertise and centre our teaching and learning around primary pedagogy, borrowing from all the richness this area has to offer, and then apply it to the FL context. The Languages Framework has done an excellent job of just this.

All children have a right to experience the learning of a FL in a formal setting. This can help them unpick the process explicitly, supporting their independence as language learners – as much of the FL as of their mother tongue – as well as providing them with a view of the different world of possibilities out there.

Recommended reading

Deutscher, G. (2010). *Through the Language Glass: Why the World Looks Different In Other Languages*. New York: Metropolitan Books/Henry Holt and Co., 2010.

McLachlan, A. (2009). Modern languages in the primary curriculum: Are we creating conditions for success? *The Language Learning Journal*, 37:2.

Rowe, J., Herrera, M., Hughes, B. and Cawley, M. (2012). Capacity building for primary languages through initial teacher education: could specialist and non-specialists student teachers' complementary skills provide a winning combination? *The Language Learning Journal*, 40:2, 143–56.

Tierney, D. (2016). *Foreign language teaching in the primary school: meeting the demands – In Applied Linguistics and Primary School Teaching* – Cambridge University Press (2016).

Chapter 3
Languages as an Irresistible Activity

Are you in earnest? Seize this very minute! Boldness has genius, power, and magic in it. Only engage, and then the mind grows heated. Begin, and then the work will be completed.

Attributed to Goethe

Chapter objectives

- To examine and address some of the apprehensions monolingual teachers have around delivering languages;
- to explore what motivating teachers entails on the personal and school leadership level;
- to consider issues around expertise, values and attitudes that support long-term and short-term visions within language teaching in the primary context;
- to reflect on how motivating children in the right way will encourage them to become independent learners, with a lifelong love and appreciation for languages.

In this chapter we will explore the four important pillars that sustain an effective primary languages community. Our aim is to demonstrate that in order to motivate learners we need to think about motivating teachers as well – making learning a language an irresistible endeavour for all. We also warn about the dangers of viewing and reducing primary languages learning to 'fun and games', a superficial approach that may only serve the short-term engagement – or rather, 'entertainment' of children, with little impact on lasting, long-term motivation to learn languages. Some of the activities referred to in this chapter are further explored and exemplified across the book.

Figure 3.1 Working towards a primary languages community of practice

Motivating the teachers

The position of FLs in the Primary Curriculum has been in question for some time as we have seen in earlier chapters. To some extent some of these issues have been resolved. FLs are now statutory, part of the foundation KS2 curriculum, and schools need to provide at least one hour of language learning to pupils, once a week. The reality however is very different, and this section will explore what in fact may be hindering the real success of primary languages in the broader picture, and what you, as an interested party, can do to champion the cause.

A study published in 2013 by Kathrine Legg found that 66 per cent of those teachers interviewed believed that schools should endeavour to offer FL learning. The study was specifically looking at teachers' opinions on the importance and place of languages in the Primary Curriculum. After reading this, you may well ask why we have spent so much time validating FL learning in the primary, since an overwhelming percentage of primary colleagues understand its value and importance in the primary programme of learning. Part of the problem may be with the amount of support (content and pedagogy) that motivated teachers are offered in schools in order to build on that motivation. The issue lies in what Robin Alexander (1989) refers to as the 'how' and the 'what' of education. He argues that the primary community do not speak the same language to each other. That is to say that the discourse of teachers about the curriculum and its process from policy to actual programme of study in schools is scant and does not encourage or contribute to address the complexity of curriculum issues. He highlighted that unless dilemmas can be acknowledged they cannot be freely discussed. There is evidence that some primary schools (Language Trends Survey 2016) are still encountering challenges around the teaching of primary languages. These issues exist in primary schools partly due to a failure to implement systematic and consistent language teaching, and yet, a huge majority of schools which responded to the survey between November and December 2015 believe that learning of languages broadens pupils' cultural awareness and confidence, improving literacy and preparing pupils for the world of work.

> Many teachers also believe that language learning can help pupils with English as an Additional Language (EAL) to shine, and those pupils who may be doing less well in other subjects sometimes thrive in languages.
>
> (Language Trends Survey 2016)

Motivational factors are important for primary schools to consider as part of their organizational performance. What is central to Primary Curriculum organization is that teachers are effective because they are well-trained and also because they are motivated to teach the agreed curriculum. But which comes first? Regardless of these pivotal factors around motivation of teachers, it is interesting to note that there is little research into the motivational professional learning of teachers who are preparing to teach primary languages or are already teaching it.

Unless teachers are motivated and school leaders know the motivating and demotivating factors of teachers, schools cannot be effective or cost-effective in relation to the recruitment and retention of teachers (Addison and Brundrett 2008). Unless research into primary FL learning delve further into the methods of motivating staff based on empirical evidence, we will continue to rely on hearsay by popular press to determine how to manage the motivating or demotivating factors at play.

Research on general teacher motivation has thrown up some possible areas of exploration. It has shown, for instance, that teachers are most likely to be motivated when their individual needs are fulfilled (Addison and Brundrett 2008); they feel adequately remunerated (Bellot and Tutor 1990); or through 'extrinsic' factors such as rewards for good practice (Azumi and Lerman 1987), although this varies depending on more specific teacher characteristics. Another study suggested that teachers prioritize the needs which will influence their performance during teaching rather than the monetary value attached to the profession (Gokce 2010). This places school leadership decisions on the teaching and learning priorities of the school under the spot light, as they are responsible for judging the performance of newly qualified teachers.

Teaching is renowned the world over for not being a well-paid profession, therefore, those who enter it usually know what to expect to some extent, and may rely on their 'vocation' to carry them through. However, in Britain at least, the burnout rate is considerable and many leave after six years or so. Despite this, many more continue to enter through the gates.

> **Pause for thought**
>
> **Questions to encourage discussion:**
>
> - Why did you join the profession?
> - How will those reasons affect your motivation around FL teaching? – motivation to engage with things you may not have otherwise engaged with (i.e. learning a new language, PE, art or music).
> - If you consider to have 'the right reasons' which promote the right kind of personal motivation in terms of teaching and learning a language, how do you plan to sustain this motivation?
> - If you already can speak a FL, how might you help motivate colleagues who feel apprehensive about having to teach it?

Whatever the nature of your responses, and no doubt it will be different for each teacher who is asked this question, one aspect remains steady, and it is not about the paycheque or the holidays but, as Sinclair (2008) identified, it is the intellectual stimulation and challenge that the profession allows. Also, the thought of impacting on young lives in significant ways, and thus, impacting on the future of a generation can also be a motivating factor, as can be seen in many television commercials seeking to recruit teachers. There is a personal expectation that when we join the profession, we will carry on learning and growing ourselves and in the process we will sustain not just our own motivation for learning but that of our pupils too, for, whatever we do in the classroom, motivation of pupils is at the core. Figure 3.2 is one of two images, with its twin in Chapter 5, Figure 2.

What are the factors then which influence motivation around the teaching of primary languages? And more importantly, how can we support and nurture resilience in language learning in primary schools? We can start perhaps by exploring what it means to be a primary teacher who delivers a FL.

Just as we need to know something about mathematics, history or geography in order to teach it, so we also need to know something about the FL we intend to teach. In the same way that we do not have to know all the primary geography or science curriculum at once and perfectly, we do not need to become fluent nor intermediate speakers of a FL in order to engage with it. What we are saying though is that we do need to be enthusiastic and interested in those areas of learning. We need to be prepared to be good beginners at least, and if we already speak a FL, we need to understand primary languages pedagogy as well as providing support and encouragement to those colleagues who do not speak the TL. This is one of the conditions upon which we chose to become primary teachers.

So what does a primary language teacher do? Just like for any other subject, we learn and we continue to learn. In fact, teaching is a profession where, unless you keep on learning, you will leave your passion behind. In the image below, some of the clues as to how we might engage with languages are staring us in the face. This is because, unless you are a linguist at heart, motivation may not be found in the foreign words themselves, but in the cultural context the words are in.

Figure 3.2 Motivating teachers to meet the challenge

Within the literature delving into the motivation of teachers, words such as 'morale', 'commitment' or 'satisfaction within the profession are often used to jolt discussion on the subject, however, this multifaceted issue of motivation remains hard to pin down.

> Whatever term is used, motivation is not just about being 'happy' or 'satisfied' (Dinham and Scott 1998); it is, as Molander and Winterton (1994) indicate, about the willingness of a member of staff to expend effort in the fulfillment of his/her role.
> Addison, R. and Brundrett, M. (2008)

This 'effort' will be more willingly spent when motivation is high, and in order to do this in an unthreatening way, we need to open windows before opening the door. This is to say, giving teachers the opportunity to appreciate the TL culture before we ask them to learn its words. Following the rationale for intercultural understanding discussed in the previous chapter, to teach a language successfully you will need to get acquainted with some of the cultural elements of the target country that may interest you (its music, art, customs, literature, etc.). By reading the literature in translated form for instance, you will learn a great deal about the TL culture which you can then bring into the classroom through the use of discussion, video, drama, art, etc. (we will also give some examples of this in the next chapters). It would be rather concerning then if teachers were not outward looking or interested in the world around them; making explicit links to the interconnected and globalized society children find and will continue to find themselves in, despite Brexit and the sad current climate of intolerance.

Motivating teachers then is one of the first pillars in the school language community, and it will involve an awareness of, and openness towards teachers' likes and dislikes, interests and passions. If we see languages as a vehicle of expression, then we must be careful to encourage all relevant forms and not to censor or dictate the content of that expression too much, lest we risk an atmosphere of demotivation instead. This is one of the greatest assets of languages after all; serving as a medium and not the message itself opens up endless possibilities – for teachers can use their own passions as content. Many teachers, for instance, love history. Understanding who we are in terms of our past and the past of others can be challenging (as much research in the teaching of history shows), and it will inevitably take us on a present and historical journey out of England and out of Europe.

Languages have always evolved in an atmosphere of controversy, of the triumphs and of humiliations of different people, a very current topic in our times, and perhaps when hasn't it been so? Human movement whether physical or in ideas has invariably led to conflict in some form or another. If we look at our social and political climate we can appreciate that children are often the unwilling victims – directly and indirectly – of conquests and invasions, present and past, and it may help them to realize that adults do acknowledge and are able to contain these issues, that teachers are capable of dealing overtly and critically with them, as exemplified in the activity below (Ambrossi 2014), designed to encourage teachers to see the bigger picture of languages.

The activity is meant to prod teachers' curiosity about language by linking it with history. It can be done with a younger audience too. It shows how the movement of people (through conquest and invasion) impacts on language. We usually ask students to do this in groups while listening to 'La Pastora' by Spanish group Radio Tarifa (available in YouTube). We give them about five minutes to do question 1 (with a prize for the most correct answers!). We then discuss point 2 in groups and as a whole class. We look at the last point (Hindu-Arabic numbers) as an example of how we take for granted our own origins and the origin of everyday concepts (and shapes), like numbers.

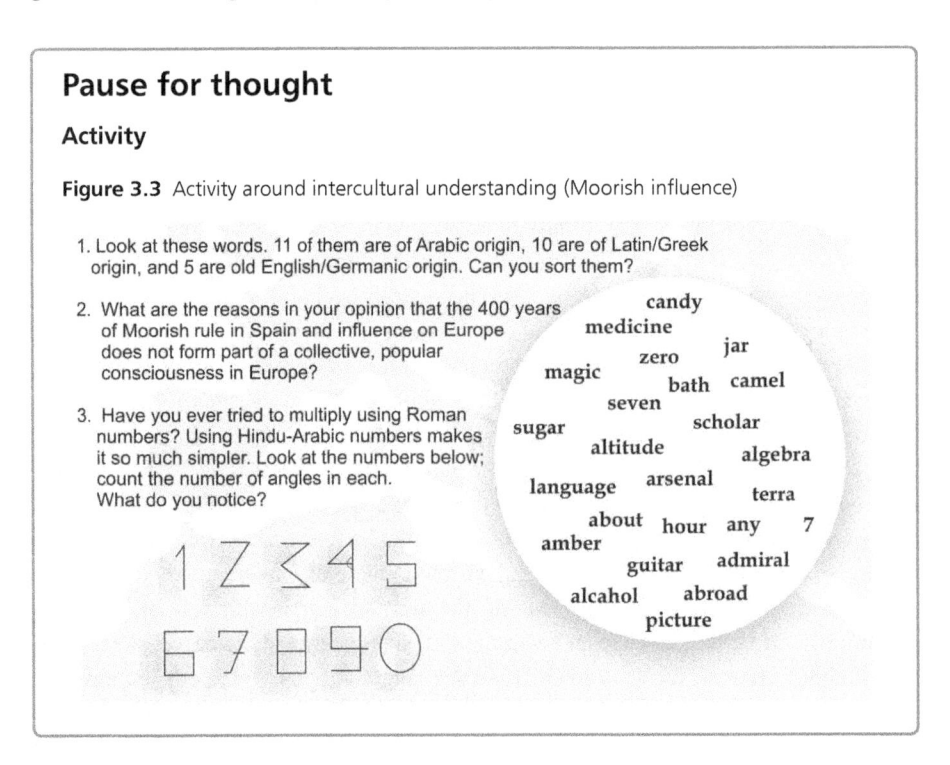

> **Pause for thought**
>
> **Activity**
>
> **Figure 3.3** Activity around intercultural understanding (Moorish influence)
>
> 1. Look at these words. 11 of them are of Arabic origin, 10 are of Latin/Greek origin, and 5 are old English/Germanic origin. Can you sort them?
>
> 2. What are the reasons in your opinion that the 400 years of Moorish rule in Spain and influence on Europe does not form part of a collective, popular consciousness in Europe?
>
> 3. Have you ever tried to multiply using Roman numbers? Using Hindu-Arabic numbers makes it so much simpler. Look at the numbers below; count the number of angles in each. What do you notice?
>
> 1 2 3 4 5
> 6 7 8 9 0
>
> candy, medicine, magic, seven, sugar, altitude, language, arsenal, about, amber, guitar, alcahol, abroad, picture, zero, jar, bath, camel, scholar, algebra, terra, hour, any, 7, admiral

You would have probably needed to do a bit of online research to sort these words out had we not provided the answers at the end of the chapter, but you will, for instance, notice that the number 7 is a Hindu-Arabic number, and yet its name, 'seven' is of Latin origin (in Spanish-speaking countries this number is often written, 7).

Teacher motivation then can be a very personal issue, but it is also affected by organizational factors. We will look at how the school organization can promote language learning presently, but let us mention another important element. Talking to many primary colleagues in schools, the constant and repeated barriers reported to impact negatively on language delivery are to do with performance-orientated ethos in schools. This means that many schools insist on the notion that they need to teach 'to the test'; maximizing test performance by supporting more able pupils to move to the next level and hence making a difference to the school's league table position for the core subjects. The main knock-on implication of this is that languages (or any other foundation subject) may be pushed aside to make room for 'more practice for maths' or 'more input for Literacy'. You will soon notice your school's take on this by their attitude towards the foundation subjects. The second implication may be the danger of approaching assessment for languages in similar formal styles. There is no fixed assessment procedure for primary languages yet, but we need to think carefully about ways of assessing FLs that do not discourage, discriminate, humiliate, stress out or put off learners and their teachers. We will explore these issues on the chapter on assessment.

As teachers our role is to enable children to build on their existing knowledge as well as develop new understandings and skills, but we need to start with ourselves; the significant adults around. What better opportunity is there than to tap into what is of interest to us as adults, and see how we may turn our knowledge into a fountain

Figure 3.4 Motivation acting on teaching and learning

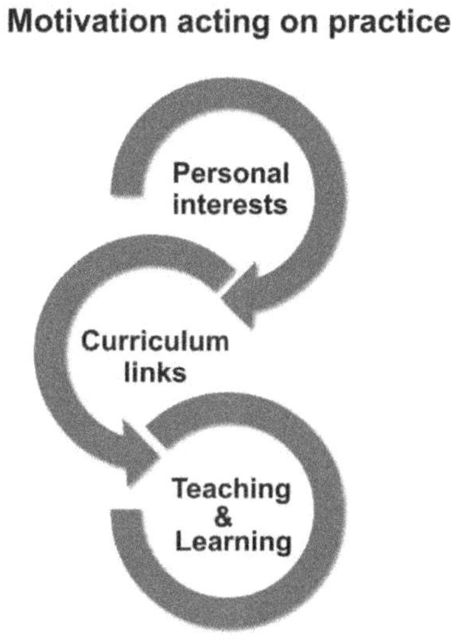

Motivation acting on practice

- Personal interests
- Curriculum links
- Teaching & Learning

of motivation for children in relevant ways. This will involve creative and cross-curricular thinking (we will explore cross-curricular activities in depth in Chapter 5). The diagram and case scenario below exemplify how this process may begin.

> ## Case scenario: Teacher's personal interests
>
> A teacher who is very keen on the Arts wants to use this media to deliver languages (French), which she once did at GCSE (but needs to refresh a great deal). She wants to bring Art and French together and allow the children to have effective learning experiences of both. She is particularly keen on Paul Cézanne and hopes to base a small until of work around his work. Hers is a class of 10-year-olds, who have been doing some French for the last two years.
>
> Starting from a personal comfort zone gives her a sense of control and ownership over the possible outcomes. The text below shows how this process might begin, and Chapter 5 will explore how it can unfold in greater detail.
>
> She loves Paul Cézanne because, when she was a little girl, it had been the first real painting she had ever seen while visiting a French gallery with her father during a holiday. It always made her think of summer and bright colours. As an adult she later learnt that Cézanne is considered the 'father' of artists like Matisse and Picasso, by both French people and artists themselves. Apples and oranges were Cézanne's favourite objects to paint. He is reported to have said that while he was painting fruit he was trying to get closer to the promise land. The 'promise land' is perhaps, Cézanne's way of saying he was after what is true and authentic in nature as well as in people. Remembering his paintings from childhood, she also remembers how seeing the fruit gave her then the sense that she too could draw and paint these solid forms from observation. While researching online, she comes across a book called 'Mon petit Cézanne' by Marie Sellier, as well as a story called 'Cézanne and the Apple Boy' by Laurence Anholt, which portrays the kind of father Cézanne might have been. She thinks that perhaps Cézanne's paintings appear simple to children because they portray objects or human figures easily recognizable by them. It is almost as though children can get lost in this world which acknowledges the life they are used to seeing around them transformed and preserved for ever in a painting. As adults we can recognize some of this as, 'still nature'.
>
> Questions to aid discussion
>
> - What do you think might be the teacher's next step in this process?
> - Can you think of any possible directions this personal interest might take in terms of classroom activities/discussion related to the five strands in the Languages Framework?
> - Can you do a similar thought process around a particular interest of yours?

While tapping into this teacher's own bank of knowledge and resources, there will be an element of raised self-esteem for both teacher and pupils. Through the teacher's enthusiasm for the topic, there is the shared understanding between them that learning goes beyond the immediacy of the learning objectives and that in fact learning about

Cézanne in the language classroom provides context and meaningful connections so that pupils can transfer their knowledge and understanding into other contexts of learning or of simply living.

We are motivated to create meaningful learning when we have at least part of ourselves in a comfort zone, when we have something to grab onto. It is our experiences after all which form the essence of who we are, and which can feed into our confidence and motivation to reach just a little bit further. We need to use our personal experience to inform our motivation, which in turn can frame our practice, allowing our interests or passions to come through, giving us the possibility of creativity.

A teacher's motivation is as multifaceted as the motivation of pupils. With that in mind, we ask you to boldly go where your interest lies, because the only risk you face is to engage learners in something new.

We began this section by looking at the four pillars that support an effective community of primary languages practice, and we will conclude by reframing the concept in terms of the sequence of events, or the hierarchy that allows this in more precise ways; what we believe needs to be in place for primary teachers in order to successfully deliver primary languages while at the same time feeling nurtured, and able to sustain their own motivation. As Anna Lise Gordon (2016) highlights and queries:

> Do we have a clear sense of direction for the language teaching and learning in our school? How well do we communicate this sense of purpose? Do pupils share our purpose? Do we feel supported by senior management?
>
> Gordon, A. L. (2016)

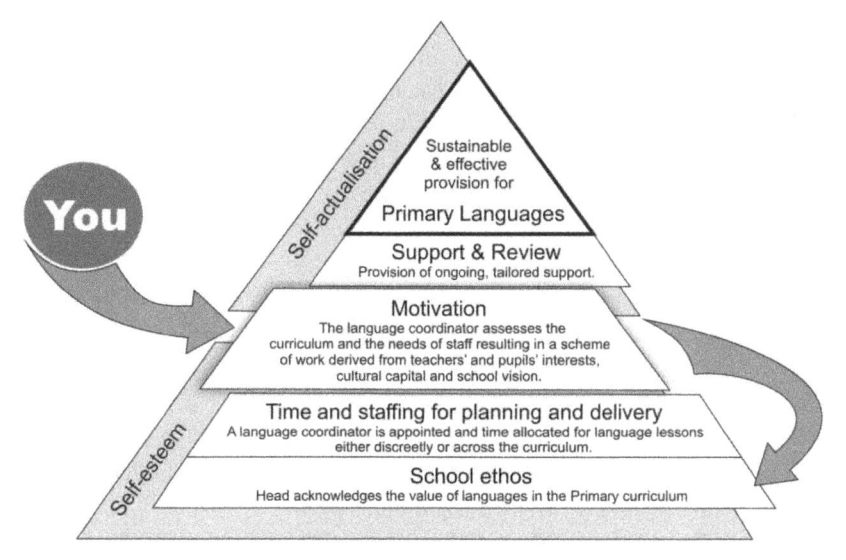

Figure 3.5 Building an effective and sustainable community of practice for FL teaching and learning

Together with these points above, you may think that a school that has not been proactive in their FL delivery is a somewhat disappointing situation to find yourself in. Well, it depends. One of the advantages of not finding an effective language delivery system in place is the possibility it gives you as a motivated language teacher, to start one yourself. Where there are no clear structures there is room for creativity. You need to envision the language community of practice that you would like to be part of, and work towards it. Maybe even become the language coordinator yourself (a clear vision and good professional relationships with colleagues really are more important than the language skill) and present your initial three-year plan to the Head.

Superimposed on Maslow's top two sections of the hierarchy of needs, the triangle above highlights the organizational and practice conditions we believe are prerequisite to the successful teaching of primary languages by class teachers. Until primary schools begin to prioritize the motivational needs of their teachers, confidence in teaching languages will remain an issue. However, it can take just one, highly committed individual to make a difference and change an entire organization. It could be you.

Children's right to explore new worlds and new visions

Our question in this chapter thus far has been how to motivate teachers to engage with languages, exploring how school ethos and attitudes to supporting them can be best approached. The ultimate aim of course is to empower teachers so that they may create opportunities to engage and motivate the children about languages, particularly by nurturing their curiosity. A difference will be made between looking at motivation to participate in class as opposed to motivation to learn a FL, for they are not necessarily the same thing.

Research on motivation is vast. Most teachers are familiar with the terms intrinsic and extrinsic motivation, a dualism approach that sees motivation as something that is triggered internally or externally. 'Numerous studies, based on self-determination theory, have linked intrinsic motivation to learn – a child motivated to learn for their own private reasons, with positive emotional health, persistence, academic engagement, mindfulness, and achievement' (Froiland, Mayor and Herlevi 2015). Externally motivated children, on the other hand, are motivated solely either by outside incentives (a reward) or by the nature of the situation they find themselves in (i.e. playing a game,) which could be seen as entertainment rather than intellectual engagement. However, this is not quite so black and white. How might we classify, for instance, the motivation to please adults or a strong desire to get a good grade? Another dualism approach that more adequately responds to the challenge is that of instrumental and integrative orientations to motivation.

> An instrumental orientation referred to the practical reasons for language learning without strong interest in getting closer to the community of speakers of that language, whereas integrative orientation was defined as openness to identification with the speaking community (Masgoret and Gardner 2003).
>
> (Young 2015, p. 370)

The issue however, is much more complex still, and a different, multifaceted approach to motivation is now more in favour. How does, for instance, socio-psychological factors like community/family or anxiety impact on motivation? There are many things that contribute to the motivation 'on display' that teachers can appreciate in the language classroom.

Take the following affective and cognitive, personal and interpersonal variables below, and think how they may affect your pupils' motivation to 'participate' (if we take participation as a measure of motivation, whether listening, repeating or producing language) and contrast it to their motivation to learn a language (how likely they are to want to continue learning languages beyond primary). In other words, does motivation to participate necessarily translate into motivation to learn a language? What behaviours would you expect from one or the other? You may tick as you judge.

Notice that we are not measuring motivation in terms of grade attainment, as this is seen as a rather instrumental orientation, particularly favoured by policy

Variables that may act on motivation to...	Participate	Continue learning
Competitiveness		
Goal setting		
Opportunity for dialogue (from content)		
Self-esteem		
Self-perception of low/high ability		
Beliefs around language learning (from school/home)		
Peer interactions		
Classroom procedures (expectations, routines, homework)		
Classroom context (teacher, groupings, use of resources, ethnicities)		
Testing		
Formative feedback		
Other (there are many)		

requiring an easy unit of measurement which throws little light on actual learning and motivation.

From the list above, what variables are more likely to determine a long-lasting motivation for language learning? More importantly, how can we, as teachers, pursue longer-term motivation for languages as well as participation in class? The answer is as complex as each individual case, but this in turn contains a tantalizing clue, for it is our individual selves, our unique histories and experiences (as teachers and children), which, with imagination, can be used to make a difference.

General Strategies
social and emotional learning
collaborative learning
peer tutoring
talking about learning
feedback

The items above have been shown to be among some of the most effective general pedagogical tools (EEF 2016). Bearing these in mind, where would they fit within the list above? The key question for us is, does delivering languages in the primary classroom, solely through 'fun and games', gets children motivated to learn languages, particularly in the long term? If the extensive research carried out by the EEF is anything to go by, we believe that we need opportunity for dialogue within our language lessons in order to engage children rather than entertain them. The theme of a language lesson can in fact be anything (learning about public transport is not more important than learning about the solar system), and this, 'anything' is an opportunity to find the right and relevant content that children would benefit from discussing as well as an opportunity for novel or different ideas that may challenge them. For instance, themes that revolve around social and emotional well-being could be used to introduce language of emotions where words are not just learnt through a game but also discussed or explored to their fullest. Social and emotional learning (SEL) approaches, which look at school ethos and how children relate to others, have shown that

> On average, SEL interventions have an identifiable and significant impact on attitudes to learning, social relationships in school, and attainment itself (four months' additional progress on average).
>
> EEF 2016

Take the French and Spanish word for 'sad', *triste*, pronounced slightly different in each case (Google translate is currently the easiest online tool to hear pronunciation).

Figure 3.6 Search engines can be used as a quick access to FL audio files

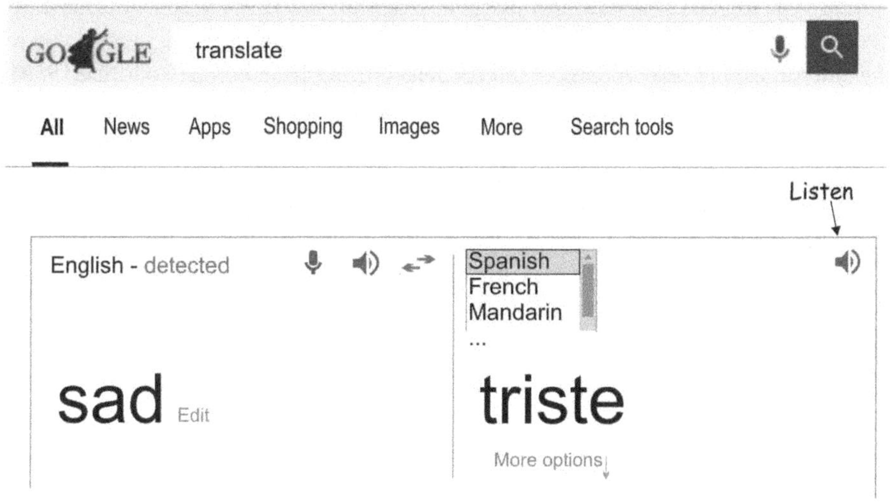

You might want to mindfully experience the 'feel' of this word in your mouth as you say it, and think that, for the French or Spanish, this sound has negative connotations or associations. What does this mean? Can the mere sound of words carry a feeling? Maybe you can get the children to borrow these new words when they feel particular emotions and in this way you get them to pay attention to these emotions.

Language learning strategies (the art of learning) which implies metacognition and self-regulation should involve dialogue as much as it can involve rote learning, and it helps children become independent learners,

> Self-regulation means managing one's own motivation towards learning. The intention is often to give pupils a repertoire of strategies to choose from during learning activities.
>
> Meta-cognition and self-regulation approaches have consistently high levels of impact, with pupils making an average of eight months' additional progress. The evidence indicates that teaching these strategies can be particularly effective for low achieving and older pupils.
>
> EEF 2016

Motivating children then needs to be a multifaceted endeavour too, where games do have a place, but only a place – not the whole stage. In order to motivate language learning rather than just participation in any given activity, we need to engage children's powers of reflection, imagination and wonder. It is the content of discussions (as opposed to the form) that can allow this to happen.

In the light of recent events like the polemic return to a grammar school culture, it is worth reflecting on the fountains of knowledge that were opened to all those children who learnt the grammar of Latin and ancient Greek (hence the name 'grammar' school). Much of this ancient knowledge has now been translated 'en mass' into

English and various languages, allowing anyone *so inclined*, to access, read and ponder over it, and subsequently possibly even act under its influence. We draw attention to the phrase 'so inclined' because it hides an enormity of issues related to the cultural capital that children – and teachers – bring from home (Bourdieu 1986). We refer mainly to 'relational' cultural capital as described by Tramonte and Willms (2010), which involves the cultural interactions and conversations between children and parents, rather than their economic status. There is a similarity between languages and technology which exemplifies the impact of relational capital on people's attitude to learning. Both FLs and technology offer access to information, and information or, 'intelligence' as it used to be called, carries power. In both cases, it is the attitudes of the user that make the difference. Technology, for instance, claims to have brought an equality of 'opportunity to access knowledge' (power) to the masses. It is, however, not so very many that make use of these opportunities (Selwyn 2007).

Why might this be? Why is it that those taking advantage of the opportunity for equal access to knowledge are the same who, before computers, would go and get information from the library? In other words, not the masses. Of course, in countries without easy access to libraries – but equal amount of curiosity – technology may have been a life changer. With FLs something similar happens in that the fact that translation, like technology, has made it possible to have easier access to certain type of information, it only seems to work in principle, that is, access in itself does not guarantee usage. It is the desire to access knowledge in the first place that makes the difference. How is this relevant to motivating children? It is simply the fact that for those children who do not have a rich relational capital at home, the desire to want to learn and to challenge their intellect may not get a chance to flourish. The teacher then can take a central role by encouraging their curiosity and modelling the desire to learn. The desire to know (our motivation) is linked to our sense of curiosity, which we all applaud in children, but which somehow so many manage to lose by the time we are adults. More on this issue in the chapter on creativity, but suffice to say for now that curiosity needs to be nurtured if it is to be turned into the act of seeking further

Figure 3.7 Availability of information does not imply usage

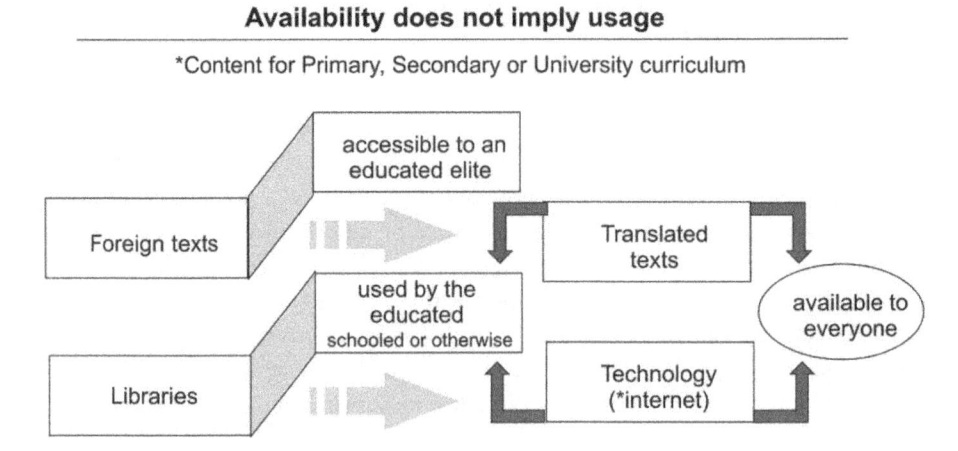

Availability does not imply usage

*Content for Primary, Secondary or University curriculum

knowledge as adults, because it is the way in which we are brought up and educated, by either parents or school, which will impact on our approach to life's experiences, including our motivation to learn and to keep on learning (the art of being).

When we speak about motivation to learn or acquire knowledge, it becomes important to differentiate 'knowledge' from 'information' in the modern context. The line dividing knowledge from information is not easily drawn in these times of ever-increasing interconnectivity between fields, subject areas and methods (Where does Chemistry end and Physics begin?). For the ease of discussion in this book, we see 'information' as units of facts about any particular topic. By knowledge we mean the act of understanding, internalizing and manipulating this information from personalized viewpoints. Thus, although ten people may have the same information, each may use it or interpret it differently, even if they have a similar agenda, depending on their previous understandings and information bank. A *guru* would be a typical example of someone with vast amounts of a particular kind of knowledge to a positive and altruistic end which some may call wisdom. The internet, an example of vast amounts of information, for better or worse, real or fake, often referred to as a 'sea of information' but with no arrived-at wisdom (not yet).

It is the difference between information and knowledge that seems to divide how teachers approach motivation in language (or any subject) teaching. Knowledge-based activities require dialogue and reappraisal, favouring a constructivist approach to teaching and learning. Information-based activities, on the other hand, lend themselves to behaviourist approaches; the 'passing down' of key facts or words, like learning phrases and vocabulary through games.

As mentioned earlier, games do have a place in the primary classroom (in any classroom in fact), as they are a very clever disguise for rote learning. There is no shortage of ideas on games for the classroom in books and online, and the trick is to

Figure 3.8 Games get children excited about the game

find the right one for your purposes. As a beginning teacher you will have come across different games that seek to motivate learning in different areas of the curriculum, and you can always adapt some of these games for the language classroom.

Games employed to motivate learners come in the following contexts:

- Starter activity (consolidating/checking previous learning necessary for current lesson)
- After main introduction (to consolidate or assess new learning)
- Plenary (to check understanding/ assess learning)
- Homework (online games to deepen or consolidate learning)

It is useful to have in mind the five strands of the Framework for Languages (next chapter) in order to classify games. In this way we can make sure that we are considering – within any unit of work – all the different aspects of language learning. In this section, we will consider the value of games rather than the games themselves (for varied example on games and resources refer to Chapter 8). Thus, seen through the lens of the Languages Framework, games can involve,

Literacy and Oracy:

1 Listening (spotting sounds or words in songs, poems, videos);

2 Speaking (repeating the above, Chinese whispers, audio making, etc.);

3 Reading (spotting patterns, scanning for words/information);

4 Writing (copying with a purpose, simple poetry, blogs, posters, etc.)

Intercultural Understanding:

1 Playing a typical French or Spanish game or activity (inside or outside the classroom)

Knowledge about Language, and Language Learning Strategies

1 Games involving grammar rules (sorting, matching, adjectival agreement, etc.)

2 Games involving dictionary use (translation, gender, spelling, etc.)

Games can be individual, in pairs or in groups. Many of the game areas above can be done through the media of technology, which children tend to gravitate towards. However, technology changes faster than school practices and it is better to consult with the ICT coordinator in your school to see what is available, and more importantly, what is relevant to, or best supports the learning you are after. Children can be greatly motivated by the use of computers, but as some research suggests, this does not necessarily translate into a motivation for (or learning of) the subject content itself (Burnett 2010).

Whatever the motivating game may be, whether traditional or through the use of technology, you need to think carefully about the features and affordances of the game and how these support the particular learning you are after. Almost any game will keep a child busy, but your objective is to facilitate learning above all, and to this end your game needs to be carefully chosen and adapted.

Case scenario

Games can be competitive or collaborative. Which do you prefer? Which do the children prefer? Can they be both at the same time?

Below are four examples of how activities can motivate children.

- Spelling Bingo (Literacy).

    Pupils in pairs or individually have a card with all the foreign vocabulary (just learnt) written down. Teacher begins to say, one by one, in English, some of the same vocabulary. If the pupils spot the right word (the translation) on their card, they can put a cross over it. The first pupil to have a complete line wins.

- Homework (Listening).

    Children have to log into the site *PiliPop Español*, and play a game related to recognizing numbers.

- Pronunciation (Oracy).

    One child volunteers to leave the room. A red object is hidden somewhere in the classroom. The class has been instructed that as soon as the volunteer walks back in, the class has to start chanting the word 'red' (in Spanish) over and over, changing the volume based on how near or far the volunteer is to the hidden red object as he or she looks for it (whisper when far, loud when near). No other clue as to the object's whereabouts is given. The volunteer is invited to come back in and the game starts.

- Spelling and grammar (KAL, LLS and Literacy).

    Children have to use the dictionaries in order to find as many words with the letter *ñ* as they can, BUT, you divide the class in two; one side can only collect **feminine** nouns and the other half can only collect **masculine** nouns. No other word class is accepted. They only have five minutes.

- Intercultural Understanding (with Oracy).

    Children in pairs have to create a short animated video using a software called Puppet Pals. The setting (background image) can be anywhere in a French-speaking country. The dialogue is a simple greeting of characters (name, plus age or any other information in French children can recall or obtain), and a simple reason for why they are in that particular location (i.e. J'adore la plage). At the end of the session, they watch each other's productions.

Discussion points

- Which of the activities above would you call 'a game'? Why?
- Are the activities entertaining, engaging or both?
- Go back to the previous small table of 'general effective strategies' and see how they match to these activities.
- Which activities are more likely to motivate children to want to continue learning languages?
- What have you seen done in your school?

The first example is a simple bingo game which children love in general, regardless of language or subject. Its aim is simply to recall meaning of foreign vocabulary in written form.

The second example asks children to use the Spanish game software *PiliPop Español*, where they can hear Spanish instructions and numbers, and drag items to find treasure. There are many commercial apps that help develop Oracy and Literacy. They're particularly good for pronunciation and vocabulary acquisition.

The third example seeks to get children to practise the *r* and *j* sounds in the Spanish word *rojo*, as well as encourage memorization. It is basically drill and rote learning made fun.

The fourth activity seeks to highlight various things such as the use of dictionary; a new letter (ñ); masculine and feminine gender, and nouns (by consciously discarding adjectives, verbs, adverbs, prepositions, etc.). This game has more possibilities still. You could ask the children to copy each found word, or even give them extra points if they use it in a simple sentence. Children can then divide tasks among themselves. This activity has an extra positive and very important aspect in that once finished you can discuss it with the children; What did we learn? Why might this or that be? Did they know that the European Union once proposed removing the letter ñ from keyboards in order to make Spanish more international? How do we feel about that?

The fifth activity uses ICT (a quick animation app) as a motivational tool. Children will be very engaged with this application as it is extremely easy and effective. Using user-friendly software will enable you to focus on the learning rather than on the technology itself. For this activity children have to discuss and plan. They have to search among the images you may have provided for them and choose one they like, during which they'll be exposed to images from abroad which hopefully will not be stereotypical. They will also have to record their voices, speaking some French in a non-threatening format, where they can edit and re-edit until satisfied. They can watch each other's productions and critique them. Interestingly too, they can upload their animations onto the school website platform and share them with parents, turning the children into authors.

The power of technology and the internet in particular is not really on the endless amounts of information it can contain; its power resides in the relational opportunities it offers (Lankshear and Knobel 2007), as in communication, distribution and authorship. These are issues beyond the remit of the school. Social media is not allowed in the classroom, but children are well acquainted with it and highly motivated to use it. However, what is partly within the remit of the classroom is how children engage critically with it and the type of information they choose to distribute and author. In other words, teachers have some say on the type of knowledge children may want to access online; have some influence on children's desire to know. Thus, a grammar schoolboy may have learnt ancient Greek through rote learning, but this act opened the gates of knowledge for him (usually a him back then), particularly if he had a good teacher or parent. Now, when his own children enjoy watching the film Percy Jackson and the Lightening Thief, and if there is a good relational capital at home, he knows exactly how to broaden the child's horizons and enthuse their curiosity further, by sharing with them – in story form, fragments of the real article (Homer's *Odyssey*).

The question is, does knowledge (not just information) in itself turn us into effective or motivating individuals? Not necessarily. The issue is in how it was developed. Was knowledge developed through our curiosity and sense of wonder or through exams? Through dialogue or repetition and analysis? In the context of languages, it is through our social interactions that we learn how to use language effectively. The linguist Dr Daniel Dor, affirms that 'language is something that is bigger than the individual person ... the essence of language is in society – not the brain itself' (Dor 2011 talk). Mastering expression through language comes when our knowledge of social interactions allows us to choose the right kind and amount of words for a given moment or context. Words by themselves will not suffice. Words serve a higher purpose, and mastering a FL is no different; it requires knowledge rather than mere information (words). It is the art of learning.

There is a fine line between entertainment and engagement. In primary education, there is a danger that by constantly making activities 'fun' we are teaching the children that unless something is fun it is not worth learning. Is this what we want children to learn? How can we transmit the notion that hard work is also worthwhile? What does 'hard work' look like when learning a language? Motivation is the key. Often when we are engaged or engrossed in an activity that to others may be quite complex, we may seem in their eyes, hard at work. It is a matter of perspective, and only motivation and true engagement can make light of hard work.

Summary

ITT and schools have a responsibility to motivate teachers as much as they must motivate children. Learning a language is an activity vulnerable to be seen as a land of 'words and rules that need to be learned', and this in turn, brings about the notion of games as the best media, as children appear 'engaged', but where memory is the muscle mostly exercised. There is nothing wrong with this, but it cannot be the only approach.

When it comes to motivating children some activities lend themselves to more than just drill or passing the time. They can be a starting point for dialogue. Socio-constructivist approaches in the language classroom look at 'what we are doing, how and why', that is, the teacher and the children together, exploring and interrogating language, starting from children's curiosity, from their current perspectives and understandings. We will explore what this approach looks like in more detail in the next two chapters, for we believe that in order to motivate teachers and children beyond a moment in time, we must encourage their capacity to make connections across the curriculum, and to involve their creativity and sense of curiosity in some way, wherever possible.

Figure 3 answers on the origin of words,

- **a** Arabic origin: candy, jar, zero, sugar, algebra, arsenal, amber, alcohol, 7, guitar, admiral
- **b** Roman/Greek origin: medicine, magic, camel, seven, scholar, altitude, language, terra, picture, hour
- **c** Old English: bath, can, about, abroad, any

Recommended reading

Ambrossi, P. (2015). Language and Culture in Foreign Language Teaching. In *Exploring Education and Childhood: From Current Certainties to New Visions*. Taylor and Francis Inc., pp. 117–29.

Laird, E. (2007). Crusade, Historical fiction, Macmillan Press (excellent book to aid discussion for a year 5/6 audience).

Loo, Sai (2008). Teaching knowledge, work-based learning and life experiences – Paper presented at the British Educational Research Association Annual Conference, Heriot-Watt University, Edinburgh, 3–6 September 2008.

Pattison, E. M. (2014). 'It's important to put yourself in any lesson that you teach': Self-efficacy in action in the primary modern foreign languages classroom. *The Language Learning Journal*, 42(3), 334–45.

Tramonte, L. and Willms, D. (2010). Cultural capital and its effects on education outcomes. *Economics of Education Review*, 29(2), 200–13.

Chapter 4
Languages as a Practical Activity

Chapter objectives

- To appreciate how IU can underpin our language delivery, giving depth and context to the words and sounds children learn.
- To explore the different ways we can engage children meaningfully with listening, speaking, reading and writing in the TL.
- To explore how KAL can help children make sense of foreign grammatical structures by becoming aware of features and patterns across languages, and viewing grammar in a different light.
- To be explicit with children in terms of how we can use LLS to make us as independent as possible in our learning.

In this chapter, we will introduce you to the Languages Framework, (DfES 2005) not merely as it stands, but rather, we will use it as a starting point for discussion as we unpick the different areas that make up language teaching and learning. Thus, our departure from the framework will be one of overall vision rather than of content, that is to say, for us, IU is the most significant strand in the framework, the one in which all other strands nest in terms of purpose and motivation.

Offering children an enriching cultural purpose to language learning, a reason to want to understand and respond to something in the first place beyond behaviourist approaches, should be one of the most important aims in languages teaching and learning. In other words, the ultimate purpose of learning the words and sounds of an FL is to give us the opportunity to experience another culture from within. IU can motivate us to learn a language, and Oracy and Literacy can help us complete that journey.

Let us begin by reminding ourselves of the original purpose of this comprehensive document, which defines the areas children need to know and understand, 'in order to learn another language and reach a recognised level by the age of 11. It will also make a contribution to children's personal development, fostering their interest and understanding in their own culture and that of others' (DfES 2005, p. 3).

The introduction of the Framework for Languages in 2005 was a pivotal moment for primary languages. It gave form, direction and momentum to what was beginning to happen in some schools through the effective initiative of enthusiastic teachers and

Figure 4.1 Representation of the five strands within the Languages Framework

5	FRAMEWORK FOR LANGUAGES
O	ORACY — Listening and Speaking
L	LITERACY — Reading and Writing
IU	INTERCULTURAL UNDERSTANDING Learning about others' culture, examining our own.
KAL	KNOWLEDGE ABOUT LANGUAGES Examining patterns and structures (grammar).
LLS	LANGUAGES LEARNING STRATEGIES Acquiring skills that help us learn a new language.

Figure 4.2 Reconceptualization of the Languages Framework

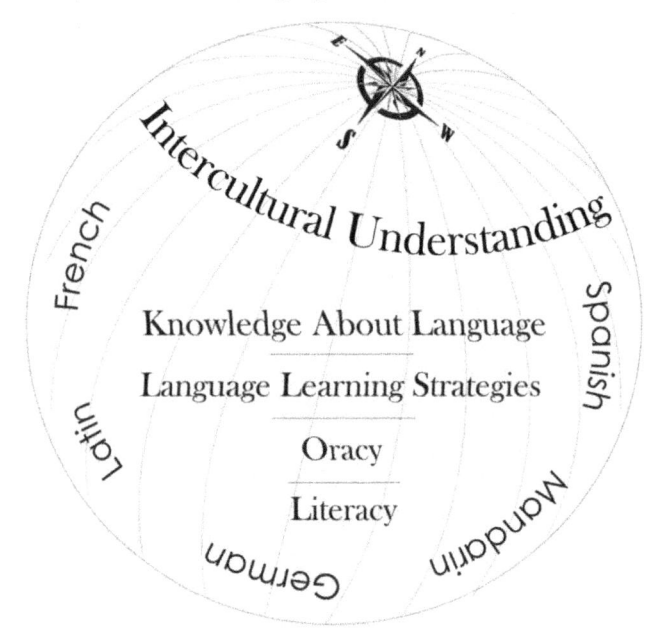

Heads. The framework brought together theory and practice around language learning and primary pedagogy, creating thus, an extremely useful guide for practitioners and primary language specialists. It also helped us view primary languages as not just a watered-down version of secondary pedagogy, but of a pedagogy of primary languages in its own right.

Much like Jones and Coffey propose, 'We embrace a broad vision of MFL and believe that it is only where language learning is narrowly defined as technical skill that pupil disaffection results.' (Jones and Coffey 2006, p. 138). Attempting to reconceptualize the framework from the outset will give you an idea of how the authors of this book view the interactions between the different strands, and how the chapter will unfold. Below is just one example of possibilities, but it offers a vision at a glance, strongly based on Byram's work in 1997 around cultural competencies – *savoir être* in particular – which we looked at in Chapter 1.

Intercultural understanding and the art of being

There is an incredibly vast set of literature around culture (Valdes 1986; Sercu, Bandura and Poloma 2005; Nunan and choi 2010 to name a few). The definition that best approaches our individual conceptualization of culture will depend on our life experiences. However, as teachers, our definition of culture needs to be broad and well informed, based on experiential as well as on codified knowledge. Our definition of culture needs to give us an awareness of, and make us sensitive to the experiences of others, less or more fortunate than ourselves. Where does, for instance, culture end and stereotypes begin? To what extent does our understanding of culture impact on our sense of identity or on the identity we impose on others? In this respect, it is also important to understand the interaction between 'culture' and 'identity', as these two terms are often used interchangeably but have, nevertheless, significant differences. The following quote gives a concise and effective definition of these two terms and their interaction, in terms of how we see them in this book,

> Culture, as we have said, has to do with the artefacts, ways of doing, etc. shared by a group of people. Identity is the acceptance and internalization of the artefacts and ways of doing by a member of that group.
>
> (Nunan et al. 2010, p. 5)

We could ask ourselves therefore, whether our sense of identity matches the culture we find ourselves in, and what it means to be, 'an outsider' compared to 'feeling' like an outsider. Internalizing the artefacts (elements) and ways of doing of a given culture could in fact be done remotely by members of a different culture who have been exposed to particular aspects of that 'more looked-up to' culture.

Pause for thought

Activity

Take a look at the following questions. Taken as 'themes' to work around, which child age-group would you say they are most appropriate for?

- What is culture?
- What is identity?

- How have cinema, television and the internet exported the artefacts and ways of doing of Western-European cultures?
- How has this impacted on non – Western-European cultures?
- What does 'globalization' mean in terms of culture and identity?

These are tough questions which would not be out of place in a citizenship or philosophy lesson, and while you may think that these are issues for older children only, you will find that the Primary Curriculum has plenty of opportunity for such topic during PSHE (personal, social, and health education), as well as primary philosophy which some schools deliver. It is important to realize that we can discuss almost any topic with young children, and that it is only in HOW we do so that marks the difference in terms of age appropriateness. As far as languages go, talking about other cultures cannot – should not – be avoided, unless the teacher is only interested in developing linguistic competence in the children, which would be a rather old-fashioned and poor approach to languages as well as unfair to the children who live in a more interconnected world. Focusing only on linguistic competency brings us to the tension between the use of TL in the classroom and the act of promoting dialogue and the exchange of complex ideas between teacher and children, and between children themselves. If the school's policy is to use an 'immersive' approach as far as possible (where only the TL is used during lessons), children will not be able to understand nor express curiosity or complex ideas about culture and identity. The primary classroom offers, however, the enviable possibility of cross-curricular approaches (explored in detail in Chapter 7). This means that, if there is a well-coordinated curriculum delivery design, children can discuss aspects of the target culture during other lessons (art, history, geography, PSHE, etc).

Culture occurs from within too. It is easier perhaps to see other cultures in the guise of 'other languages', but any one society has many mini-cultures within it – and we do not refer to different ethnic groups, but to any societal group that runs its day-to-day business in particular ways; having their own systems of doing things, communicating with each other, engaging in activities, etc. This has become known as 'communities of practice', the origins of which came from Lave's Situated Learning Theory. This theory views learning as an unintentional and situated event which takes place within authentic activity, context and culture. For instance, training to be a teacher and starting your first job as a teacher imply different types of learning. The rules for the second instance will not be written down anywhere (how you address your colleagues, what you may wear, where you may sit in the staff room, how you present an idea, professional etiquette, etc.). These rules are implicit in the practice, and you may find colleagues saying things like, 'This is not how we do things here', which alert you to a 'faux-pas' you may have made. In short, you learn these rules and ways of being by experiencing the authentic situation, through collaboration and interaction, having started from the periphery of a community of teachers and moved into its core, where you become a full member. This process of

Figure 4.3 Primary classroom in Spain

legitimate peripheral participation was coined by Lave and Wenger in 1991, and it is a useful tool for understanding the complexities of culture at a small scale. How do children, for instance, new to a school, manage to become one more member of a community of practice which may be quite alien to them (depending on where they come from), and how do we, as teachers, enable or hinder such process?

Pause for thought

Case scenario:

A teacher from England is participating in an exchange programme with Spain. On entering the Spanish school, where she will teach English as an FL, she notices children running and shouting in the corridor on their way to class and adults ignoring this behaviour. She also notices that when the teacher asks the class a question, children tend to shout-out the answer, with no hands-up. After a few days she has the opportunity to do an activity with the class, which she carefully prepares with the aim of moving away from the children's usual textbook learning. She asks the children (ten-year-olds) to work in groups so as to solve a word challenge. All children listen attentively and seem excited, but once the activity starts, chaos ensues and their usual class teacher has to intervene.

Questions:

- Why are the adults letting children run and shout in the corridors?
- Why is there not a hands-up system to answer questions?

- Why were children unable to work in groups even though the activity was interesting, clearly explained and understood?
- What can we learn about this particular community of practice as well as about our own?
- How can we bring these issues to the fore without appearing judgemental?
- Why might the first two questions seem rather odd to a Spanish person?

The behaviours of teachers and children in the Spanish school context are very different from English ones, and it can be easy to find fault when seen through a narrow lens. If limited by experience, we risk assuming that 'our way' of doing things is the 'only' or 'best way' of doing things, without a real understanding of underlying cultural practices. The questions above will encourage you to challenge any judgements implicit in your observations of others. Children running in corridors may just be 'children being children' to a Spanish person (children's exuberance is less restricted in Spain, making them appear perhaps, 'less polite' to an English person). The area of ethnography (the study of other cultures) has much to offer in the FL classroom, as it can bring light to what might otherwise be a stereotyped observation followed by uninformed judgements. Nunan already warned us about avoiding a 'tourist type' approach to exploring other cultures when superficially examining their customs. Thus, applying an ethnographic approach to IU can help us see behaviours and practices within context,

> The whole physical and social event as well as the bodily movements, pacing and rhythm of speakers' turns, and so on have to be apprehended and then (tentatively) links made to wider social knowledge and practice.
>
> Robert et al. (2001) p. 59

A mastery approach to language teaching will require an enquiring and open mind, willing to critically engage with culturally diverse artefacts and ways of doing or being. This will necessitate some retrospection and the challenge of current beliefs about self and others. Teachers need to be able to anticipate misunderstandings and misconceptions that children – and sometimes teachers themselves – can bring into a discussion, seeing these as opportunities for learning and exploring diversity and culture, particularly in light of recent events which have seen Britain leave the European Union.

Children can demonstrate a kind of cultural awareness at a very young age.

CASE STUDY

One of my students was once getting a group of five-year-olds to practice simple greetings from around the world with. The discussion soon lead to the different languages people speak, and what followed from one of the children was rather telling, and although amusing to our ears it shows nonetheless, his willingness to be part of the discussion and of what constitutes 'otherness' to him – as well as our society's share of the responsibility for such utterance.

Figure 4.4 A five-year-old wanting to engage with IU

> Sir! I speak Chinese food!

As the teacher, where would you take this exchange? This young voice shows us that the lines that separate language from culture and from experience itself at such a young age are quite tenuous if present at all. 'I speak Chinese food' makes reference to the act of engaging with one's experiences, of recognizing 'otherness' as something that could actually be lived 'en carne propia' [in the flesh]. Perhaps this anecdotal evidence can serve as a metaphor for how young children experience language, as in, 'the taste of words'. However, therein lies a danger, for in our well-meant attempt to discuss other cultures, are we not introducing children to the notion of 'them' and 'us'? The trick is how to explore other cultures without building a wall around our own. It should not be about making a contrast and drawing lines between different peoples, but rather exploring different experiences. This is why starting by looking at 'communities of practice' rather than 'other cultures' can be beneficial, as it highlights the fact that we can be very different within our own society and communities or very similar across different cultures.

Never has a framework for IU been so well contained as by Byram and Doye (1999) which we presented in Chapter 1. They developed the concept of the five *savoirs*, which are the necessary skills that need to be acquired in order to communicate successfully in an FL – beyond linguistic competence. These savoirs (French for 'knowing') will be reinterpreted here as, 'the art of'. We call it *art* to reflect a Foucauldian stance to this issue, 'Couldn't everyone's life become a work of art? Why should the lamp or the house be an art object but not our life?' (Foucault 1991, p. 350). We refer here to the impact we can have as teachers – our agency, on children's development; creating opportunities for them to shape themselves in both breadth and depth, and encouraging them, by example, to be at least interested in the art of being, of observing, of interpreting and of interacting.

IU then, gives children a platform on which language learning makes sense, because there is something we can actually discuss and feel passionate about. There are some examples of IU in action in subsequent chapters.

The taste of words: Knowledge about language

When we think of KAL in the primary context, grammar forms an important aspect of it, but is not the whole story. We need to think about the type of language we are exploring, for instance, is it written or spoken? Is our interlocutor within sight or remote? Each of these scenarios brings different possibilities and context to language.

> **Pause for thought**
>
> **Activity**
>
> Examine the written language given in Figure 4.5.
>
> **Figure 4.5** Written symbols
>
> - What can we infer about this language system?
> - Think about at least three characteristics that this language seems to have.

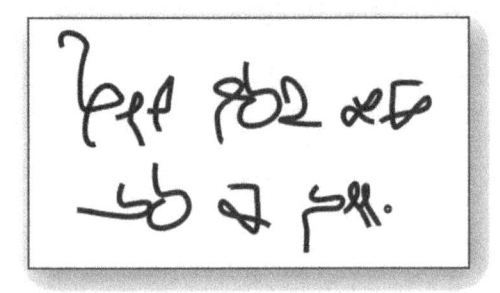

You will find that the items you came up with are based on your current understanding of what constitutes language (direction of writing, use of full stops, capitals, spaces between symbols/words, repetition, patterns, etc.).

If you were to show an FL text to a group of seven-year-olds, and asked them to list as many things as they could about that language, just by exploring its visual landscape, the children will reveal their own understanding of language, mapping their knowledge of English language onto the new presented language (i.e. if no one mentions full stops, what might this tell you about possible gaps in their knowledge?).

If we repeated the experiment using only audio, different aspects might come to light, pulling on a different kind of knowledge on our part, for instance, our breath of experience of hearing (or even speaking) other languages (if we have heard Greek before, we might recognize it again when we hear it). In short, your knowledge about language allows you to explore and infer meaning and structure in a different language, including body language (certain gestures can go with certain words, as in, 'I don't know', where we can shrug our shoulders). This knowledge, when made explicit, can form part of a strategy for language learning which promotes independence, and it is therefore an important tool.

> **Pause for thought**
>
> **Activity**
>
> Have you ever wondered at what age children can recognize written English from other written languages?
>
> **Figure 4.6** Different written languages
>
> Vor einem großen Walde wohnte ein armer Holzhacker.
>
> Había una vez un ratoncito llamado Pérez.
>
> Once upon a time there was a little girl called Goldilocks.
>
> كِتَاب أَلْف لَيْلَة وَلَيْلَة
>
> 狐狸精 這是故事的名稱。
>
> Булочка вскочил на морде лисы и пели ту же песню
>
> - Ask children (in pairs) to pick out English.
> - If they can, ask them which other language is most like or unlike English.
> - You could try this in your school. Notice how children go about their choice (which languages they discard first).

For many trainee teachers, their first encounter with English grammar – in its explicit form – has been through the study of an FL, usually at secondary. It is possible that the most overt use of English grammar in our lives is when we learn a new language. For instance, I might say to you that in Spanish, the noun usually preceded by an article, is always placed before the adjective, modifying this last in terms of gender and number in what is known as adjectival agreement. This information would be very useful if you had a secure understanding of each grammatical term used.

Pause for thought

Activity

Knowledge of grammar can enable you to do the following activity, without necessarily understanding all the meaning.

Figure 4.7 Using knowledge about language to structure a sentence

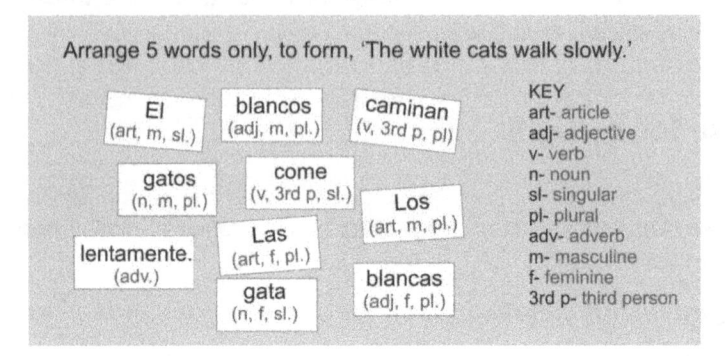

Arrange 5 words only, to form, 'The white cats walk slowly.'

El (art, m, sl.)	blancos (adj, m, pl.)	caminan (v, 3rd p, pl)
gatos (n, m, pl.)	come (v, 3rd p, sl.)	Los (art, m, pl.)
lentamente. (adv.)	Las (art, f, pl.)	
	gata (n, f, sl.)	blancas (adj, f, pl.)

KEY
art- article
adj- adjective
v- verb
n- noun
sl- singular
pl- plural
adv- adverb
m- masculine
f- feminine
3rd p- third person

You do not need to know what the words actually mean in order to arrange them correctly thanks to the grammatical information provided (*Los gatos blancos caminan lentamente*, where 'gatos' means cats, masculine plural noun, and 'blancos' means white, the corresponding adjective for masculine plural, with the verb 'caminan' needing to be in the third person plural). No other formation would have made grammatical sense, unless it had poetic licence.

Knowledge of these terms can allow us to talk about language and its rules and characteristics. For instance, how many other languages use gender to classify its nouns? What other criteria are there to classify nouns in other languages?

At the primary level you will need to understand the basic terms in the box above, which form part of the compulsory element in the English curriculum. How confident do you feel in your grasp of grammatical terms and their function within structures? We would encourage you not to 'get married' to definitions, or to assume that to memorize a rule or definition equals understanding. Children are often asked to learn that a noun is 'a naming word', yet, 'she eats greedily', names an action but has no noun. It has instead a pronoun, a verb and an adverb.

CASE STUDY

Varied examples speak louder than definitions.

A class of seven-year-olds were involved in an activity where they needed to produce a variety of descriptions using 'adventurous' adjectives. They had been to the woods the previous day as part of their topic work. When asked what an adjective was, some were able to say 'a describing word', yet hardly any were able to produce more than one or two adjectives in their paragraph. The teacher stopped them at various points and asked them to think carefully what an adjective did.

Read the following responses. Which do you think were made by the children?

An adjective is …

- It's a colour.
- It's something that is not real.
- What you can see and then you can say.
- A thing you use in a sentence.
- An adjective makes the sentence longer.
- A type of word that we can use in a sentence.

Teacher: But what is an adjective?
Child: It's a describing word.
Teacher: Good. Can you describe a squirrel for me?
Child: (thinks carefully) It has fur on its back!

This was actually a very good lesson in terms of child engagement, and the beginning teacher was able to learn a great deal from it, demonstrating a very good level of critical reflection (one of the most important assets a teacher can have). In fact, all of the responses above were uttered by the children during the activity. It is interesting to note that all the statements are, in a way, correct; they are all plausible characteristics of an adjective. When she asked them directly, 'How would you describe a squirrel?', a little boy thought hard and said, 'It has fur on its back', which, although correct, was not the response the teacher was looking for.

One of the ways one might have narrowed the gap between the acquisition of explicit grammar (the grammatical term 'Adjective' in this case) and the use of words, such as soft, furry, fast, and cute, in the case study above, was to have made this connection more explicit to the children 'in action' rather than in terms of definition. For instance, during their visit to the forest, the children could have been asked to find as many 'adjectives' as possible. They could have gone out on a Noun-hunt and an Adjective-hunt, and see which terms were easiest to find; collect them on special Noun Books and Adjective Books (or bags); filled in texts that were ready-made with Noun-gaps or Adjective-gaps, etc. The main idea is to get children accustomed to hear the grammatical term in connection to varied examples. The objective is to get children to 'play' with grammar on a daily basis, so that they are given opportunities to internalize meaning and consolidate these connections as opposed to memorize definitions that are too abstract (and open to alternative interpretation) for them.

> **Pause for thought**
>
> **Activity**
>
> When is an adjective a noun?
>
> **Figure 4.8** How words change their grammatical function (Eng/Sp)
>
> | NOUN | VERB | Grammatical musical chairs | ADJECTIVE | ? |
>
> What class of word is 'playing' in the following sentences?
>
> The children are **playing** card games. (where 'playing' is part of the verb, present progressive)
>
> It's the **playing** that concerns me. (where 'playing' functions as a noun)
>
> We saw the **playing** children. (where 'playing' functions as an adjective)
>
> As is often the case with English, one word can serve many functions. Compare both languages below. What can we learn about Spanish (and English) just by looking at this Venn diagram?
>
> | ENGLISH | | SPANISH |
> |---|---|---|
> | SILVER a ∩ n | | a PLATEADO |
> | FALLEN v ∩ a ∩ n | VERBS   ADJECTIVES | v ∩ a ∩ n CAIDO |
> | COLD a ∩ n | V   a | a ∩ n FRIO |
> | TABLE n ∩ v | n | n MESA |
> | BIG a | NOUNS | a GRANDE |
> | SINGING v ∩ a ∩ n | | v CANTANDO |
>
> So what can this tell us about learning an FL? Having a secure understanding of the basic grammatical terms (noun, adjective, verb, adverb, article, verb tense, etc.) can, as mentioned earlier, facilitate the learning of some of the different nuances of these terms in other languages (word order, gender, number, adjectival agreement, verb conjugation, etc.). We will explore in Chapter 6 how we can play with grammar in FLs in a creative way in order to consolidate learning and enjoy the taste and texture of words, as well as their sound.

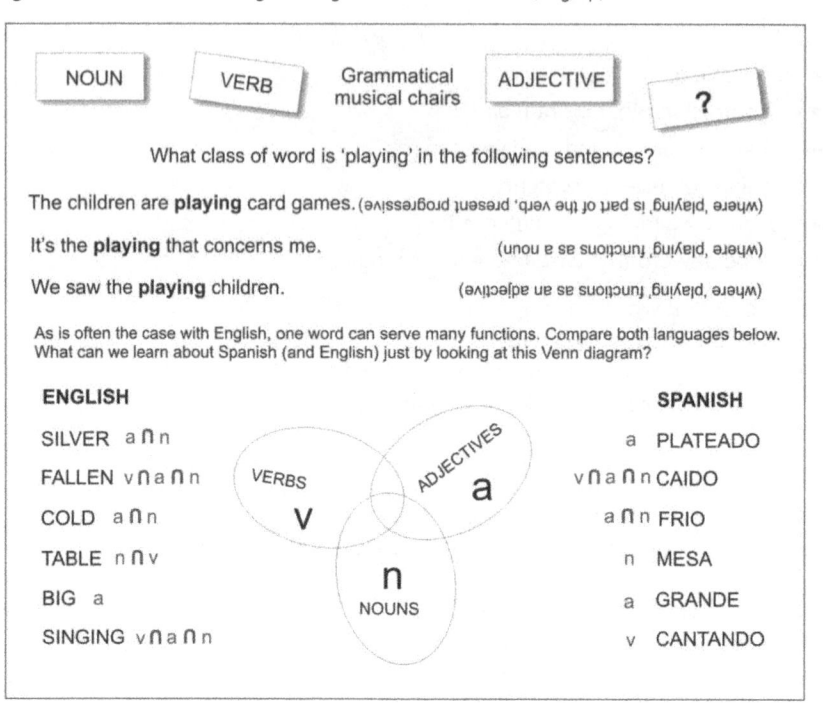

Oracy

When talking about Oracy we refer to the skills of speaking and listening. The National Curriculum places great emphasis on the English language for pupils throughout the primary years and beyond. This is reflected in all areas of the curriculum. Teachers teach the subject as well as the language required to understand the subject, and to create

Figure 4.9 Broad features of Oracy

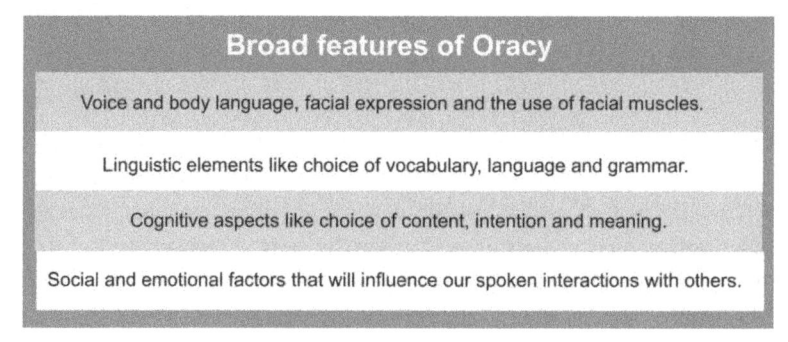

Broad features of Oracy
Voice and body language, facial expression and the use of facial muscles.
Linguistic elements like choice of vocabulary, language and grammar.
Cognitive aspects like choice of content, intention and meaning.
Social and emotional factors that will influence our spoken interactions with others.

new ideas from that subject using language. All primary class teachers are teachers of language, because they are the core professionals who will teach pupils to speak and to write fluently so that they can communicate their ideas and emotions and through their reading and listening they can communicate with others too. The ability to express oneself and to understand speech is not only essential, but also necessary to be able to participate effectively in society. Oracy then is about both listening and speaking and implies an interaction between at least two speakers. The features of Oracy can broadly be categorized into four areas (Faculty of Education, University of Cambridge).

> **Pause for thought**
>
> **Activity**
>
> Think about your speech and verbal interactions with others as a native speaker. Are any of the statements below applicable to you? Consider which of the aspects in Figure 4.9 are relevant to each of the following statement.
>
> - My speech is fast, moderate or slow.
> - I think of my choice of vocabulary before I speak.
> - I am conscious of grammar when I speak.
> - I speak literally or I include metaphors in my verbal communication.
> - I take account of the level of understanding of the person I am speaking to (age, language proficiency).
> - I manage my interaction with others. For example, I give the person I am speaking with the opportunity to respond/talk and my response, in turn, reflects this.
> - I consciously include humour in my verbal interaction with others.

We can see that spoken language is more than words being strung together to convey meaning. It is ineluctably linked to our thinking processes. It is therefore important to take stock of what happens when we teach language to children in primary school and beyond:

> We have known for a long time that talk is essential to children's thinking and learning, and to their productive engagement in classroom life, especially in the early and primary years.
>
> Alexander, R. (2012)

Furthermore, the Primary National Curriculum reflects the importance of spoken language in pupils' development across the whole curriculum and the emphasis schools should place on assessing these skills. Spoken language underpins the development of reading and writing. Teachers have an obligation to assist learners in making their learning clear through talk. They need to develop pupils' capacity to explain their understanding of passages, stories, books and to use discussions to probe and develop their misconceptions.

So what does Oracy look like in the FL classroom? First we need to understand what Oracy means in terms of FL learning. How can we, for instance, engage learners in the type of Oracy that allows them to become familiar with the rhythm and the pattern of a given FL?

If the physical aspect of spoken language deals with the pace, volume and pitch of our speech so that we can engage our listeners by altering these and by allowing them the time to process what we are saying, then we need to pay due attention to the skills involved in listening as well.

Introducing new language to a class is always an important moment of 'first contact' (a new taste) with a particular sound or spelling. It is worthwhile thinking the process through. Should children be exposed to the written form of the word at the same time they hear it, or beforehand, or after they have heard it and repeated it? It depends. Let us use the teaching of ten colours in Spanish, to a class of seven-year-olds. We will use a kinaesthetic approach involving gestures, body movement and the use of the imagination (getting the children to imagine a blue sky, or touching fresh green grass while repeating the new words, etc.). To assess their understanding we will employ a method called Graded Questions, which, as the name suggests, teaches, targets and deals with children's level of understanding in a graded way. Graded questions are also a very inclusive way of teaching new vocabulary, as the system always guides a child's response or contribution, whatever it may be, to be ultimately correct and of value.

Oracy also involves the phonics and phonology of a language. This includes the relationship between phonemes (sounds) and graphemes (letters). For instance, in Spanish there are only four graphemes that have very different phonemes to English, and it may serve the children best, not to see the written word until they have internalize the sound. Spanish Vowels and other consonants are similar, but unlike English they are very regular, with a 1:1 correspondence between grapheme and phoneme. This means that one letter equals one sound only.

There is a little bit more to pronouncing Spanish, but if the letters shown in Figures 4.11 and 4.12 are pronounced correctly you will be understood. The rest of the letters in Spanish can be pronounced as you might pronounce them in English, and although you may have an English accent, you will be perfectly understood.

Figure 4.10 Graded questions

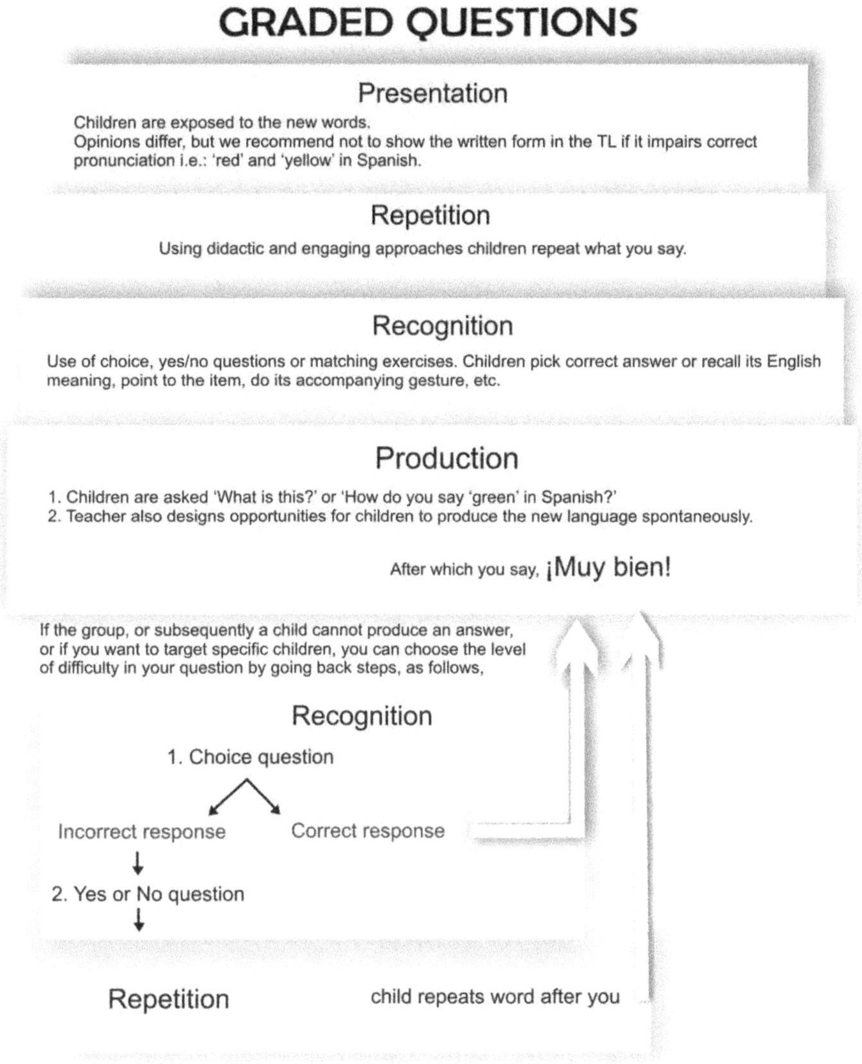

GRADED QUESTIONS

Presentation
Children are exposed to the new words.
Opinions differ, but we recommend not to show the written form in the TL if it impairs correct pronunciation i.e.: 'red' and 'yellow' in Spanish.

Repetition
Using didactic and engaging approaches children repeat what you say.

Recognition
Use of choice, yes/no questions or matching exercises. Children pick correct answer or recall its English meaning, point to the item, do its accompanying gesture, etc.

Production
1. Children are asked 'What is this?' or 'How do you say 'green' in Spanish?'
2. Teacher also designs opportunities for children to produce the new language spontaneously.

After which you say, ¡Muy bien!

If the group, or subsequently a child cannot produce an answer, or if you want to target specific children, you can choose the level of difficulty in your question by going back steps, as follows,

Recognition
1. Choice question

Incorrect response   Correct response

2. Yes or No question

Repetition
child repeats word after you

It is then, during Oracy that we can support children to become more familiar with the sounds and letters which make up the FL. It is a given that children in KS2 would already know the sounds of their own native language and indeed some would be matching familiar words from the aural to the visual, from the sounds to the symbols blended together to form words on a page. However, we cannot take for granted that all children would be sufficiently aware of the different sounds that exist in their native language. As the mother tongue serves as a template that influences the way we go on to hear the sounds of other languages, we need to break down the sound patterns of the FL if we are to help them to learn, remember and apply the

Figure 4.11 Spanish letters with very different sounds to the English equivalent

graphemes & phonemes

as in the word jump
Ll dʒ
Me llamo María
amarillo

As in the word lasagna. ɲ
Ñ
lasaña
niños
ñ

Strong sound as in the Scottish lo**ch**, or in **h**ot
J x
/j
Un pájaro rojo

Español

Hola
ahora
H-
h
The letter H is always silent.

letters & sounds

Figure 4.12 Vowel sounds in Spanish

vowels	Always pronounced as in:
a	pat
e	pet
i	ski:
o	pot
u	put

No exceptions

sound system to other words. Cheater and Farren (2001) pointed out that children will benefit from being drawn to look at the way the mouth is being shaped and where the tongue ends up as the word from the FL is being pronounced. '*Rojo*' is such an example (you can easily find and listen to any word online by typing, 'How to pronounce (word)'). You may want to consider the different ways in which you can support a pupil who is having difficulty pronouncing any given sound. For instance,

- Touch under your chin as you say it.
- What is your tongue doing?
- What facial muscles are being used? (use a mirror perhaps)
- What happens when you cover your ears as you say it?
- What happens when you place your hand in front of your mouth?

As far as rhythm and flow is concerned, children need to have plenty of opportunities to hear the FL in use. It takes time to tune into the new language, where one word ends and the next one begins – the intonation of questions, exclamations or statements, etc. What listening opportunities can a teacher give the children? There are many listening games and audio files online which can be used to support text (see Chapter 8 for such resources). As an example, you can play Edith Piaf's song 'Milord' to the children and get them to count how many times she says the word 'milord' in the song.

There comes a point when children listening to FL audio or film clips notice that some words have stopped sounding incomprehensible, which in fact they can pick them out even if the whole sentence is not completely understood. Children get a great sense of satisfaction when they can pick out a word in an FL sentence. However, they do not arrive at this point without hearing the TL and being encouraged to focus on language content relevant to them.

Target Language

The use of TL has been discussed at length in many other language resource books and the conclusion is that unless children hear the language, they will not become familiar with the sound patterns, rhythm and intonation of the new language. Kirsch (2008) confirms that primary school teachers worldwide enhance the exposure to the FL by using it as a medium of instruction in the language lessons. It is without doubt a way to encourage pupils to make sense of the overall meaning of what is uttered in the FL without attempting to translate single words in order to understand the gist of the communication. Jones and McLachlan (2009) point out that children cannot embed the new language unless they have encountered it first, have processed it and are in an environment, where they can use it in different contexts.

Krashen's *comprehensible input* is where learners are encouraged to guess words and infer meaning from the context, that is, learners understand the message in the TL because the teacher deliberately *selects* language slightly above the level that pupils already understand. Krashen's theory of language acquisition derives from a meaning-based or natural approach, where communication is the main objective. Production of the new language emerges under the right conditions which have been created by the teacher. This is also where pupils will develop their understanding of the grammatical structures of the new language and may begin to use the language creatively by the end of their primary years if progression has been considered effectively. Thus, using TL in the classroom, from giving simple instructions to asking for reasons or opinions, not only supports children to process meaning, but also presents them with a chance to reproduce language learnt previously. Learners in the primary classroom can be taught how to use TL, to ask question, to say they don't understand and to ask the teacher to repeat what has been said. Learners not only recognize language being taught but they can also be motivated to use the TL immediately and eventually use language independently of the teacher.

While the use of the FL in the classroom must be carefully planned (and non-native speakers are much better at this as their language may be limited), absolute control is not necessary. Native speakers tend to vary their language and vocabulary a great deal, which can make familiarization with certain phrases more difficult for the children. A mixture of styles seems effective.

Case scenario

You are teaching French to your class and the children are already quite familiar with basic classroom vocabulary such as:

- *Écoutez* – listen,
- *Écrivez* – write,
- *Jouez avec un partenaire* – play/work with a partner.

After which you add:

- *à vous maintenant* –

Your class remains watching you and it looks like they are waiting for more instructions.

- What is happening?
- How do you bridge this gap in their knowledge?

(Think about all the hand and body gestures that can accompany language. One basic rule is: if you can mime it, you should use the TL. '*à vous maintenant*' means, over to you.)

Promoting a TL-rich environment entails core learning content. For example, if you are teaching the topic of clothes, choose the context of '*Que portes-tu? De quelle couleur est ton pantalon?* (What are you wearing? What colour are your trousers?). By getting pupils to answer questions which encourage them to describe what they are wearing and the colour of the items, you are embedding language in the context that they might encounter in real life. From the above 'Over to you' scenario, it is clear that introducing new vocabulary within structures which children have not encountered before may render them unresponsive the first time; it is nevertheless, important for children to get used to listening out for new language. Indeed we will argue that systematic and authentic use of TL is necessary for learners in primary schools. We don't advocate learning through the medium of the FL exclusively, although, we do believe that our practice is more inclusive when we attempt to use TL whenever feasible. Developing a classroom environment where the TL is used and supported through facial expressions and gestures will support all learners to succeed on an even-playing field.

Paralinguistic features of language learning

Paralinguistic features are the components of language teaching which are not verbal, but rather have the role to communicate without the use of speech, such as gestures and facial expressions. Daniela Sime's (2003) research on learners' perceptions of their teachers' communication strategies showed that gestures used by teachers were perceived by learners as valuable to their cognitive learning processes. Participants observed that speech was used in conjunction with nonverbal communication and maintained, and it supported their understanding of new language and their learning. However, that said, Macaro, Graham and Woore (2016) while clearly endorsing paralinguistic features in the classroom warn that there could be a risk of learners becoming over reliant on facial expressions and gestures at the expense of actually listening to the language itself.

Neuroscience studies are being carried out with hearing babies born to deaf parents to find out which modality (spoken or signing) those babies are receiving their communication input in. For example, are they receiving information through

Figure 4.13 (Let's go!) Spanish speakers use b/v sound indiscriminately

the eyes (signing) or are they receiving the information through the ears? In an FL learning context in the primary, we are fortunate enough to know that pupils invariably can do both. It is this practitioners' knowing that leads us to put forward the notion that because children are still developing, they are using both modalities to receive the information input: the spoken word through the ears while processing the association of facial expressions and gestures through the eyes. If you type 'the McGurk Effect' in YouTube, you will see how important what we see is in terms of what we hear – or think we hear. It also goes some way towards explaining why Spanish speakers do not differentiate (although they can) between the 'b' and 'v' sounds, which plays havoc with their spelling! We suggest you teach children to distinguish between the two, by pronouncing 'v' when they see a *v*, and 'b' when they see a *b*, as this will help with their spelling and it will make no difference to a Spanish speaker listening to them.

There is an explosion of neuroscience research examining how the brain processes language and language learning. It can now tell us that it is the part of the front of the brain called Broca's Area and part towards the back of the brain called Wernicke's Area which are very important for processing language. Although neuroscience has a road map of how language is processed, they are not yet able to tell us, the level of presentation of language that is happening in those parts of the brain. We suspect it is only a matter of time before they will be able to do so. In the meantime what we do know is that watching someone speak in an FL just as hearing-impaired people who communicate through signing watch the facial expressions as well as the signing, so will miming and gestures enhance the understanding and cognitive processing of acquiring the new language. Experimenting with your own 'paralinguistics', by making use of gestures, miming, etc. can be an effective investment in your pupils' learning.

Language learning strategies

'Language learning Strategies will help children become more independent learners in any language.' The Key Stage Two Framework for Languages may be categorical in its ambitions for encouraging pupils in the primary, to become familiar in discussing their LLS with other children and with their teachers while expanding their range of strategies, as this quote suggests. Nevertheless LLS is not short of controversies, in fact, as Griffiths (2004) points out the concept of LLS is surrounded by 'fuzziness'. Griffiths goes on to explain that even though LLS are considered 'an extremely powerful learning tool' (O'Malley et al. 1985); the field of LLS continues to be marred by a lack of consensus. The confusion lies with various researchers and is around the notion and inability to pin down what exactly LLS are and how do they differ from other types of learning strategies. Oxford (1990), cited in Griffiths, (2004) summarizes it for us quite concisely and highlights that classification conflicts are inevitable in this area of language learning:

> There is no complete agreement on exactly what strategies are: how many strategies exist; how they should be defined, demarcated, and categorised: and whether it is – or ever will be – possible to create a real, scientifically validated hierarchy of strategies.
>
> Oxford R. L. (1990) – *Language learning strategies: What every teacher should know*

Nonetheless, LLS remained of great interest for teachers because of their potential to improve language learning. The Framework makes great use of these potentials by highlighting a range of strategies for primary school children to become familiar with, such as remembering rhyming words and making use of gesture or mime to show they understand, repetition, looking for visual and aural clues, etc. It is clear that the intention is for the teacher to engage pupils with LLS in the hope that learners will adopt them and expand on their own method of learning languages. Reassuringly, Maynard (2012) states that although some of these strategies will be new in the context of FL learning, they will be completely familiar to the primary practitioner, particularly in the phonics and reading lessons. The objectives for LLS are not only for learners to progress over the four years of primary schooling, but it is also hoped that they will support learners to learn languages beyond the primary.

In terms of vocabulary acquisition, one strategy that has stood the test of time is the keyword method (Carney and Levin 2008), where students are encouraged to associate part of the sound of the foreign word with a known word (the keyword) in their own language, and combine the two images in some meaningful – hopefully comical or extravagant way, thus making it memorable in sound and meaning.

Pause for thought

Take, for instance, the number 14 in French, 'quatorze', which can sound like 'cat' and 'horse' put together (different people may hear different things). Now combine these two images, inserting the number in some way, as below.

Figure 4.14 Playing with mnemonics (the keyword method)

Literacy

Literacy refers to the ability to read and write. We know well that there is more to it than being able to decode words. We also need a phonological awareness, phonics, fluency, comprehension and vocabulary. Mastering all those subskills is important in becoming a proficient reader and writer. As we discussed in the Oracy section above, learners need to hear as much as the TL as possible so that they can become familiar with the rhythm and patterns of the language. During a TED talk, Chris Lonsdale, renowned psychologist, linguist and educator, mentions that the brain filters only sounds of the language we know and are familiar with, and filters out those sounds which are not. As language teachers, we cannot expect that learners will have the phonological awareness of the language we are teaching them. We must clearly plan to introduce the sound and letter system of the FL to them.

Children's existing knowledge of phonics in their first language will help them understand and attempt different pronunciations in the TL. They will come across relationships between phonemes and graphemes in the new language that will not be familiar to them such as in the examples provided further above for Spanish letters.

Some research has demonstrated that many deaf children find it difficult to learn to read regardless of their ability. This seems to show that reading, on the face of it, appears to be visual, but when we read, what we are actually doing is reading the **spoken language** written on a page using symbols. So the challenge for children learning to read in a new language is to map their knowledge of the spoken word onto the symbols on the page. We need to give children plenty of opportunities to identify and match sounds to symbols/words, thus developing their writing skills in the FL.

Kirsch (2008) makes a case for not separating oral and written language. She maintains that linguistically it is completely artificial. We caution, however, that some letters in the FL that carry a different sound to English should be introduced after the child has heard and spoken the word. We would not want a child's first encounter with the word 'red' in Spanish to be decoded using English phonics, as it will render it unrecognizable to any Spanish speaker. We also firmly believe that we will be doing learners a disservice if we delay introducing writing for too long, for children in KS2 will already have been reading and writing for some years, spending a great deal of time understanding, decoding and writing in the first language. Consistently and gradually introducing the written language gives children a visual input of the language, thus reinforcing the learning. The Key Stage 2 Framework for Languages supports not delaying reading and writing, as it states that these skills reinforce and are in turn supported by the development of Oracy.

> *Children use the skills of reading and writing to develop a basic knowledge of the writing system, the spelling and the structure of the language. In doing this, they reinforce and expand their knowledge and understanding of their own language(s).*
>
> Key Stage 2 Framework for Languages, Part 1, p. 8

The National Curriculum on the other hand expects that children will leave primary school, after four years in KS2 with the ability *to 'write phrases from memory, and adapt these to create new sentences, to express ideas clearly'*.

We propose that children could begin writing the new language they have learnt, either through copying or through a process of choosing the appropriate answer from several options. They could also be trained to answer questions by reading statements and writing responses like 'True/False' in the TL. Additionally, they could be reading instructions, dates, stories, poems, menus, recipes, letters, emails and so on. In fact, the wider the range the more empowered they will be to move from listening to speaking and from reading to writing.

Summary

In this chapter we wanted to introduce to you the Framework for Languages in terms of the ideas that underpin it, as well as our own take on issues surrounding the teaching and learning of FLs in the primary. Mostly, we wanted you to understand how language learning can be more than just words and sounds; how your knowledge of the target culture can inspire and give context to the language by giving children a reason to want to express themselves in the first place; how your knowledge about language in general can enhance children's learning by exploring the features of the new language, the taste of the new words. Finally, we hope that you are able to share your own LLS with the children, so that they may learn by your example. We hope that you consider the different aspects of the TL's phonic system in order to inform your approach to Oracy and Literacy. Ultimately, we hope you can empower children to become as independent learners as possible.

Recommended reading

The Key Stage 2 Framework for Languages (2005). *Department for Education and Skills*. Nottingham, UK: DfES Publications

Robert, C. et al. (2001). 'Theoretical Issues in language and culture practices'. In *Language Learners as Ethnographers*. Clevedon: Multilingual Matters, pp. 44–63.

Chien Kuo Lee (2010). An Overview of Language Learning Strategies – Newcastle University, *ARECLS*, 2010, 7, 132–52.

Griffiths, C. (2004). Language Learning Strategies: Theory and Research, School of Foundations Studies AIS St Helens, Auckland, New Zealand Occasional Paper No. 1, February 2004, http://www.crie.org.nz/research-papers/c_griffiths_op1.pdf (accessed on 2 August 2017).

Chapter 5
Skills to Develop in Languages

It always seems impossible until it is done.

Nelson Mandela

Chapter objectives

- To highlight that it is our intervention and interaction with children's worlds that support the building of their knowledge, motivating their participation, engagement and involvement in the world around them;
- Whether you are a beginning speaker of the TL or a native speaker, you need to reflect on issues about language learning and teaching and reformulate your existing beliefs of what can be achieved when you start making links across different subject areas;
- To enthuse you to make languages a priority in your classroom so that your pupils too will be enthusiastic and will surpass the low expectations that have been wrongly construed by the motto 'We (British) are bad at languages';
- The examples of cross-curricular planning we give in this chapter are meant to get you thinking about your own passions and how to intertwine them with the curriculum.

In this chapter we explore how you can be creative with the curriculum time you have in order to embed FL in the daily teaching and learning experiences of the children in your classroom. We are quoting Nelson Mandela, a hero who made what seemed impossible, possible. Of course we are referring to his phenomenal legacy of becoming the first black president of the then xenophobic state of South Africa, after having been a political prisoner for twenty-five years. However, the feeling of having to deliver what at times seems impossible is no stranger, but it can take just one good inspirational someone or moment to push us forward into what will be a very personal road. The connections we make across different aspects of our lives are defined by our experiences, by what we choose to observe, and the path is therefore unique in each case.

> **Pause for thought**
>
> Read the extract below, and think about a particular moment in your life when a new idea sparked a whole world of possibilities.
>
> My mind goes back to those maturing years as a teacher in the late 1980s to early 1990s when full of enthusiasm but rather lacking in ideas of how to bring the world to my classroom, I came across a primary practitioner, academic and author, called Sylvia Collicott, who introduced me to the notion of cross-curricular working. While I was very clear that it was an important approach, once I returned to my classroom it was a challenge to implement some of the ideas I had learnt from my lecturer and mentor. They did not seem easily translatable and attainable but I nevertheless persevered until one day I realised that the perfect plan did not exist then, has never existed and does not exist now. The perfection lies in the journey, and we are all capable of that.
>
> Darnelle Constant-Shepherd

In this chapter, we are speaking to the teacher who knows that high expectations is the key to learners' high achievement; the teacher who knows that the perfect plan, like an ideal world, does not exist, and that the perfect lesson will not be found in a plan, no matter how elaborate that plan may be, but in the learning experience you give the children. We are thinking about the teachers whose planning experience is like a journey that requires detours, distractions, and even going astray sometimes in order to get to the point where they are happy with the learning experience the children will live. The right delivery of these plans of activities or experiences will encourage learners to use their imagination and to involve themselves as thinkers who will question what they are being presented with. The cross-curricular approach we are referring to here has everything to do with the aspiration and ambition generated by the teacher, as he or she provides children with opportunities to use the language they will learn.

We also know as primary teachers that we can value a subject without having to know the subject area exhaustively. We can excite children's imagination and provoke dialogue which in turn encourages children to foster discovery skills and push them to explore, understand and make sense of their world. This is exactly what cross-curricular working is all about.

Below you will see a collection of photographs depicting the work achieved by pupils in the primary language classroom. They are not without small errors but it is clear that this kind of work can only be generated by a teacher who believes that language work for children in the primary can and needs to go beyond the 'greetings' stage syndrome. We can only achieve this when we begin to foster the kind of creativity innate in all of us. Now take another look at Figure 5.1, and glance at the web planning of a group of student teachers preparing to undertake a Year 3 topic of mini-beasts.

Skills to Develop in Languages 95

Figure 5.1 Nadine Chadier's pupils' work on landmarks of London, and PGCE students' cross-curricular web planning on mini-beasts for Y3

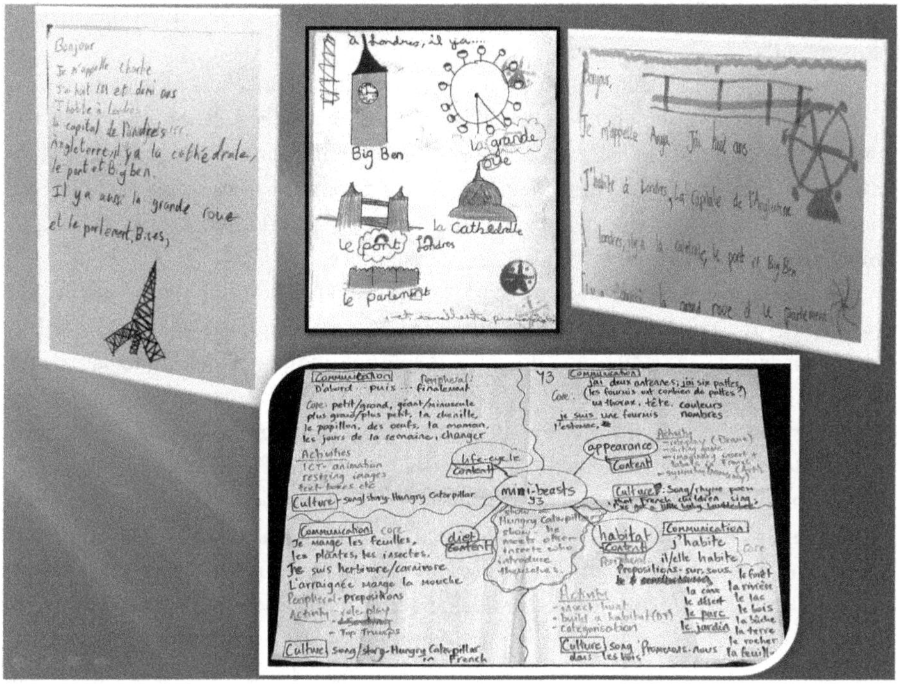

> **Pause for thought**
> - Can you imagine planning your language lessons in such a way?
> - Does this language web planning generate ideas of how you can tackle the subject cross-curricularly when you next sit down with your colleague to plan?

We want you to hold on to this thought; just because our pupils have inherited Western civilization, for the moment, the 'dominant' civilization perceived by some, it does not mean that we do not need to give them the opportunity to experience different perspectives and visions. Each aspect of experience acts as a powerful 'enabler' for the child to develop confidence in participating as an 'apprentice citizen'. Most children will not become professional linguists, writers, anthropologists, scientists, musicians, sculptors, geologists or historians, but they all do have a right to know about such possibilities.

Learning about other people's language and culture is a sure way of engaging and understanding others. While we do not dismiss the fact that the Primary Curriculum is overcrowded, we nevertheless believe that equipping our primary learners with the skills of language learning is as important as learning numeracy and literacy skills. In fact we can go further and say that FL learning enhances literacy skills specifically and generally.

Cross-curricular learning and teaching is motivating for teachers as well as pupils. It is social learning which takes account of children's world. It involves both the teacher and the pupils in a creative space to generate thinking, make progress while at the same time revisiting the values which are important to us, such as inclusion, friendship, equality, hope, confidence and meaning in addition to the skills and knowledge underlying the learning of the curriculum.

Eventually you will be in a position to draw your own map, be it within the restraints of the national curriculum, of how you will teach and what you need to teach your pupils. Whatever you do, what is implicit in the Nelson Mandela's quote above is that we are the creators of possibilities. The complete impact of your cross-curricular planning will remain unknown to you but the progress in the TL that needs to be achieved by your pupils will be very visible. Language learning and teaching is in fact, an ongoing journey which we, as primary class teachers can join, as we begin to view cross-curricular teaching as the powerful medium that it is, for providing our pupils with a rounded education. The content and the learning processes of this way of working will inevitably impact on learners and their development. All the same, owning this privilege and gradually and surely moving away from the notion of languages being simply 'bolted on' at the end of term – for the sake of covering the curriculum – will reap huge benefits for your pupils and for you as a teacher. It sends the compelling message that languages are valued and meaningful and, further down the line, pupils may appreciate that languages are essential because communication with other people living on their planet is essential and stands to create peace, address global environment issues and find solutions to world problems, such as hunger and poverty and inequality, which the world continues to face in the *twenty-first* century. Barnes (2015) highlights that meaningful education outlives temporary curriculum change. He is also right when he reminds us that successful teachers have always known how to turn restrictive curriculum into meaningful and relevant learning for children. On that note, let us guide you as you embark on this journey to provide your learners with meaningful and relevant language learning experiences.

> ## Pause for thought
> - What does cross-curricular teaching and learning mean to you?
> - Have you observed colleagues who are teaching in this way?
> - Perhaps your school has already adopted this approach?
> - What is the official guidance for teaching in a cross-curricular way in your school?

Figure 5.2 Linking FLs with other subjects

Understanding cross-curricular

Our definition is simply an approach to teaching and learning which has been with us time immemorial. It is a pathway to teaching the objectives of an area of the curriculum by linking it with another subject area of the curriculum. In this chapter we explore how we can teach or consolidate FL through other subjects of the curriculum. We use the term 'subject' and 'areas of the curriculum' interchangeably and when we refer to topic-based learning or teaching we are referring to learning which is delivered by using a theme, such as 'Materials' to teach the learning objectives of a range of subjects. So the key word for this chapter is 'integration'. To integrate FL learning with other areas of the Primary Curriculum means integrating the different strands of language learning such as IU, Oracy, Literacy as well as language learning strategies and knowledge about language. It is also about you choosing materials and interpreting the changing dynamics of the learning context and appropriately taking actions based on your pedagogical experience and your personal interests and the interests of the children you are catering for. For instance, in primary school, besides being interested in whether children in other parts of the world wear school uniforms, children will also be interested in how they celebrate special days. What happens when children go on trips such as *classe de neige/skiing trips* in France or when South American Spanish-speaking children celebrate *Día de los Muertos/ Day of the Dead in Mexico* or when German-speaking children celebrate Zukertüte

Festival/School Cone? Propel your own engine by tapping into your own interest. If travelling is the unbroken thread of your life, then use it to excite the children you teach!

Cross-curricular working has a history of its own, and we now use very broad brush strokes to provide you with a context. Some have tried to compromise it by introducing a national curriculum which on the surface claimed its aim is to create a broad and balanced education, but in actual fact, consciously or unconsciously had removed the terms *'coherence'* and *'integrated'* from the national curriculum document, and instead embedded the word 'core subjects'. Hence the civil servants who formulated the consultation document (DES 1987) on the National Curriculum for secondary education listed the core and foundation subjects using 80–90 per cent of curriculum time, with no mention of primary education and leaving a mere:

> 10–20 per cent for a second modern language, classics, home economics, business studies, careers education, PSE and a whole range of cross-curricular material.
>
> Hargreaves, D. H. (1991), p. 36

Others, on the other hand, have embraced it and in the primary, there is evidence to support the fact that when children experience coherence in their learning it is because their primary teachers are in fact more alert to problems of between-subject experiential coherence system (Hargreaves 1991). In other words, the primary teacher makes absolutely sure that connections are made explicit between subjects through teaching and the created learning experiences they eventually deliver.

Alan Bennett, quintessential English playwright and author of 'The History Boys' being interviewed by Andrew Marl (BBC – Start of the Week, 31 October 2016), spent part of the interview lamenting the fact that he wished he had a teacher like Hector. Hector is a fictional character in 'The History Boys', a teacher in a boys' grammar school in the north of England who delights in knowledge for its own sake. However, Bennett continues the conversation by telling us the unfortunate fact that his teacher was more like an Irwin character, the cynical history teacher, brought in the school to coach boys to pass examinations so that they could go to Oxford or Cambridge. Bennett is not the only person though, you only have to pay attention to the media reporting on education, to realize that there are many head teachers and experienced practising teachers who remind us that the success of their schools lies in how well their pupils can link the different strands of learning during their primary school career.

In 2009, the publication of the Rose Primary Review made it clear that in primary some of the most effective learning occurs when connections are made between subjects. The review proposed a new curriculum framework in which these connections are more explicit and made planning for teachers more accessible. Unfortunately it triggered an outcry about the danger of cross-curricular learning as proposed by the review. It claimed that, subjects like art, music, history, geography will play a subservient and submissive role. We would argue that from a practical point of view, far from these foundation subjects being categorized as 'inferior', in fact, cross-curricular approaches to teaching and learning leads to a powerful experience for both teachers and learners. We would also dismiss the idea that foundation subjects play second fiddle to English and mathematics, on the contrary we firmly believe, along with an array of practitioners starting from Alan Blyth to Ted Wragg that foundations subjects are important in their own right and it is they which bring spice and joie de vivre to the Primary Curriculum.

As a new teacher you need opportunities to play with ideas of the subject discipline you are planning to teach. Barnes (2011) makes a convincing case for teachers to be allowed to experiment and to have opportunities to frame and explore questions and answers relevant to the subjects they are being asked to teach. He argues that only then a teacher can successfully plan progression in her pupils learning.

We are not suggesting that you will achieve cross-curricular teaching overnight, like others, Boyle and Bragg (2008) after charting the chronicle of changes in curriculum planning for the period 1997–2007, arrived at the conclusion that primary teachers are rightly reverting back to cross-curricular teaching, but it is a slow process because of the political nature of curriculum reforms. Clearly the Cambridge Primary Review (2009) has yet to be heard for its plea that Westminster loosens its grip on education. But we do reassure you that if you want to create a climate for children to explore, learn and apply their knowledge in a purposeful and original way, then this is worth the investment of your time for as Barnes (2015) affirms; well-being can be achieved through intellectual stimulation of every subject.

Making a start

Pause for thought

Consider the teacher's realia collection shown in Figure 5.3. How could you use coins, foreign postage stamps, plastic bags, postcards, etc. in your language classroom?

Figure 5.3 Realia items for FLs

The different levels of teaching languages across the curriculum

One of the benefits of teaching languages across the curriculum is that it encourages the use of the TL beyond classroom instructions. Doing the register in the TL is quite common and learners are keen to respond in the TL, but you need to increase the challenge gradually and purposefully. An example which works really well to focus and settle the class while you do the required administration of registration is to ask pupils to give you verbally or in written form one or a few TL vocabulary of the previous language lesson. The more of the TL they hear the more likely they will acquire proficiency in listening. Teaching through other subjects however takes it to a different level.

Hood and Tobutt (2009) identified four different levels of teaching language across the curriculum, which we will look at and exemplify in turn.

1. *Surface-curricular linking.* Teachers with less confidence in their language skills in the TL might begin with this approach.
2. *Integrating language and semi-familiar content.* This approach uses teaching language through a content-centred base, meaning working on a topic and drawing from other areas of the curriculum.
3. *Integrating language and new content.* In this way languages are taught by introducing new content in the TL, but this will imply a more challenging linguistic ability, as the material previously learnt will come into play.
4. *Immersion* is the fourth level of cross-curricular teaching and learning of language and this is also referred to as CLIL.

We will now focus on (1) surface-curricular linking, then (3) integrating language and new content and finally (4) CLIL.

Figure 5.4 Representation of Hood and Tobutt (2009) levels of integrated learning

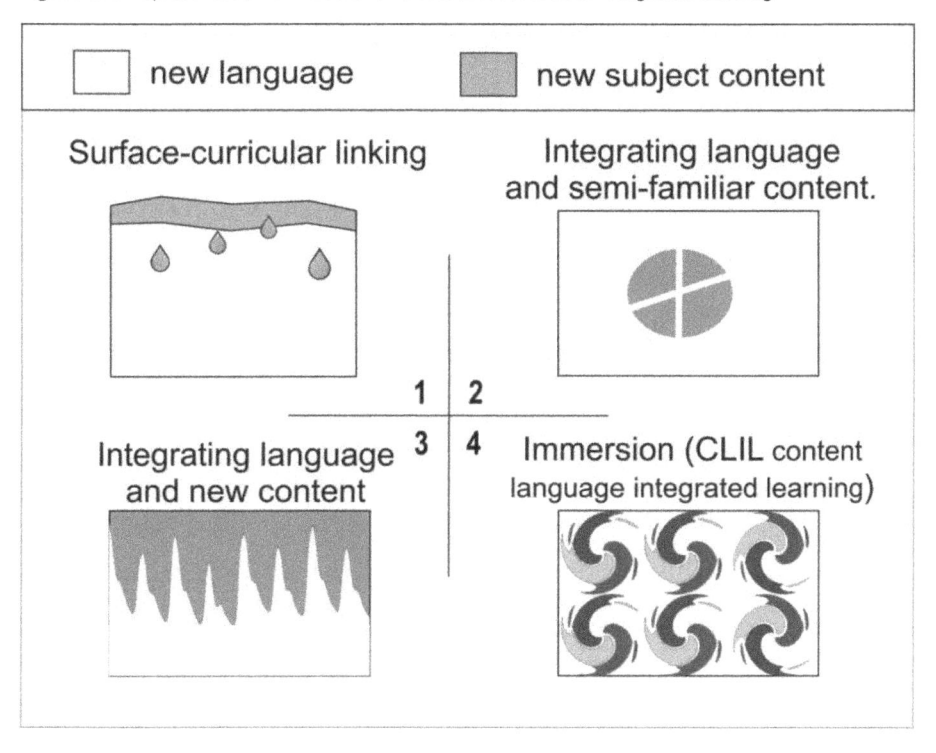

Surface-curricular linking

The surface-curricular linking is a topic and vocabulary-based approach where the teacher plans and links with another area of the curriculum.

Below are the aims from the KS2 Framework for Language for children to achieve by the end of Year 3 in Speaking and Listening. These can be easily covered as exemplified in the subsequent scenario.

- Enjoy listening to and speaking in the language.
- Listen and respond to familiar spoken words, phrases and sentences.
- Communicate with others using simple words and phrases and short sentences.
- Understand conventions such as taking turns to speak, valuing the contribution of others.
- Use correct pronunciation in spoken work.

Maths and Spanish example

The class teacher has some Spanish. This Year 4 class had no FL input in Year 3. So far they know greetings and they can introduce themselves. They have learnt some classroom vocabulary and are confident with colours.

The teacher wants to use his 45 minutes Spanish lesson to consolidate their knowledge and conceptual understanding of shapes – maths learning objective. His Spanish learning objective is to consolidate colours and introduce 3D shapes in the context of simple words and phrases.

He first builds children's confidence up by introducing the seven shapes (Figure 5.5) through an interactive guessing game, using near cognates. Then learners are invited to reproduce the names of shapes through the use of graded questions, which revise, practise and consolidate the new vocabulary, finally arriving at the production stage where, in response to, *¿De qué color es el triángulo?* the children will say, *el triángulo es amarillo*. Each shape is linked with a colour, following the same pattern.

Song activity:

El círculo es amarillo … amarillo, es amarillo.
El cuadrado es rojo … rojo, es rojo.
El triángulo es verde … verde, es verde.

Children go on to listen to the above rap shape song in Spanish and then sing along to consolidate. (Use learners to come up with the rhythm of the rap.)

Further consolidation of shapes and learning is for children to work in partners with small packs of cards of the shapes or draw shapes using their mini whiteboards – practising asking and answering the above question.

Figure 5.5 Seven 2D shapes in Spanish

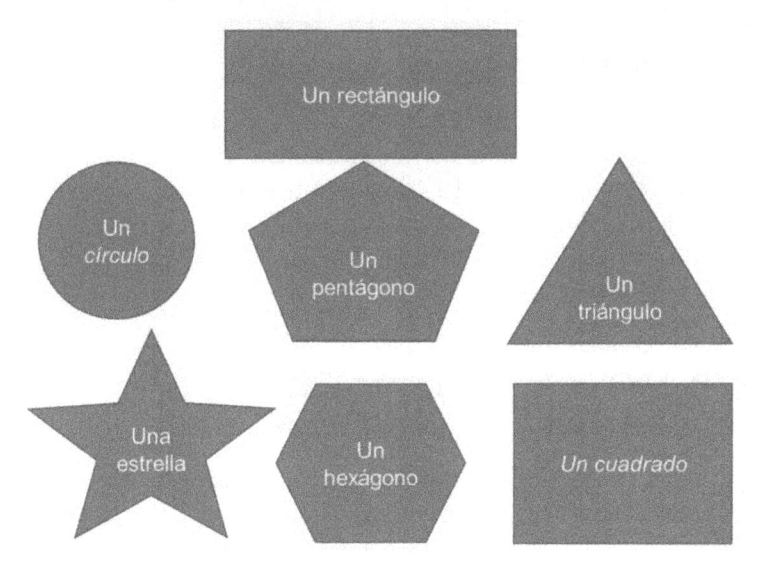

- Un rectángulo
- Un círculo
- Un pentágono
- Un triángulo
- Una estrella
- Un hexágono
- Un cuadrado

As a written activity, children model their writing from examples on the board after they have created a shape-monster/fun figure which they will use next lesson to tell each other stories. The book, *Oso Pardo, Oso Pardo, ¿Qué ves ahí?* [Grizzly Bear, Grizzly Bear, what do you see over there?], by Eric Carle will be used to model storytelling, revise colours and animals and inspire children to write their own stories using their shape-monster in a further Spanish lesson the following week.

The lesson ends with pupils pointing out objects in the classroom and naming their colours using simple words, phrases or short sentences.

https:// www.youtube.com/watch?v=DmKl9on5Jfo

There are many fun songs for practising Spanish shapes on YouTube. This one below is particularly good for articulation:

http://www.youtube.com/watch?v=43i4ereGxHo

Resources: 3D and 2D shapes, PowerPoint presentation of shapes in different colours with the Spanish names of shapes clearly visible on each slide.

http://www.youtube.com/watch?v=99zPboqO3sw

The two links above will help you with your presentation of shapes in Spanish as well as rehearsing your pronunciation before the lesson if you decide to try this out.

In the above Spanish lesson, children have been provided with the opportunity to manipulate language (and shapes), which is part of the goal of creatively being able to produce something new of their own (the story).

Integrating language from semi-familiar to new content

Integrating language, going from semi-familiar to new content is a way of working which draws from a range of areas of the curriculum, when semi-familiar or new content from another subject can be introduced during the language lesson. This approach will gradually increase vocabulary and expand usage of vocabulary for learners. Learners would already have encountered some aspects of the learning during the specific subject lessons.

History through French example

The history topic for a Year 3 class is Stone Age. The class has already been introduced to the topic. The teacher has studied French up to GCSE. Her degree was in archaeology and it is a passion. She wants to bring this passion in the classroom to help pupils understand what archaeologists do and to help children to think of themselves as detectives. At the same time, in French, the class is learning about parts of the body. Read what happens next…

The teacher uses the resource pact (freely available online) The History Detectives

- *The class will collaboratively create their own cardboard cut-out detectives providing him /her with a name, attributes and characteristics (patient, observant, determined, and intelligent). The character will then be used throughout the history topic, to focus attention on investigating and to find out information.*

- *In the language class the teacher revisits parts of the body and tells the children the learning objective of the lesson.*

- *The teacher also introduces the idea of cognates to the children explaining that cognates are words which are easy to read and remember, when learning a language because they look the same and have the same meaning. In pairs children have to list as many cognates as they know or see in the classroom.*

- *Teacher then plays a five-minute clip from YouTube, introducing them to Hercules Poirot, Agata Christie's Belgian famous detective. This follows discussion in English to briefly summarize who and what Poirot is and does. The discussion will continue later on, leading children to distinguish differences between a crime detective and a history detective in the TL.*

- *In French the teacher introduces Hercules Poirot: C'est un détective. Il s'appelle Hercules Poirot. Il est belge. Il cherche des preuves et fait un plan pour découvrir le criminel et le met en prison. Poirot est un détective de crime.*

- *The teacher now turns to the class and says 'Mais vous, vous êtes un detective aussi. Vous êtes archéologue … un détective de l'histoire.*

- *The teacher stops and ensures understanding by getting pupils to speak in pairs in English or French – Maintenant discutez avec votre partenaire – La différence entre un détective et un archéologue. The teacher takes feedback and addresses misconceptions.*
- *The teacher asks children how many cognates they notice on the slide she uses to introduce Hercules Poirot.*
- *Next, the class is placed into small groups to draw around one member lying on the floor and then to label all parts of the body in TL, to name the archéologue (archaeologist) character made up by the children.*

The class will then come together for a final plenary to consolidate on Il/elle est anglaise(e). Il/elle archéologue Il/elle cherche des preuves pour connaitre la vie des personnes de l'histoire.

In the above lesson the class has been introduced formally to the idea of cognates. Cognates are words which look the same, have similar pronunciations, meanings and spellings. For example, in French *collège/college, difficile/difficult, retourner/return, apprécier/appreciate, gigantesque/gigantic, astronaute/astronaut, bébé/baby, calculatrice/calculator, électricité/electricity, etc*. Making use of cognates in your language class is a long-term investment. Cognates support understanding and reading skills. Making learners look at a short passage in the TL which has cognates embedded will empower them from the beginning to use what they already know to infer meaning, make connections and comprehend the gist of what's in front of them. Below, the use of words such as *détective/adore/résoudre/ mystères/ patient/ intelligent* etc. is deliberate.

- Voici Hercules Poirot. Il est belge. Il est détective. Il adore résoudre des mystères. Il est patient et intelligent.
- Voici Howard Carter. Il est anglais. Il est archéologue. Il aime creuser la terre pour trouver des trésors de l'histoire. Il est observant et très intelligent.
- Voici Dame Kathleen Kenyon. Elle est anglaise. Elle aime creuser la terre pour trouver des trésors de l'histoire. Elle est intelligente et elle adore l'histoire. Elle a découvert des choses merveilleuses à Jéricho. Savez-vous où est Jéricho?

Above is the additional text the teacher uses when introducing the common ideas between both detective and archaeologist. Notice that the class is presented with examples of both male and female famous archaeologists and it provides learners with opportunity to make further connection with the field of archaeology and the people who brought clarity to our understanding of how our ancestors lived. The children will most certainly meet Howard Carter when they start learning about the Egyptians, but it takes the teacher's interest in women scientist and a cross-curricular opportunity, in this case a language learning lesson, to meet the most famous English woman archaeologist of the twentieth century.

To consolidate on the language structures introduced and practised in this lesson, children can be further encouraged to do their own internet research about other male or female archaeologists and to come ready to introduce them at the beginning of the next lesson. This could be for all learners but it could be for learners who are speakers of the TL or those learners who need to be extended further.

Rigour and challenge can be maintained fairly easily when our cross-curricular teaching learning involves two areas of the curriculum. It can be taxing and rather challenging we believe, if we take on more than two areas of the curriculum at any given time. The promotion of creative thinking while learning the skills and knowledge of two subjects through a single lesson is more manageable for both the teacher and the pupils. Barnes (2015) makes a case for achieving progress in one subject by also teaching aspects of another. Progression of all subjects involved is essential. There needs to be clear progression in language skills as learners are led from listening skills to reading, to eventually writing linked sentences in the TL to describe a geometrical shape, its colour, size and properties or to write a short profile of an archaeologist either from the content of the lesson or from their own research. In both the above scenarios, maths and history are the weaker, if you choose the subsidiary subject partner in a language lesson. However, we can also appreciate that in both lessons, there has been a great deal of opportunity for learners to consolidate on their previous learning because they have been provided with a creative and original space in which to think about their previous learning and to see

Figure 5.6 Ancient French map showing Jericho

it in a new light through the medium of another language. Those learners who need further consolidation in their developing English language skills, and/or may not have attended school previously will surely benefit from the broad approach.

Cross-curricular learning is highly motivating and energizing and provides learners with a context to further their knowledge and understanding of the world they live in. Cross-curricular learning also promotes values such as love, hope, community, positive relationships, sustainability, health and well-being. Using your language lessons to work on the content of the PHSE programme of study, such as promoting the attributes of being a good friend, is an interesting way to engage learners with themes of emotional and mental well-being. Figure 5.7 will be a good opportunity to explore, clarify and if necessary challenge children's and others' values, attitudes, beliefs, rights and responsibilities while engaging them progressively with the process of using the TL to exploring the important themes of well-being and relationships with others.

> **H6.** to deepen their understanding of good and not so good feelings, to extend their vocabulary to enable them to explain both the range and intensity of their feelings to others.
>
> KS 2 PSHE Programme of Study (2017)

Figure 5.7 French/English checklist of what friendship should mean

Un bon ami doit... ✓/✗ A good friend should...

Qualités	vrai/faux	Qualities
Être honnête		Be honest
Vivre dans une grande maison		Live in a big house
Savoir écouter		Be a good listener
Faire tout ce que je veux		Do whatever I want
Avoir beaucoup de jeux et jouets		Have lots of toys and games
Porter des beaux vêtements		Wear nice clothes
Être gentil		Be kind
Me parler seulement		Only talk to me
Avoir d'autre amis		Have other friends
Pardonner et oublier		Be forgiving
Prendre soin des autres		Be interested in other people
Avoir beaucoup d'argent		Have lots of money
S'intéresser aux autres		Care about others
Faire ce qu'il faut		Do the right thing
Être toujours d'accord avec mes idées		Always agree with what I say
M'apporter toujours des cadeaux		Bring me presents all the time

Content Language Integrated Learning

CLIL is a pedagogical model of teaching and learning languages. It emerged in the 1990s, and it is evidenced based and well documented for its success in Canada. CLIL has had considerable success in European countries too, due to its impact on language learners. It is an immersion model of language teaching and learning where subjects of the school curriculum are delivered through learners' non-native language but through the medium of the FL being learnt. It is a view of learning which maintains that you learn swimming by swimming, not by reading about it and you learn a language by using it. There is evidence to support CLIL effectiveness in terms of language proficiency, pupils' engagement and retention.

In the last decade, the development of CLIL has been mostly found in English secondary schools. However, there is no reason to believe that it is not possible to develop CLIL in primary schools. Massler, Stotz and Queisser (2014), Cross and Gearon (2013), Hood and Tobutt (2009) reinforced the fact that the dual subject approach of teaching and learning can work equally well in primary schools.

Coyle (2007) asserts that CLIL is a new era for languages. It is a more holistic approach to learning which will transform classroom into a language-rich environment and a cultural space where language can thrive while offering learners opportunities to engage in meaning-making and language progression through activities which are cognitively challenging and culturally enriching.

However well-documented CLIL is, there remain issues of implementation here in the UK, as elsewhere. The potentials of CLIL are difficult to realize because a universal model for CLIL does not exist; however, as Coyle points out, the nature of learning theories are ever-changing and the multiple research accessible to inform our pedagogies within the classroom is leading us to one conclusion and that is, it is our mindset that needs shifting to accommodate the extending goal of our teaching and learning.

We are in agreement with Coyle (2015) and Hood and Tobutt (2009) that the greater changes must be directed at classroom practices, the underlying pedagogic principles used to guide teaching and learning and the shared ownership of a vision for those leaders of learning and teaching. There is positive evidence in schools in the UK to suggest that where the individual is an effective teacher with deeper understanding of CLIL, the evolution of a CLIL approach is more likely to be secure.

Here are the steps of how CLIL can be realized in the classroom setting using our example from Chapter 4, on the painter Cézanne.

Remembering that the two important principles of a CLIL lesson are:

- We use language to learn and to communicate.
- The topic we teach determines the language we need to learn.

After a first lesson children would know something about the French painter and his paintings, its relevance to children in French-speaking countries as well as to famous subsequent artist who were influenced by him. We propose that the next step be the five-question grid which we have created based on NCSL's paper on personalizing learning. (NCSL – National College for School Leadership. p. 14)*. The children can write their ideas on colourful post-its which you can use to create a classroom display.

The language lesson

What am I going to learn?	How am I going to learn it?	When am I going to learn?	Where is it to be learnt?	Who is going to help me to learn?
• French artist Cézanne. • What kind of pictures did he paint? • Researching and Presenting in French.	Use books and internet to research	In my French, Art and Computing lessons	National Gallery Art lesson French lesson Library At home	My class teacher and my class mates My parents

It can support the teacher to negotiate and advise on the appropriate individual answers to these questions. Conversely we are embedding this in the constructivist learning model whereby we are engaging learners in challenges, problem-solving and research, with peers and with the teacher. This kind of learning can be creative, motivating, and easy to differentiate and open to multiple forms of assessment. A Year 5 learner can be guided to research independently. Here we draw on Vygotsky's theory of learning of Zone of Proximal Development (ZPD) where a pupil can achieve independent learning and/or seek help from a significant other, a classmate or the teacher/the (MFL) teaching assistant.

As far as the actual language content goes, after two years of regular French input, we would assume that most children would be able to confidently introduce themselves and another person, hence using the third person singular (il/elle).

French and Art example

Key vocabulary, phrases and concepts

'Avec une pomme, je veux étonner Paris !' Paul Cézanne is claimed to have said 'I want to astonish Paris, with an apple!' (Explain this to pupils).

1 http://www.ina.fr/video/CAC95050595 Play this film clip (under three mins) to the class. It provides pupils with visual input of Provence, the place where the artist lived and painted. After viewing, assess overall understanding by asking pupils general questions about the place rather than about what was said about Cézanne.

2 To stimulate reading in the TL and build confidence, introduce Cézanne using the sentences below with pictures from the internet through a PowerPoint presentation.

Il s'appelle Paul Cézanne.
Il est français.
Il est peintre.
Il aime peindre les beaux tableaux de la nature.
Il adore peindre des pommes, des oranges et quelque fois des poires.
Il est timide et aime la montagne mais il n'aime pas beaucoup être avec les autres gens.
Il a un fils qui s'appelle Paul aussi. Sa femme s'appelle Marie.
Son fils et sa femme habitent dans la ville de Paris. Son fils visite souvent Cézanne à Aix en Provence.
Si vous visitez Provence, vous pouvez visiter le beau studio de Cézanne et sa maison à Gardanne.

3 Use these questions/or your own after the presentation through shared reading with the whole class:

Qu'est-ce que vous voyez dans cette image? Comment s'appelle cet homme ? Quel est son métier? Est-ce qu'il est français ou anglais? Pourquoi? Où habite-t-il ? Et son fils? Dans quelle région de France est Gardanne?

4 Make grammar points: *habitent* – third person plural. Difference between *peintre* and *peindre* – painter *and to* paint

5 Children work in pairs to play *running dictation*: it is a race, the text is at one end of the room and competing teams send their partner to read it, remember it and recount it back to the writing partner. They agree on the final correct version.

6 To stimulate writing use the original text as a writing frame with gaps for pupils to fill in either from memory or with words provided.

7 Finish lesson by viewing Cézanne virtual gallery or Pinterest's Cézanne – invite pupils to speculate why Cézanne may have said that he wanted to astonish Paris with an apple?

- http://www.cezanne-en-provence.com/galerie/les-natures-mortes/
- https://uk.pinterest.com/explore/paul-c%C3%A9zanne-919898039381/
- https://www.theguardian.com/artanddesign/2017/oct/23/cezanne-portraits-national-portrait-gallery-review
- http://www.telegraph.co.uk/art/what-to-see/art-show-year-cezanne-portraits-national-portrait-gallery/

The scenario above contains the language we want to reinforce or introduce and practise in the first language lesson while at the same time we will be telling the class of how we will follow this up in the art class. Throughout this first language lesson, since the focus will be on language, we will be asking pupils differentiated

Figure 5.8 Key interactive language around colour and technique

Art Lesson-Learning Objective: develop knowledge about great artists in history
FL lesson- Learning Objective: Use key words to describe paintings and colours
Resources: IWB/ a printed copy from the internet of **Still life with Apples and Oranges (1895)**
Key vocabulary, phrases and concepts:

Que voyez vous?
Qu'est-ce qu'il y a dans cette image?
Quel est le sujet?
Quelles couleurs? Pourquoi ces couleurs?
Quelles formes? Pourquoi ces formes?
Quelle est la technique dans ce tableau?
Quelles sont les couleurs primaires?
Combien il y a-t-il? (jaune, rouge, bleu)
Quelles sont les couleurs secondaires?
 (rose, blanc, noir, marron, gris)
Comment fait-on une couleur secondaire?
 (orange, violet, vert)
Quelles sont les couleurs chaudes dans cette image?
Quelles sont les couleurs fraîches?

J'aime la couleur
J'aime ...parce que
Je n'aime pas ... parce que
C'est super... c'est bien... c'est nul...
Je vois la couleur (*jaune*) parce que ....
Il n'y a pas de
Je ne vois pas la couleur
Ici les couleurs et les formes sont ...
La technique est la même que ...
La technique n'est pas pareil ...
C'est du style de la nature morte
La couleur rouge est plus foncée que normal
La couleur rose est un melange de rouge et de jaune/ de blanc
If faut deux couleurs ...

questions in French to ensure they are secure in their understanding. By the end of the first language lesson, we will be providing the children with an opportunity to consolidate the new language they have learnt and to ensure they have grasped the gist of who Cézanne was. After the general collective introduction of the painter and some independent research, pupils can put together what they have found out and how to present this in the TL.

We have purposefully kept the illustrated presentation above, in the present tense, but there is no reason why some children in the classroom whose first spoken language is French cannot at this point be using the perfect tense, formally/informally, in order to acknowledge their language skills and provide the children in the class with an example of rich language.

Figure 5.9 Forms of the imperative mode for the classroom

Instructions words:

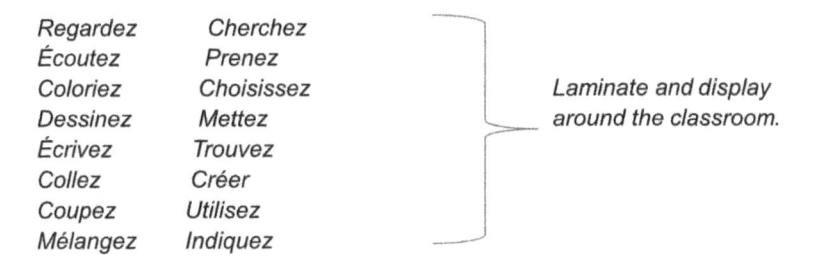

Regardez   Cherchez
Écoutez   Prenez
Coloriez   Choisissez   *Laminate and display*
Dessinez   Mettez   *around the classroom.*
Écrivez   Trouvez
Collez   Créer
Coupez   Utilisez
Mélangez   Indiquez

Painting vocabulary:

du papier, un crayon, un pinceau, une brosse, de la peinture, des pastels, des croyons a la cire, une palette.

While children are introduced to various paintings, Cézanne's historical time period and his location, they are also being encouraged to create their own artwork. They can gain confidence in the notion that they too could become great artists. There will be many ideas for activities, but the above can introduce learners to the process needed to create a darker or lighter shade of colour using the TL to consolidate the language already learnt.

Ask pupils to add red to black to create a darker shade of red. Add yellow to red to create a lighter tint of yellowy red. This process will be applied to their paintings which will be similar to Cézanne's *Still Life with Apples and Oranges* painting.

Pause for thought

Activity 1

Highlight the grammar point of the imperative mode: three ways to give orders or instructions using *tu, vous or nous*, but we never actually see those pronouns (as the conjugated form is for that pronoun only) like in:

(Tu) Ajoute rouge au noir. (Tu) Mélange les deux couleurs. (Instructions to a single person)

or

(vous) Ajoutez rouge et noir. (Vous) Mélangez les deux couleurs. (Instructions to several people at once)

or

(Nous) Ajoutons rouge au noir. (Nous) Mélangeons les deux couleurs. (Instructions to all of us)

Remind learners when to use these: instructions, commands and exclamations (as in a speech). Play an interactive game in groups – pointing game – an elected member of the group indicate/touch the correct instruction as the teacher calls them out.

Introduce the expression *il faut (to have to/ you need to))an impersonal expression indicating that something is necessary.* Practise with:
Il faut des couleurs primaires. Il faut le rouge, le jaune et le bleu.
Il faut des couleurs secondaires. Il faut le vert, le brun et le rose.

Activity 2

- Discuss Cézanne's art, including the still life, 'Apples and Oranges'
- Use books, internet, maps, etc., to discuss where and when he lived, alongside other historical events.
- Dress a table in white cloth, and arrange apples and oranges as in the painting, or do your own version of still life.
- Discuss some key words (artist, inspiration, imagination, technique, etc.).
- Model some basic colouring techniques (colour shades)
- Children can evaluate their own and each other's paintings in their language portfolios (if appropriate)

Figure 5.10 Mixing colours in French

To achieve **rouge foncée**

Il faut mélanger _____ et _____ (en français s'il te plaît.)

Dessine un exemple

To achieve **rose**

Il faut mélanger _____ et _____ (en français s'il te plaît.)

Figure 5.11 Wordle of cross-curricular planning in languages

Summary

The core of an excellent curriculum is not only what learning it delivers but also that it instils in children a love of learning for its own sake. The Wordle image shown in Figure 5.11 reminds us not only how enriching language learning can be for all, but also how much primary children can benefit from the experience of cross-curricular learning. While they are learning how to learn, they engage in a lifelong process of learning to make connections which then support breadth, balance as well as excitement in the classroom for both the teacher and the pupils.

Recommended reading

Barnes, J. (2015). Cross Curricular Learning 3-14 (3rd Edition).

Coyle, D. (2015). Strengthening integrated learning: Towards a new era for pluriliteracies and intercultural learning. *Latin American Journal of Content and Language Integrated Learning,* 8(2), 84–103.

Freire Institute: http://www.freire.org/paulo-freire/

Hood, P. and Tobutt, K. (2009). Modern Languages in the Primary School.

Kirsch, C. (2016). Using storytelling to teach vocabulary in language lessons: Does it work? *The Language Learning Journal*, 44(1), 33–51.

Morgan, C. (1994). Creative writing in foreign language teaching. *The Language Learning Journal*, 10(1), 44–7.

Chapter 6
Children's Ideas – Promoting Curiosity

Curiosity is, in great and generous minds, the first passion and the last.
Dr S. Johnston

Chapter objectives

In this chapter we highlight the relevance of the cultural, relational capital of teachers and children and its impact on our sense of curiosity and approach to learning, and thus, children's curiosity and creativity. We discuss one of the most relevant theories on creativity in the context of education, ending with an exploration of how creativity can look like in the FLs classroom.
The objectives are:

- to explore the different aspects that seem to maximize creative potential in the language learning classroom through the promotion of curiosity;
- to unpick what we mean by curiosity in languages and its relationship to creativity;
- offer examples of creative outputs that stimulate and trigger your own creative processes which in turn, should find their way to the children.

In terms of creativity and language learning, we hope to encourage you to boldly go where only the privileged have gone before.

Creative minds seldom realize how motivated or curious they are and the curious mind seldom sees how creative its strategies and outcomes can be. Like the two sides of the same coin, they do not exist but in relation to each other, for better or for worse. Creativity is one of those concepts that evade clear definitions or formula. Creativity itself (as opposed to creative outcomes) will not be contained, boxed or published for others to 'put on' so to speak. Yet, we continue to unpick creativity in order to understand it and manipulate it to some extent, offering ideas on why and how we are creative, but the definitive book on creativity can never exist, as creativity is intrinsically linked to our individual sense of self and diverse perceptions and cultures.

We need to differentiate creativity from other confounding aspects like engagement, entertainment, art or even the verb 'create' itself. We would like to question a statement made in Chapter 1, 'The creative adult is the child who survived,' a quote attributed to Ursula LeGuin, American author and essayist. There are so many assumptions in that statement regarding popular views on creativity and childhood that it makes a good starting point for reflection. Do we really feel we have lost something on our journey to adulthood? A quote attributed to Picasso says, 'It took me four years to paint like Raphael, but a lifetime to paint like a child.' It supports this notion of childhood as having some secret insight into what art and creativity is all about. Quotes on creativity are easy to come by, but they often tend to reaffirm popular, romanticized views of childhood rather than reflect what may be really taking place in the creative process. For instance, some studies have recently suggested that boredom and creativity are linked. Boredom it seems can allow for the creative process to get started.

Figure 6.1 *The Guardian* newspaper excerpt on boredom

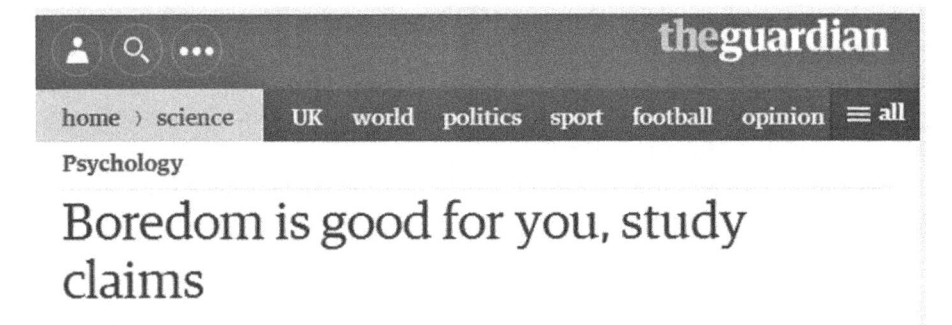

These studies see boredom as a precursor of creativity. We do not mean to say that boredom in the classroom is necessary in order to encourage creativity. Most of the research points towards perceptions of boredom having a negative impact on academic achievement (Mann and Cadman 2014), so, perhaps pinning down the right kind of boredom may be as difficult as pinning down creativity – although Herger (2014) does this very well as he discusses the types of boredom most conducive to creativity. What has been suggested is that it is the daydreaming effect boredom brings about that gives creativity an opportunity. This would seem to oddly suggest that if our lessons are boring enough, then the child's mind will wander off in search of more stimulating material, leading possibly to a creative outcome. Perhaps. However, boredom is not what we strive for as teachers. What is of greater value from these studies is the acknowledgement of the impact that daydreaming can have on the creative process, and daydreaming is a reflective event. Children constantly engaged in onscreen games and activity may have very little time to daydream.

Pause for thought — *Where is creativity?*

Consider the following 'freeze frames' and tick the ones you believe demonstrate the following possibilities (P):
    P1: evidence of a creative process taking place.
    P2: evidence of curiosity and engagement.
    P3: evidence of boredom/daydreaming.

Freeze frames	P1	P2	P3
Children sitting in a circle, all attentively listening to one of them who is saying something.			
Children working in groups at tables, where large pieces of paper and other materials can be seen.			
Children watching a video about Mexico on the IWB.			
Children, in pairs, working with iPads.			
Children standing by their desks, following the class teacher's lead, in a game of movements and foreign words.			
Children sitting at their desks, reading in silence.			
Children sitting at their desks, writing.			

> | |
> |---|
> | Children during PE, playing football using French vocabulary. |
> | Children sharing their Spanish homework with a partner. |
> | Children play-acting in French, videoing their performances. |
> | Children talking loudly with each other, waiting for teacher to get started. |
> | Children walking to or from school on the day of their language lesson. |
> | Children introducing themselves in Spanish using hand puppets. |
> | Children talking with an equivalent French class via Skype. |
> | A child, quietly watching the raindrops running down the window outside during their French lesson. |
> | Children as whole class, memorizing numbers in Spanish (chanting). |
> | Any other activity you can think of. |
>
> - Independently, number the activities above in terms of which are more creative (1) to which are the least creative (17). Share and discuss with a partner.

The list above provides different snapshots of possible activities that can take place in a language classroom. That is all they are – activities. There is no possible way we can sort this list in terms of how creative or boring each may be. A child walking to school has the time to reflect about a design, a story or any project he or she is working on in their language lesson, so the walk to school turns into part of a creative process. Children working on a colourful poster may be just following the most confident member's instructions, trying to copy some famous artist's design without any thought on expressing their own meaning and understanding, rendering the activity an engaging event at best, but it shows no evidence of creativity necessarily. This is because creativity happens in the mind, in the intentions, in the purpose. It cannot be photographed or 'put on scene' as such; we can only subjectively judge the various outcomes.

Each single activity above can potentially be evidence of a creative process – or not. If you look back at the list, what extra information would you need about each activity in order to assess it in terms of creativeness? For instance, 'children sitting at desks, writing' could be part of a creative process *if* they were engaged in say, writing a short, simple poem, possibly haiku (three-line observation about a fleeting moment involving nature), inspired by a relevant activity and based on their own experiences. Or, they could be filling in a worksheet, matching or writing from memory, which would not be part of a creative process even if they could colour in. However, it is important to know that not all learning needs to involve creativity.

Some theories on creativity are somewhat deterministic (i.e. intelligence) and difficult or impossible to manipulate in a classroom environment, and will not form part of this chapter. However, other theories are more relevant in terms of teaching and learning. Investment theory, as the name suggests, sees creativity as the outcome of some considerable investment (knowingly or not) on the part of the individual. This is a good way of thinking about creativity in the classroom because it allows for agency; that is to say, there are actual things we can do that might directly affect our creative potential. This theory was developed by the cognitive psychologist Robert J. Sternberg (2006), who considered both types of creativity; big C (creativity that advances the human cause in some way, as in inventions and discoveries), and little c (the type of creativity that allows most of us to find/express meaning in our own lives, as in hobbies). For Sternberg, creativity can occur when six particular characteristics 'converge', or meet and interrelate.

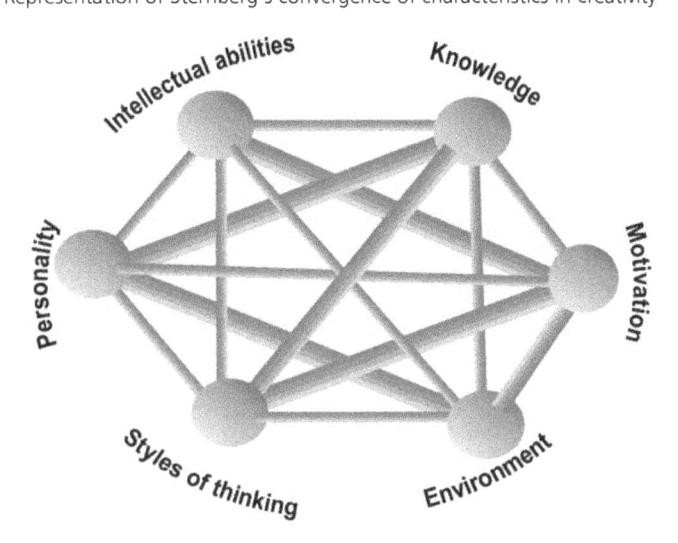

Figure 6.2 Representation of Sternberg's convergence of characteristics in creativity

Sternberg unpicks these further and goes on to suggest ways in which we can actively support the creative process. I would like you to read the following list and think about the aspects which you, as a teacher, can actually manipulate to enhance both your teaching and the children's learning in the language classroom.

a- redefine problems,
b- question and analyse assumptions,
c- not assume that creative ideas sell themselves: sell them,
d- encourage the generation of ideas,
e- recognize that knowledge can both help and hinder creativity,
f- identify and surmount obstacles,
g- take sensible risks,
h- tolerate ambiguity,
I- believe in oneself (self-efficacy),
j- find what one loves to do,
k- delay gratification,
l- role-model creativity,
m- cross-fertilize ideas,
n- reward creativity,
o- allow mistakes,
p- encourage collaboration,
q- see things from others' points of view,
r- take responsibility for successes and failures,
s- maximize person–environment fit,
t- continue to allow intellectual growth.

Sternberg (2006)

You may be surprised to see 'knowledge' as both a hindering and an enabling factor in the creative process. Sometimes 'too much' knowledge or focus on one aspect can prevent you from seeing things from different perspectives. For instance, a linguist who knows a great deal about grammar, and grammar only, and does not engage in many of the other characteristics mentioned above may not be interested (due to her extensive knowledge) in finding alternative ways of seeing or understanding or playing with grammar in order to learn something new or to represent it to others. On the other hand, a linguist who does engage in those types of behaviours may well come up with novel ideas in their field, which advance understanding for others. A good example is Noam Chomsky and the way he developed the theory of Universal Grammar, in debate to this day.

There is little point in reinventing the wheel in terms of synthesizing the research on creativity in the primary context. The Qualifications and Curriculum Department (2004) drafted a very good report entitled, 'Creativity; find it, promote it', which can help you do just that, in general terms. We will look at some of the points raised in that document in terms of how they might look like in the FL classroom.

In the necessary absence of an all-encompassing definition of creativity, we can learn to spot creativity by its effect on us and our society.

CREATIVITY ENRICHES PUPILS' LIVES. By promoting creativity, teachers can give all pupils the opportunity to discover and pursue their particular interests and talents. We are all, or can be, creative to some degree. Creative pupils lead richer lives and, in the longer term, make a valuable contribution to society.

QCA 2004, p. 9

When pupils are thinking and behaving creatively in the classroom, you are likely to see them:

- questioning and challenging
- making connections and seeing relationships
- envisaging what might be
- exploring ideas, keeping options open
- reflecting critically on ideas, actions and outcomes.

QCA 2004, p. 10

These are difficult things to see, but not impossible. Only a teacher or observer who takes the time to really listen and interact with children can actually spot these events taking place. In other words, you need meaningful dialogue with children.

Pause for thought

Activity: Let us arrange the statements above in terms of three possibilities,

- **P1**: questioning and challenging/reflecting critically on ideas, actions and outcomes
- **P2**: making connections and seeing relationships/envisaging what might be
- **P3**: exploring ideas, keeping options open

With a partner, go back to the list of freeze frames and see which of the P statements above are more likely to be potentially taking place in each frame.

Keeping options open demonstrates flexibility of thought; the idea that there is more than one way of approaching something. As teachers it is important that we are aware that creativity exists in many different contexts and fields, and therefore, can be appreciated and approached in many different ways. We must not give children the impression that the arts (and art-related activities) or fiction-writing hold the monopoly on creativity. We might need to differentiate in our minds between 'artistic' and 'creative'. Not all creative people are artistic, and not all artists are necessarily creative. Of course, this will depend to a great extent on your definitions of 'artistic' and 'creative'. You may have a very generous view on what creativity entails, and might think that anyone who is good at drawing for instance, must be creative. However, for many, creativity even in drawing must display some of the characteristics above mentioned before it can be called creative. This is why Picasso is viewed as a creative artist (questioning and challenging our views or assumptions on the portrayal of the human form). But where does this view leave children? Do we believe that children are creative? Do they possess the P1, P2, P3 characteristics by default? It may be that they do so in abundance, disproportionally and indiscriminately so. After all, babies need to keep their options open until they learn to understand the different disciplines and rules in which humans organize the world. However, once they internalize a particular viewpoint, it is almost impossible to go back to that blank slate of perspectives and open possibilities which Picasso sought.

Some say that our current education system does not lead children into creativity, but out of it. You may want to listen to Sir Ken Robinson himself on YouTube, eloquently arguing for a necessary revolution in the way we educate our children. More recently he points out that education so far has been following a linear, conformist, product-based route, instead of an organic, agriculture-like approach where we prepare the ground for children to reach their potentialities and guide their creative nature.

Dalí was another famous Spanish artist known for his creative take on how our subconscious minds can play on our dreams and imaginations. However, getting children to copy Picasso or Dalí's paintings is not really engaging children's creativity. No matter how well you copy something, if you are not making new meaning (that comes from your own experiences and understanding), you are not really being creative. You would be, nevertheless, acquainting children with a Spanish painter, and this in itself can be a very worthwhile experience for the children, particularly if you discuss the paintings with them. It can be inspirational and open up new avenues for their curiosity to explore.

Pause for thought

Activity: Being Dalí

How might an activity around the works of Salvador Dalí encourage creativity in the language classroom, within the three possibilities above, particularly P2 and P3? This will involve some research on our part. It is not in vain that people often speak of success in terms of '1% inspiration, 99% perspiration' (hard work). First, what do we know about Dalí? How did he approach his work? What does it all mean?

When Dalí was a little boy he was obsessed with pebbles on the beach and would spend hours looking at them. He also had a curious fascination for ants, and you will often find these 'significant objects' somewhere in his paintings. Dalí was also greatly impressed and intrigued by Freud's work around the subconscious mind and the interpretation of dreams and this also comes through in his paintings. So, we have two concepts we can explore: significant objects and dreams. We need to think how we might put them together; copying Dalí's possible creative process rather than one of his paintings.

You can give children an opportunity to 'make connections and see relationships' between elements, thus 'envisaging what might be'. You can do this yourself, now. All you need to do is to think about a significant object in your life. Children are often asked to bring a shoebox for show-and-tell, and they can bring things (or photos of things) they hold dear. Then you need to share the most bizarre or

Figure 6.3 A child's drawing of a dream containing a significant object

beautiful dream you can remember (or you can make one up!). The trick now is to put these two things together: the significant object and a scene from a dream. How you go about it is entirely up to you. Drawing is one possibility.

- What activities could follow that would encourage children to interpret or share their drawings?
- What Spanish vocabulary might you introduce, why and how?
- What do you think the children are really getting from this activity?
- What impact can teaching cross-curricularly have on enabling opportunities for creativity?
- Think about your own school. Could this activity be carried out in your setting? Why/why not?

This theme would belong to the Language Framework strand of IU, but you can also incorporate some simple Spanish vocabulary by asking children to label some of the items in their paintings/drawings, getting them to use a dictionary, etc., as the drawing shown in Figure 6.3. In this way they get to read/hear language that is meaningful to them. If you look at the top right-hand corner, the child drew a cat as the significant object, and labelled it (gato), with a backdrop of a scene from' The

Snowman', which the child said he had dreamt about. It does not matter if the image comes from a dream, daydream or something the child saw.

This activity can be easily differentiated by including grammatical structures, from simple phrases to whole sentences. Afterwards, children could present their piece in front of the class or make a multimedia project including sound and narration, which could be uploaded to the school website. I strongly encourage you to do the activity yourself, with the children, modelling interest and passion in what you do. Ultimately, if you manage to broaden children's repertoire of possibilities in terms of what can be interesting and what can count as a resource for the imagination (encouraging creativity), then you will have done an important job, and if, on top of this, you manage to waken their curiosity and expand their knowledge about Spanish culture, even better. If a child, spontaneously says a Spanish word to you (from their painting), then you need to reward them somehow. Explicitly valuing creativity and spontaneous production of foreign vocabulary can send a strong message to children.

Role-modelling creativity

We cannot underestimate the impact that parents and significant adults have on children's intellectual development which includes their curiosity, motivation and creativity. The conversations and verbal interactions children have at home impact greatly on children's narrative powers and styles (Peterson et al. 2004). If not possible at home, school ought to be the place where children should have a right to access ways of seeing that may not be available to them otherwise. Are we, as teachers, nurturing children's curiosity by example and deed in our daily interactions with them?

> **Pause for thought**
>
> **Activity:** A letter to a son
> I will not forget your commission. As soon as I get to Leeds I shall scream out in the middle of the street, *Ironmongers* – Ironmongers – Six hundred men will rush out of their shops in a moment – fly, fly, in all directions – ring the bells, call the constables – set the town on fire. I *will* have a file and a screwdriver, and a ring, and if they are not brought directly, in forty seconds I will leave nothing but one small cat alive in the whole town of Leeds, and I shall only leave that, because I am afraid I shall not have time to kill it.
>   Then what a bawling and a tearing of hair there will be! Pigs and babies, camels and butterflies, rolling the gutter together – old women rushing up the chimneys and cows after them – ducks hiding themselves in coffee cups, and fat geese trying to squeeze themselves into pencil cases – at last the mayor of Leeds will be found in a soup plate covered up with custard and stuck full of almonds to make him look like a sponge cake that he may escape the dreadful destruction of the Town.

> At last they bring the things which I ordered and then I spare the Town and send off in fifty waggons and under the protection of 10,000 soldiers, a file and a screwdriver and a ring as a present to Charles L. D. ... from his affectionate Papa.
>
> **Questions:**
>
> - Which very famous children's author do you believe may have written this letter?
> - What impact may it have had on his son, short and long term?
> - What sort of imaginative interactions do you remember having with the adults in your childhood?
> - What sort of imaginative interactions do you, or might you have with the children in your class? (where you are part of the essential resource)
>
> We will return to this extract further down.

Our role is often a compromise between meeting the child's needs and the government's demands. Within this, we need to find room for the stimulation of creative thinking. As mentioned earlier, not every activity can or must necessarily be creative, but what it can be is a source of inspiration. Think of lessons as opportunities to provide children with the resources necessary for creativity to take place at some point. This will involve lessons around information (vocabulary and phrases) and processes (interpretation, sentence construction, discussions). Together these will contribute to a child's knowledge bank. Role-modelling creative thinking for children is crucial as they will want to copy adults' thinking styles (in order to please them). If you value creativity enough to make room for it, so will children. This means getting children involved in something that you, the teacher, are also part of not just as guide, but as full member; otherwise there is the danger of children becoming 'unreflective spectators' of your modelling as opposed to 'reflective participants' of it, as well as our 'entertaining' learners rather than 'engaging' them with the given task (Piazzoli 2012; O'Neill 2006). Following from this premise, we can say that, during FL lessons, students can easily turn into 'unreflective participants', and it is this lack of reflection that can hamper creativity, as the learning environment is too busy with frantic games (involving sound, visuals, movement, quick actions and reactions) that even though the children are actively participating, there is no time to reflect and/or think alternatively around anything.

> **Pause for thought**
>
> - What sort of language learning activities have you mostly seen in your school?
> - What type of participation did they promote (reflective or unreflective)?
> - What exactly made it one thing or the other? (subject matter, the nature of the activity, the teaching style, something else)
> - How compatible are, in your opinion, giving children room for creative processes and getting them to learn new vocabulary? Can we do both at the same time? Can the act of memorization ever be a creative process?

The most beautiful experience

The most beautiful experience we can have is the mysterious. It is the fundamental emotion that stands at the cradle of true art and true science. Whoever does not know it and can no longer wonder, no longer marvel, is as good as dead, and his eyes are dimmed.

Einstein 1930

I have a valid reason for quoting Einstein in this chapter. Einstein is often used as a model of the creative mind, yet few of us can truly clearly understand his contribution to science. No one argues with the fact that he was highly creative. He said he came to his equation in the spare time he had during his job as a patent's clerk (maybe we have boredom to thank for this!). As a child, Einstein was given a book about 'thought experiments', and he said he then got used to carrying them out. Thought experiments are case scenarios that run through one's mind and help us predict or understand a particular event or concept. The use of VR (virtual reality) headsets is now beginning to do this in schools for geography, science or cultural field trips. Einstein's most famous thought experiment was the one about the train station and the travelling beam of light (you can find out more about it online). Thought experiments however, are not the sole preserve of physics; we also have them in philosophy, where they are described as 'devices of the imagination used to investigate the nature of things'.

Thought experiments can take many forms, from simple case scenarios to full stories that end up with some kind of understanding or revelation, private or shared. They happen in the mind, when you have or make time for them. What might this look like in terms of language learning? Children will often ask questions that seem 'pointless' or simply 'unanswerable' to adults. For instance, you may be asked, 'Sir, why is everything in Spanish masculine or feminine?' and I am wondering what your response might be (it is interesting to think that Spanish native children would rarely ask this). It is good to give time and room for these questions as opposed to just ignoring or dismissing them because we don't know the answer. It is fine not to know, as this gives us an opportunity to model what to do when confronted with what we do not know or understand. What better lesson than learning to overcome or deal with our own ignorance? Even when there are no decisive answers the question can be of great benefit, and perhaps particularly so, for it is when we are confronted with an inexplicable mystery that our minds can really soar in search of answers and possibilities, impelling our creativity to explain the inexplicable.

One such mystery deals with an issue from a previous chapter, when we looked at a game of finding masculine and feminine nouns. Let us go back to that point on nouns and gender. As it happens, many languages like French, Spanish, German,

Arabic, etc. have gender. Some, like Spanish, have only masculine or feminine nouns, while German also has neutral gender nouns. There is no reason for this. Sanskrit, the ancient language from which most European languages are derived, also has gender. Nobody knows why. It is a great mystery. There are no criteria that could allow one to guess the gender of a noun – it has nothing to do with traits or characteristics socially attributed to masculinity or femininity. However, gender is not just a detail of a word. Gender dictates how we use the rest of the language around that word (its grammar) and it can permeate how those speakers conceptualize or imagine a certain word according to its gender (Boroditsky 2009).

Grammatical gender is a big deal. How might we get this across to children? Simply stating the fact will not be enough. Like we discussed in a previous chapter around 'knowledge about language', children need to play with concepts in order to internalize them. Giving out dry information about grammar and getting children to memorize rules is not particularly engaging. Getting them to use their memory and teaching them how to be analytical is important, but doing so in creative ways, to promote creativity in them, is the most interesting challenge and bears the greatest fruit. 'In other words, to the extent that one's goal is just to maximize children's memory for information, teaching for creative as well as analytical and practical thinking is still superior. It enables children to capitalize on their strengths and to correct or to compensate for their weaknesses, and it allows children to encode material in a variety of interesting ways.' (Sternberg 2006, p. 94)

Another Nobel Prize winner in physics, renowned for his creativity (and particularly his pedagogy) was Richard Feynman. It was his father, he says, who taught him to question the world, to look at it anew in order to understand it, and with this, his natural child's curiosity was sparked and developed into an adult sense of enquiry and continuing wonder. 'It [enquiry] has to do with curiosity. It has to do with people wondering what makes something do something. And then they discover that it has to do with answers that relate to each other; that things that make the wind, make the waves; like the motion of air, the motion of sand' (Feynman 1973).

A thought experiment: Turning information into play, and play into knowledge

When I was seven years old, and just like now, I used to lie in bed at night, before sleep came, and I would think all sorts of things. One night I had a vengeance thought. During the day my cousin had destroyed one of my favourite playthings; the dream that I would one day become a sailor. He was older than me and knew more things. He told me that I could never be a sailor because I was a girl (you see, back home in those days girls were not allowed to join the navy). I felt crushed. He had, in one simple sentence full of nouns and verbs (strangely enough there were no adjectives), made me realize that I would never be able to wear that lovely sailor's uniform – which is all I really wanted.

That night I stared at the ceiling in the dark and had my vengeance thought. If being a girl meant I couldn't be a sailor then I would part from all things male forever – even words. Yes, in my new world, no boy words would exist. I would only keep those words that belong to the girls. You can do things like that in Spanish because all things in the Spanish universe are either boys or girls. Everything that you can see and feel is either **m**asculine or **f**eminine. Miss had talked about that in school on Friday. She had called those words **n**ouns (sustantivos). 'Nouns are either masculine or feminine', she had said in her high pitched voice as she divided the board in two with a thick white chalk. For homework, we had to write 10 masculine nouns and 10 feminine nouns. Children still do that homework back home, in their books, in neat writing. I'm pretty sure they still do.

Figure 6.4 'I want to be a sailor'

Figure 6.5 Drawings of feminine nouns and masculine nouns

So, that night I knew just what I should do; I began to divide the universe into feminine and masculine nouns. What would it look like? I began to see it in my mind. 'The girls will have the moon and the stars. The boys will keep the sun ... but girls will have the light. Boys can keep the rivers and the oceans but us girls can keep the currents, the waves and the sand.' I went on and on until I fell asleep. What a strange world it was turning out to be, 'a sea without a shore and a sun without a sphere'.

I knew that for my homework I should keep as many naval nouns away from boys as possible. I remember sitting at the kitchen table writing all the feminine nouns of the navy that I could think of. 'Water!' – water is a feminine noun (*agua, n,f*). Men will just have to carry their ships on their shoulders!

Figure 6.6 is a photograph of my actual homework which I kept after all these years.

> **Pause for thought**
> - What games can you think of for the classroom around the theme of gender?
> - How does this thought experiment (story) enhance vocabulary learning?
> - Do nouns retain the same gender across languages? Look up 'nose' in French and then in Spanish.
> - What kind of learning might you be modelling to children through this?
> - What is it that you are actually modelling?

Figure 6.6 Paula Ambrossi's homework on masculine and feminine nouns

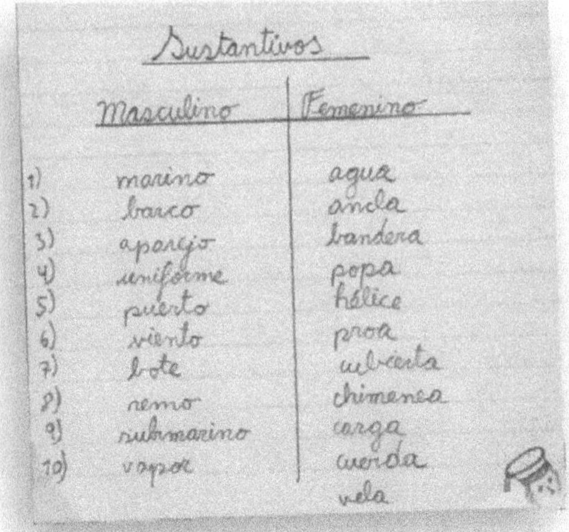

Nouns	
Masculine	Feminine
1) sailor	water
2) ship	anchor
3) rigging	flag
4) uniform	stern
5) port	propeller
6) wind	prow
7) boat	deck
8) oar	funnel
9) submarine	load
10) steam	rope
	sail

This thought experiment is actually a narrative, and narrative is how we make sense of the world. You can use narrative to make abstract concepts more accessible to children, so that they may play with the concepts. The narrative used to support abstract information (like grammar) must enhance the salient features and not distort the basic rules of the language (I could not have pretended to change a word's gender for instance, as this would have broken the rule: inert nouns do not change gender). Narrative can be very powerful as we tend to be good at remembering stories. The thought experiment above is actually true (I did do that as a child), but I have narrated it in a story-like manner in order to communicate it effectively.

> Narrative imagining – story – is the fundamental instrument of thought. ... Rational capacities depend on it. It is our chief means of looking into the future, of predicting, of planning, and of explaining. ... Most of our experience, our knowledge and our thinking is organized as stories.
>
> M. Turner (1996, p. 5)

The story about nouns and gender serves to illustrate how we can 'play' with information in order to make it familiar and open to examination. We need to let our own imagination free, and loosen up the ties we may have been bound in during years of unimaginative teaching. We can still do it, and more importantly, model it for the children. The letter to a son that you read earlier on, about, 'getting a file & a screwdriver' was actually written by Lewis Carrol's father. This might perhaps allow us to understand how Lewis Carrol's own imagination was encouraged (his real name was Charles Lutwidge Dodgson). It shows us that we see the world in the way we were taught to see it, as Richard Feynman poses earlier. As teachers, this can be very powerful information to have.

We need to learn to allow for the impossible to be real, just for long enough so that we may contemplate it in wonder and reflect.

> Alice laughed: 'There's no use trying,' she said; 'one can't believe impossible things.'
> 'I daresay you haven't had much practice,' said the Queen. 'When I was younger, I always did it for half an hour a day. Why, sometimes I've believed as many as six impossible things before breakfast.'
>
> Lewis Carrol, Alice in Wonderland

Pause for thought

Activity 1

In order to get some practice at seeing things differently, try this with a partner. I call it, 'confused nouns'. The idea actually comes from a theatre warm-up game meant to get actors to loosen up their imaginations before improvisation work. You can also do this on your way to places.

1 Look around you. Name every single object you see BUT with the wrong name (avoiding the names of things nearby but without too much thinking), thus you might call a 'tree' a 'glass', and a 'wheel' might be a 'tooth', etc.

2 It's harder than you might think, but if done frequently it leaves your mind ready to approach things differently. Look up improvisation techniques to find out more (Johnstone 2007).

Activity 2

1 Think about and answer the following question (which I once heard somewhere). Do not to fight the question (which some students tend to do) but just to go with it.

   Are you a regular or an irregular verb? – Why?

What is actually being asked is if you are a regular or irregular kind of person, making us think about characteristics of regularity and irregularity. When I get the 'irregular' students to put their hands up I ask the rest to pay close attention, because these are the people we cannot trust (everyone laughs). We cannot predict them in any way possible; we don't know what they did yesterday or will do tomorrow; what they may have done or would do; etc. In short, they're so irregular that we have to take them one case at a time and learn them by heart; they are irregular verbs. We all like being special and unique like irregular verbs so we are all tempted to call ourselves irregular. However, when it's the 'regular' students' turn, many more hands usually come up because we also like to be seen as dependable and trustworthy people. I tell the other students that these 'regular' people are the ones we can truly depend on. We can predict them entirely; we know what they did yesterday; what they'll do tomorrow; etc. just like regular verbs. Some students say that they are not a verb at all, but a noun

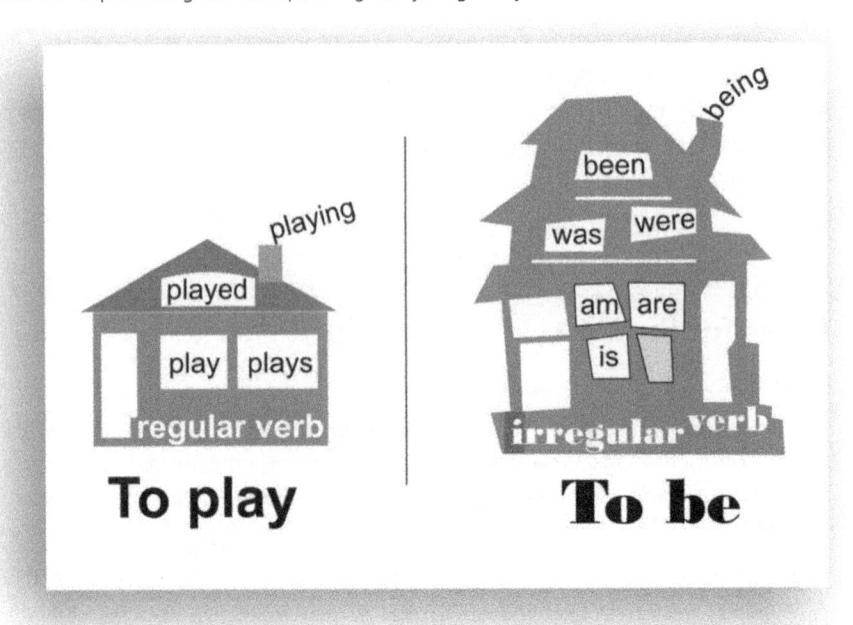

Figure 6.7 Representing the concept of regularity/irregularity in verbs

(true). But then, if we are nouns, how come every time we look in the mirror we see an adjective? (We describe – judge – our appearance whenever confronted by it!)

The point here is to play with grammar. The next step may be to think that if verbs were people, where would they live? How can we 'characterize' grammatical terms according to their behaviour within a structure?

If verbs lived in houses, this is what English verb houses would look like, with the most irregular verb 'to be' accompanied by the ordinary, regular verb 'to play'. Each form has a room of its own.

If we were to compare the houses shown in Figure 6.7 to the Spanish version, for the same irregular verb 'to be', we would not have enough room in the page. Spanish verbs live in high-rise buildings of about ten floors (excluding compound forms), with between five and six rooms in each floor (one room per conjugated form). Let us just look at the first three floors, and then skip to the roof and chimney!

> **Pause for thought**
> - Can you think of other ways we could represent the fact that verbs change according to time and pronoun (conjugation)?

We can also characterize other grammatical terms, like nouns. In Spanish for instance, nouns have gender and number, and are always placed before the adjective. Nouns are rather bossy (they tell the article and adjective how to behave). Seen from this

Children's Ideas – Promoting Curiosity   133

Figure 6.8 Representation of Spanish irregular verb To Be

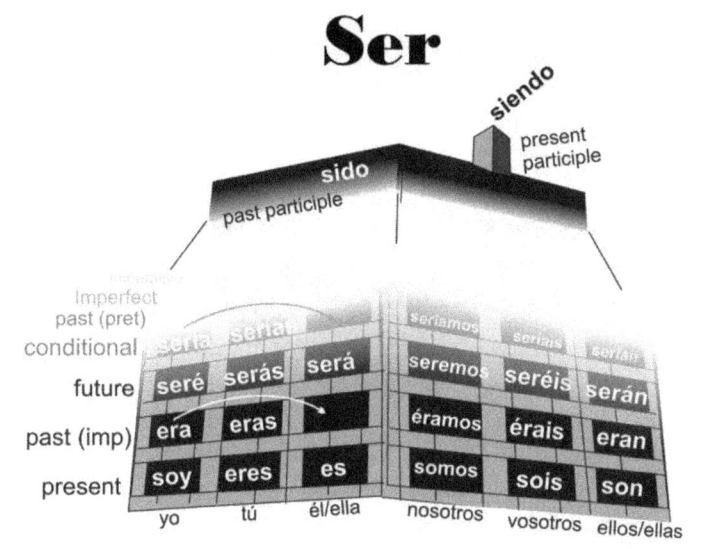

Ser

siendo
present participle

sido
past participle

Imperfect
past (pret)
conditional: sería, serías, sería, seríamos, seríais, serían
future: seré, serás, será, seremos, seréis, serán
past (imp): era, eras, era, éramos, erais, eran
present: soy, eres, es, somos, sois, son

yo tú él/ella nosotros vosotros ellos/ellas

Regular AND Irregular verbs in Spanish
are conjugated differently for every pronoun.

point of view, we could say that in the Spanish universe, nouns are the masters. We have the He-noun and the She-noun, with articles and adjectives acting as mutant slaves, doing whatever the noun decides.

Figure 6.9 Spanish nouns dictate gender for article and adjective

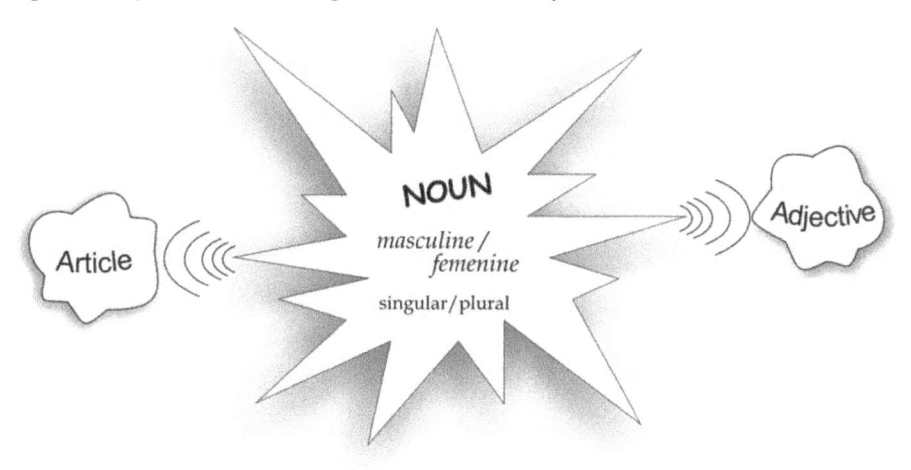

Article))) NOUN masculine/ femenine singular/plural))) Adjective

Another way in which we can foster creativity is by modelling 'making connections and seeing relationships' (and we saw this in greater detail in the chapter on cross-curricular learning). When it comes to FLs you need to play to your strengths and use your curiosity about the world and why the world is the way it is. The beauty of languages is that they are so inextricably connected to our history and culture that they have a great abundance of contexts to explore. For instance, children learn a great deal about the Romans in their primary years, but what can the Romans really do for us?

> **'What have the Romans *ever* done for us?'**

That is what a character from Monty Python asked at a secret meeting in ancient Jerusalem, trying to raise the fervour against the occupying Roman army. 'What have the Romans ever done for us?', he repeats, uninterested in the myriad of answers given to him by members, who cry – out: arches, columns, concrete, highway systems, aqueducts, thermal baths, law, Roman alphabet, etc. 'Yes. Yes', he rebuffs, 'But apart from all that, what have the Romans *ever* done for us?' There are many answers to this question, for knowledge is not absolute, and we need to be open minded because ambiguity can be a good thing; there is always another possibility, another interpretation, another dialogue that can be had. One might easily say that the one thing the Romans did for us, above all others, was to copy the Greeks.

Figure 6.10 Greek Gods and their Roman denomination

ARES   ZEUS   CRONOS
ARTEMIS HERMES APHRODITE APOLLO
Diana Mars Mercury Jupiter Venus Saturn Apollo

ΟΔΥΣΣΕΙΑ
Α

Ἄνδρα μοι ἔννεπε, μοῦσα, πολύτροπον, ὃς μάλα πολλὰ
πλάγχθη, ἐπεὶ Τροίης ἱερὸν πτολίεθρον ἔπερσεν·

Ὅμηρος

Tell me, O Muse, of the man of many devices, who wandered full many ways after he had sacked the sacred citadel of Troy.

(Homer, *The Odyssey*, first line).

The new curriculum encourages the teaching of ancient languages, and many children are learning some Latin. Figure 6.10 shows some of the Greek gods (with their Latin names below). When the Romans encountered Greek culture, they gave the Greek gods Latin names. Then, considering the stars, they named the known planets after the same gods, thus, the Greek god Zeus (most powerful) became Jupiter, and consequently the largest planet was named Jovis. When the eighth and furthest (known) planet from the sun was discovered in 1846, it was Poseidon, the Greek god of the sea, in Roman form, whose name would be taken, 'Dark, cold and whipped by supersonic winds, Neptune is the last of the hydrogen giants in our solar system' (NASA). How is this connected to primary languages? Can these fragments of information at all enhance language learning and inspire children? A more apt and relevant question to pose in our classrooms may well be, what have the Moors ever done for us? After all, when the Romans left, Europe sunk into the Dark Ages, but after the 500 years the Moors were in Europe – through Spain, Europe was able to experience the Enlightenment, after breathing in all the wealth of knowledge from the Islamic Golden Age, curtesy of the Moors (see Figure 3 in Chapter 3).

Languages used to belong to an elite; to those who could afford to buy an education and maybe use the knowledge to inform their policies or strategies, feed their artistic imagination, etc. They may have learnt Latin and ancient Greek grammar, but more importantly, through this act they were able to read works like *The Odyssey*. Anybody can now buy an English translation of *The Odyssey*, cheaply in print or online, and read it, and yet, how many actually do so? Many will have seen films like *Percy Jackson and the Lightning Thief* (2010), or *Jason and the Argonauts* (1963) with many references to the original text by Homer, but how are we using this rich material (if) in the classroom? Can we use it effectively if we don't understand its precedence and relevance? It may require some basic research on our part so as to fill in the gaps in our knowledge, and we can find the information easily if we look for it, but we need to have the desire to look for it. In other words, it is the expression of our own sense of curiosity that we need to transmit and model to and for the children.

Making connections across the curriculum allows us to envisage new things, to consolidate understanding by integrating information within different contexts and possibilities. Thus, we enable ourselves to at least have a choice; we can either spend twenty minutes on a game so as to help children memorize seven famous words, or we can have a unit of work that takes them through a journey to show them the wonder of ancient cultures, the universe itself, our place within it, and the seven words that followed.

Figure 6.11 Solar system in Latin

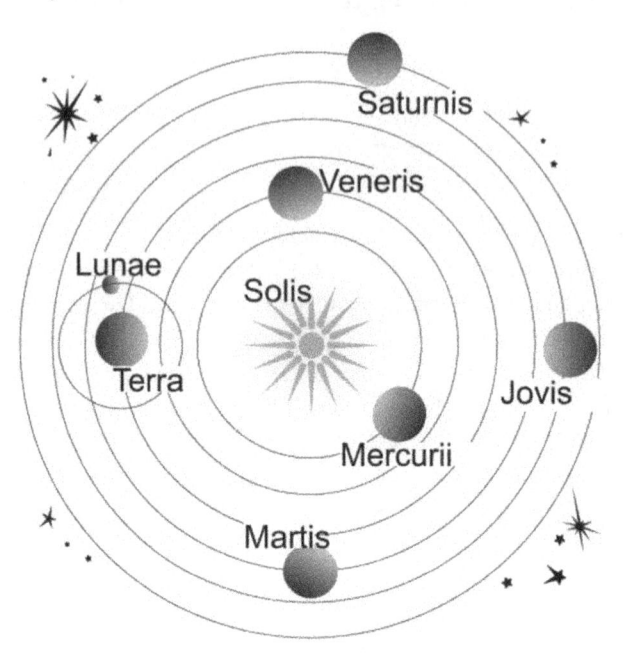

Listen to Holst's 'The Planets' during activity

> **Pause for thought**
>
> | español | français | italiano | român | English |
> |---|---|---|---|---|
> | lunes | lundi | lunedì | luni | |
> | martes | mardi | martedì | marți | |
> | miércoles | mercredi | mercoledì | miercuri | |
> | jueves | jeudi | givedì | joi | |
> | viernes | vendredi | venerdì | vineri | |
> | sábado | samedi | sabato | sâmbătă | |
> | domingo | dimanche | domenica | duminică | |
>
> - Can you fill in the last column?
> - What about the origin of the English days of the week?
> - How is this activity modelling creative thinking (rather than a creative product)?
> - If all schools taught the days of the week in this way, would it still be a creative approach?
> - Where is creativity, in a lesson plan or in the way it is delivered?

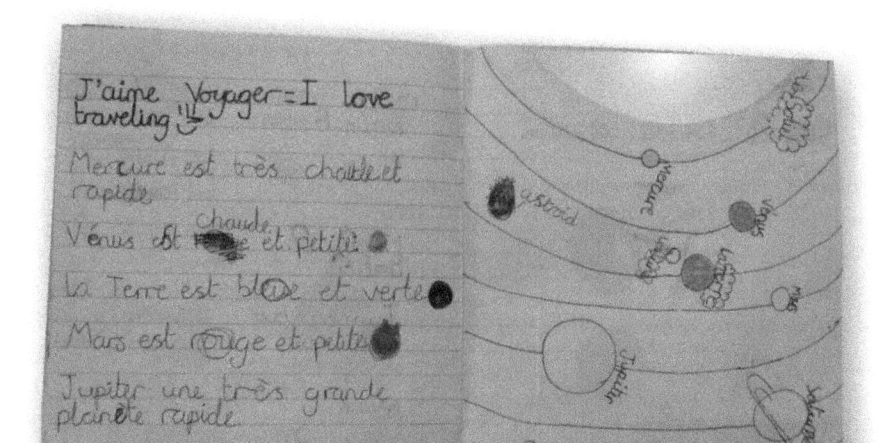

Figure 6.12 Children's work from Nadine Chadier's class

Portuguese is also a Romance language, but their days of the week are based on the word 'féria', meaning fair (festive day) which goes from the second to the sixth day (Monday to Friday). It joins Spanish for Saturday and Sunday, which, like all the other Romance languages, has 'day of the Lord' for Sunday (Latin: dies Dominica), and the Jewish 'Sabbath' for Saturday.

Children can be taught to incorporate these new visions into their developing learning identities. Both the psychologist Carl Rogers and the educator and philosopher Paulo Freire (foundational scholars of experiential learning) highlight the relevance of the direct personal experience in the motivated learner, where the goals are not fixed (tests), but rather an opening of potentialities that can be explored. What happens in the classroom has been shown to act directly on children's motivation (Graham, Van Bergen and Sweller 2016). Modelling the use of the imagination during class time can be an invaluable lesson; modelling how to be observant of things in order to feed the imagination in form and content can offer children a whole world of creative possibilities. 'Young people's creative abilities are most likely to be developed in an atmosphere in which the teacher's creative abilities are properly engaged' (ibid.). (NACCCE 1999).

We mentioned Ursula's saying in Chapter 1, 'The creative adult is the child who survived,' which we take to mean the child who managed to live through unimaginative adult input (parent or teacher) with his/her sense of wonder and curiosity intact. But maybe there is no such thing, and as Ursula says in her response to this 'attributed' saying, maybe there ought not to be such a child. Children have a right to *develop* their curiosity into adulthood, which means necessary change. We can only hope to enable children to retain their open-mindedness about the world by modelling it ourselves, through our interactions with them. Something that Ursula did actually say, which can work in defence of all the imaginative grown-ups (teachers) around, is, 'It's so much easier to blame the grownups than to be one' (LeGuin 2014), the grown-ups of our childhood. We need the power of agency that adulthood gives us over our own development rather than the helpless simplicity of childhood. What Picasso was really after – rather than being a child as such – was a way in which to view the world anew; without the constrains of received wisdom, what can and cannot be. We need to remember that after all, it takes an adult to be Picasso. In his art he was able to reconceptualize a view; create new meaning. In languages, we have the advantage of numerous contexts on which to learn and, in a way, play with meaning, but only if we are interested in the dialogue.

Summary

Teaching and learning in FLs will never be a creative endeavour if only the powers of memorization are engaged – however fun the activity may be. If we do that we are selling our children short of a world of possibilities; we are satisfying a short-term goal and depriving them of the ingredients necessary for long-term motivation and creativity. In short, we would not be nurturing their curiosity.

We can question words, be curious about them. In this chapter's quote, Dr Johnson, one of the greatest literary figures in the eighteenth century and creator of the first English dictionary, reminds us that curiosity is a lifelong affair – in great and generous minds. We need to at least try to make all the children in our class like the privileged, creative few, who have had contact with knowledgeable, curious and creative adults and learnt from their example, from their minds. That is where the privilege lies.

Recommended reading

Johnstone, K. (2007). Impro: Improvisation and the Theatre, Bloomsbury Publishing PLC, Methuen Drama, London (a free pdf version is available online)

Jones, N., Barnes, A. and Hunt, M. (2005) Thinking through languages: A multi-lingual approach to primary school languages. *The Language Learning Journal*, 32(1), 63–7.

Kalogirou, K., Beauchamp, G. and Shona Whyte (2017). Vocabulary Acquisition via Drama: Welsh as a second language in the primary school setting. *The Language Learning Journal*.

Piazzoli, E. (2012). Engage or Entertain? The Nature of Teacher/Participant Collaboration in Process Drama for Additional Language Teaching, 6(2) online at http://research.ucc.ie/scenario/2012/02/Piazzoli/05/en

Chapter 7
Assessing Children in Languages

Do not judge me by my successes, judge me by how many times I fell down and got back up again.

Nelson Mandela

Chapter objectives

- to consider that we all continually engage in diverse processes of assessment;
- to explore what assessment has looked like until now in the primary language classroom and its future directions;
- to gain an expert languages adviser's perspective on assessment, Dan Alliot will hopefully dispel some of the anxiety teachers have around assessment;
- to explore some of the resources available to help you assess your learners.

Who's afraid of assessment?

In this chapter we will explore the different ways in which the language classroom gives us opportunities to assess our learners in positive ways. First, we need to feel comfortable and unthreatened by the word 'assessment', and not treat it as some artificial skill only mastered by some.

We are all born into an extremely complex world. It is through our five senses that we are enabled to navigate and make sense of our environment, as we receive information, process it and then assess it. Thus, we take in visual, tactile, aural, olfactory and gustatory cues to understand colour, shape, distance, depth, taste and texture, etc., all interrelated. From this we come to not only understand simple events but talk about them too, from events like, 'I drop something', to more complex situations and ideas like, 'you would have dropped the glass if you hadn't noticed that the chair you were about to sit on was broken.' Both sentences are the outcome of experience, observation and interaction, but the second event goes many steps further and looks into a possible future (you might not notice the broken chair), reflects back to the past (you did notice the broken chair) and settles into the present (you still have the glass), all this from somebody else's perspective. Experience and information allow us to assess the world around us in increasingly complex ways as we grow (Groh 2014). Thus we make informed judgements on things and people by assessing not only what we see but also the intentions behind certain actions, according to the contexts that surround them. In other words, we live in a perpetual mode of assessment, and as teachers, we need to unpick this skill in terms of assessing what others know as they learn. Some types of knowledge are very easy to assess, and while all forms of assessment require particular knowledge and experience on our part, some types of assessment are much more complex to define – but still natural to perform.

> **Pause for thought**
>
> Take the following events, as the parent or teacher:
>
> - What information about the child (say, eight-year-old) do you need to know in order to assess the following events effectively and make a fair judgement on her or his performance?
>
> 1 Crossing the road
> 2 Walking home alone
> 3 Buying sweets in the shop
> 4 Deciding which clothes to wear on a cold day
> 5 Following Lego instructions to build a car
> 6 Asking for help from the teacher
> 7 Answering a question in front of the class
> 8 Matching fifteen French words to pictures on a worksheet
> 9 Understanding your spoken French instructions
> 10 Holding a brief dialogue in French with you
>
> - Which events would you say are easier or more difficult to assess? Why?
> - In order to help the child develop the necessary skills to perform the tasks well, which of the following feedback is most and least helpful? Why?
>   a. a score out of 10;
>   b. highlighting what went wrong;
>   c. emphasizing what worked well while ignoring what went wrong;
>   d. getting child to discuss possible outcomes with peer and find ways to move forward.
> - Consider events 8 to 10. What might have greater impact on your approach to assessment – your FL knowledge or your understanding of primary pedagogy?

Figure 7.1 10–11-year-olds' spontaneous writing from memory

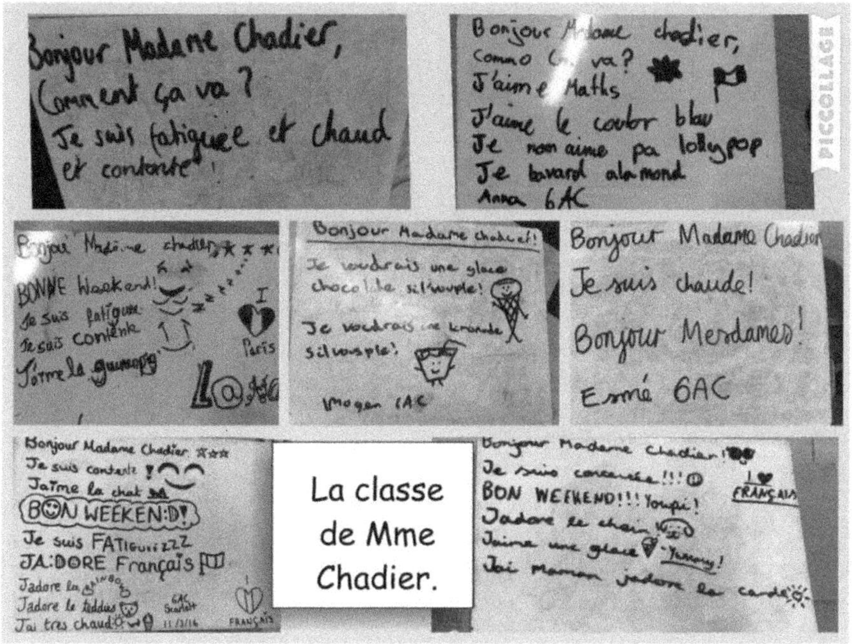

When we think about assessment in the FL primary classroom, we need to use the skills we already have, and refine them for a particular context, purpose and theme. For instance, what is the purpose of assessment in the language classroom? What counts as progression in languages? Does a child who remembers twenty French words demonstrate greater achievement than a child who remembers only ten? What is the role of memory compared to understanding, pronunciation and application?

> **Pause for thought**
>
> Look at the use of mini white-boards in Figure 7.1 and consider what you can assess from the picture. Think about the following:
>
> - Content
> - Spelling
> - Grammatical structures used
> - Quality of presentation
> - Amount of writing
> - What contextual information is missing in order for you to make the most accurate assessment?

> Do remember that assessment of children's writing focuses on just that particular aspect: writing, which may seem like the easiest component to measure, but it is nevertheless, just one of five strands.
>
> Using mini white-boards gives children the opportunity to show you what they can remember if prompted and encouraged appropriately.

We assume that you already have a basic understanding of primary pedagogy which will entail an assessment component, and of particular use in our context is assessment around English (Literacy). This knowledge will be essential in your understanding of assessment strategies in FLs, and we encourage you to make links as you read this chapter.

Our assessment of children's learning will depend directly on:

a our powers of observation;

b our powers of interaction;

c our knowledge around the topic;

d our understanding of teaching and learning (powers of intervention and interpretation).

How your school (and indeed the educational system in your country) approaches assessment will also influence how you apply it in your classroom. Generally speaking, England is a good place to be when it comes to children and assessment. The reliance on textbooks around most of the world means that children are submitted to an incredibly high amount of testing, as most textbooks come with an 'end of unit' test, usually every fortnight. If you multiply this by the amount of subjects, we have at least three or four in-house tests every two weeks, for the duration of primary school life. Not something to be envied. However, many private schools in England also follow this model.

Tests and exams fall under the umbrella of 'summative assessment' which has a purpose within education in terms of use to other educational establishments and accountability to government. It has been extensively shown however that summative assessment (grades), although it may fuel competition and motivate the 'grade-seeker', does very little for the actual learning process of the learner, as you may have observed in the activity above. English state schools tend to favour formative assessment, which can be described as a process that

> can help learning if it provides information to be used as feedback, by teachers, and by their pupils in assessing themselves and each other, to modify the teaching and learning activities in which they are engaged. Such assessment becomes 'formative assessment' when the evidence is actually used to adapt the teaching work to meet learning needs.
>
> (Black and Jones 2007, p. 4)

If we discuss assessment of and for learning we also need to be clear as to what we mean by that learning. Summative assessment tends to focus on memory and on what the pupil is supposed to have learnt. However,

> teaching is about what students learn, not what the teacher presents, and the main purpose of education is to promote understanding and not short-term remembering. Thus, if understanding is to be assessed, methods are required that involve learners in using their knowledge and linking it to real context.
>
> (Antoniou and James 2013, p. 169)

Formative assessment then gives the greatest fruits in terms of learning, and it will be the mode of assessment of choice in this chapter. Giving children a grade against their performance can have a place in the classroom, but mainly as a form of game, a mark out of a total number of items well remembered or performed. It should not however form the backbone of their assessment. This touches on issues around effective pedagogy – which assessment is part of. We make reference to James and Pollard's Principle 2, from their teaching and learning research programme (TLRP) published in 2011, which states that

> effective pedagogy engages with valued forms of knowledge. Pedagogy should engage learners with the big ideas, key processes, modes of discourse, ways of thinking and practising, attitudes and relationships, which are the most valued learning processes and outcomes in particular contexts. They need to understand what constitutes quality, standards and expertise in different settings.
>
> (James and Pollard 2011, p. 21)

Principle 5 (below) brings assessment together with teaching and learning, and gives a sound direction in terms of what we should use assessment for. In England, what used to be known as 'streaming', later became 'setting', and in primary schools is known as 'ability tables'. This system does on the surface appear to make it easier for the teaching (less effort required for differentiation in lessons), but it is a practice which this book firmly opposes, and for which there is no research evidence of success in the learning or academic outcomes of the whole class, only a tradition that has stuck, and which can have negative academic, social and emotional impact on many children.

> In ability-based grouping, pupils in lower groups are vulnerable to making less progress, becoming de-motivated and developing anti-school attitudes. There is evidence that these pupils experience poorer quality of teaching and a limited range of curricular and assessment opportunities likely to have an impact on later life chances.
>
> (Kutnik et al. 2005, p. 3)

Group or pair work can encourage peer assessment, which is fortunately a valued and well-used form of assessment in English primary schools, and can impact positively on the learning as it allows the child to 'own' their own progress and direction. However, this only works when the criteria for creating groups are predicated on cooperation and collaboration rather than on ability.

> For effective group working of any kind, children must establish positive relationships between group members (e.g. Light and Littleton 1994; Mercer 2000) that allow for sensitivity to others, trust of others and effective communication.
> (Kutnick and Manson 1998 quoted in Kutnik et al. 2005, p. 22)

Principle 5 reminds us that assessment is a tool that must be closely aligned with planning in order to be valid (consider the last point around Figure 7.1),

> Effective pedagogy needs assessment to be congruent with learning. Assessment should be designed and implemented with the goal of achieving maximum validity both in terms of learning outcomes and learning processes. It should help to advance learning as well as determine whether learning has occurred.
> (James and Pollard 2011, p. 22)

Bearing all this in mind, we can focus on what formative assessment can look like in the big picture of primary FLs. Thought has also been given to issues around transition to secondary, and how assessment can aid this process. Colleagues from the secondary and primary sector have already drafted a proposal which highlights key points around assessment.

- Effective assessment practice in language learning should foster motivation, enjoyment and progress in learners.
- Assessment should support learners to feel confident and successful and help build resilience, enthusiasm and persistence in continuing to learn languages.
- Assessment should be embedded in the language learning process, respecting that language development includes making mistakes whilst also establishing high expectations for individuals.
- All learners should be able to describe their own progress in ways that can be fully understood by themselves, their parents/guardians and other stakeholders in primary and secondary schools.
- Monitoring and describing progress in language learning should be consistent across Key Stage 2.

(Bailey and Murray-Hall (2015), p. 1)

The current Programme of Study from 2014 specifies that **we should enable pupils to make substantial progress in one language**, and that by the end of KS2, they should be able to:

- Communicate practically around familiar and routine themes
- Understand (read and listen)
- Communicate (speak and write)
- Apply knowledge of some grammar and phonology

- Express ideas, thoughts
- Write at length
- Improve accuracy of pronunciation, intonation
- Increase confidence, fluency and spontaneity

The School Inspections Handbook (OFSTED 2016) gives us clear guidelines as to what is expected from pupils' work and how this is evidenced in an inspection. However, it does not prescribe any set amount or quality of work in children's books, as this will heavily depend on the circumstances, age and ability of the child and class. Marking and feedback to pupils, both written and oral, are highlighted as necessary aspects.

> However, Ofsted does not expect to see any specific frequency, type or volume of marking and feedback; these are for the school to decide through its assessment policy. Marking and feedback should be consistent with that policy, which may cater for different subjects and different age groups of pupils in different ways, in order to be effective and efficient in promoting learning.
>
> (Ofsted 2016, p. 10).

Figure 7.2 Dan Alliot, languages adviser

In the following section we would like to guide you in a slightly different way. We will look at assessment in very practical terms. The voice you will hear belongs to Dan Alliot, a language adviser who has worked very closely with our primary student teachers over a number of years. Dan is a practising primary and secondary languages teacher, and delivers training in schools for non-specialist class teachers, at universities for student teachers, and nationally for language specialists. Dan's advisory work centres on the pedagogy of primary languages, including such aspects as the use and creation of resources, the enabling of non-specialists, lesson planning, observation, demonstration and feedback, and the monitoring of learner progress over time.

The following questions are a compilation of aspects around assessment that our trainee teachers have most frequently asked Dan. The answers are a combination of Dan's and our own approach to assessment, brought together by shared values around teaching and learning. We encourage you to think about each aspect; how it may look like in your own setting.

Dan, in your experience, how do primary schools feel about assessment and learners' progression in languages?

I think it has been seen to cause teachers undue amounts of work and concern, largely because there is a perceived lack of clarity over what should be assessed, how formally, how frequently, and whether or not the approaches are even accurate in evidencing the progress being made whilst demonstrating that the teaching is effective.

Whilst assessment is a vital part of teaching and learning, and whilst there are a multitude of considerations to be made in order to approach it effectively, it need not be an onerous task – nor does it need to be something that learners perceive to be daunting or disheartening. However, if approached incorrectly it can result in learners becoming despondent, undue work for teaching staff, and invalid data or information being presented.

At the moment there is no national assessment scheme, and no stipulation as to the approach that we should take, which affords the subject teacher the creativity to experiment and to develop strategies which can be rewarding and effective, based on their greater pedagogical expertise. In a way, this is the freedom of not having level descriptors; using your own initiative and what you know about your learners.

Pause for thought

- How does your school respond when you ask about their approach to assessment in languages?

Who do we assess for and why do we assess?

This is a very important factor to consider when it comes to assessment, as this could (or should) impact on the way in which we assess and how we present the findings.

Consider, for example, the following groups or individuals, and ask yourself what sort of information they are likely to want from your assessment and why.

Head teachers

Parents

The class teacher

The young learner

Head teachers

Head teachers or senior leaders may need evidence that our learners are making sufficient (*substantial*) progress, first because it will help them to gauge whether the teaching programme and approaches are of high quality and effective in their school, but also because they need to feel secure that they can demonstrate to others (parents, governors, inspectors) that learners make good or outstanding progress in the subject. Consequently, it may be a demand on subject leaders to report on learners' progress at regular, agreed intervals over a period of time, against criteria or statements, and some will require levels, statements or skills (measured, for example, against titles or categories such as *Emerging, Developing, Secure, Mastery,* etc.). However, even this need not be onerous or daunting to subject leaders or class teachers, and we will look at some approaches as we move on.

Parents

Parents, however, are likely to want to understand exactly what it is that their child is able to do or even say now in the FL, or how their child is measuring up to expectations and others in the school, or if there is something they can do to help their child move on to the next stages. In order to fully equip parents to receive the information you give them, it can be useful to fully appraise them of what it is you are trying to achieve through your curriculum in school, what outcomes you are hoping for, and what is important. Parents may, for example, be frustrated if they feel that their child is only able to introduce themselves, count to ten and name some colours in the FL after a term of learning. However, they will feel rightly proud of their child if they are given the opportunity to understand that the focus during these early stages has been on developing their child's ability to recall language from memory with accuracy and confidence, or on acquiring an ability to recognize and pronounce some common phonemes in the language, rather than merely on developing a substantial bank of vocabulary or phrases.

> **Pause for thought**
> - What would be the benefit of introducing parents to the Languages Framework?

Teachers

From a teacher's perspective, we must recognize that we assess every minute of every lesson, whether formally or informally, in a summative or formative way. As we teach from the front and engage in question–answers with individuals around our classroom; as we circulate the room to listen to pair-work conversations and role-plays (assisting as we go, or challenging specific individuals to go a step further); as we measure understanding and enjoyment through participation; game/project outcomes; the number and quality of responses and questions asked by the children; and as we look at the 'correct' or accurate answers on a worksheet, in a book, on a 'test' or in set homework, we are in the process of assessing whether or not our learners have met our objectives, whether our teaching and planning have achieved the outcomes we had hoped for.

> **Pause for thought**
> - How many different ways to assess were described in the paragraph above?
> - Which of them have you used in your assessment of language learning?
> - Which have you not used, and why?
> - What other ways might you assess learning?

Language learners

Language learners will want to know that their skills and understanding are being recognized, and to feel pride in what they can do. It is common to see learners turning straight to their result at the bottom of a test or worksheet, rather than focusing on the areas that they misunderstood or got wrong. Inherently, learners want to achieve and to do well, and largely we want to feel as though we are at least as good as – if not better than – our peers.

There are many ways in which we can involve language learners in the process of their own assessment and progression, without making them feel like 'winners or losers' (Stiggins 2007), and getting them to think about assessment as a process that enhances learning rather than simply monitors it. You will find the literature around formative assessment and self-regulated learning of particular interest in terms of student inclusion in this process. Both, for instance, include an element of student self-reflection.

> **Pause for thought**
> - What 'planned for' opportunities do you give your learners to reflect on the work they produce?
> - How do you use their reflections?

How do you see the relationship between the way we approach languages, and our own, personal experiences of language learning?

In England, for some time, surveys and data show that learners perceive languages to be difficult, and that when compared to other countries we have low attainment or engagement beyond compulsory level. Many adults readily declare themselves as 'non-linguists', although we are also told that many adults regret not continuing with their language studies, and blame fear, poor teaching, a curriculum that failed to engage or simply the fact that languages aren't seen as necessary. While some of this is likely to be true, it is also probable that when asked if they speak another language, most adults who did study a language at school will recall some of the words, phrases or those 'strange' rules about masculine or feminine while simultaneously declaring themselves to have been 'terrible' at languages.

Some of their beliefs might be attributed to the way in which assessment and feedback takes place, because it is all too easy for us to be aware of what we *cannot* do in a FL, rather than feeling encouraged by what we can do. Unlike some other subjects, the outcome of successful language learning is perceived as different to other subjects – after all, isn't the final outcome meant to be total fluency? If on a weekly basis we encounter a situation where we cannot say what we want to say, where we are acutely aware of all of the words and phrases that we do not yet know or remember, and where for a long time we won't be able to truly use our newly acquired small steps and skills in any meaningful situation, then of course we will always feel as though our languages glass is more than half-empty, as opposed to slowly filling up.

As we try to learn another language (as an adult or a young learner) it is easy for frustrations to build up when we fail to communicate something even simple, unless our teachers help us to understand that fluency is a long way off, not necessarily even the aim, that the small steps are enjoyable and useful, and that one of the benefits of language learning is the skills that we can take forward and develop over time, sometimes with different languages.

If a learner is presented with a page of French, for example, and overwhelmed by the amount of unfamiliar language and content, (s)he is likely to abandon the task of even trying to understand the gist or some detail. If, however, (s)he is told that some skills will enable him/her to decipher more than (s)he originally thought possible, and his/her attention is drawn to context, cognates, near-cognates, guesswork, logic, process of elimination, effective use of a bilingual dictionary, then the daunting or insurmountable 'task' becomes more of a rewarding game or challenge.

> **Pause for thought**
> - How were you assessed as a language learner at school?
> - If you learnt a second language outside of school, what are your memories around the feedback you were given? What enabled you to progress?

What is the role of planning and schemes of work in assessment?

Highly significant. Our lesson planning and our schemes of work must be the starting point for effective assessment. If we do not plan for opportunities in our lesson where our learners can progress, then we cannot effectively assess their ability to do so.

A mere 30- or 60-minute lesson filled with engaging activities does not automatically ensure that learners make progress. We have to consider in advance what we want our learners to know (K), understand (U) or be able to do (BAT) by the end of a lesson that they couldn't do beforehand, and we need to plan in a carefully thought-out sequence of activities that will lead them on that journey, as well as opportunities during the lesson to gauge whether or not we are achieving this. It helps if we consider what the specific K, U and BAT will be while planning our lessons so that we are clear about the outcomes we want for our learners.

Similarly, a sequence of lessons over a period of time (or a module or a half-termly unit) will need to be thought out in advance, that is, what will our children be able to achieve, or know or understand by the end of that unit that they didn't know before, and that will help them to advance further in subsequent learning, so that they may move from beginners towards an intermediate level at KS3?

This might all sound obvious, but the scheme of work will soon fall short if it is merely a sequence of interchangeable 'topics' whereby the aim is to teach the children the relevant nouns or phrases which are commonly deemed to be 'useful', followed by a context, question or response in which that vocabulary can be used. While it is of course progress if a child can, for example, recall ten animals and then construct a simple sentence or response around that topic (*It is a small, white cat*, or *Yes, I have a cat and two dogs*), there is no longer-term progress or increase in the child's ability

Figure 7.3 Language content from beginner to intermediate level

Intermediate level

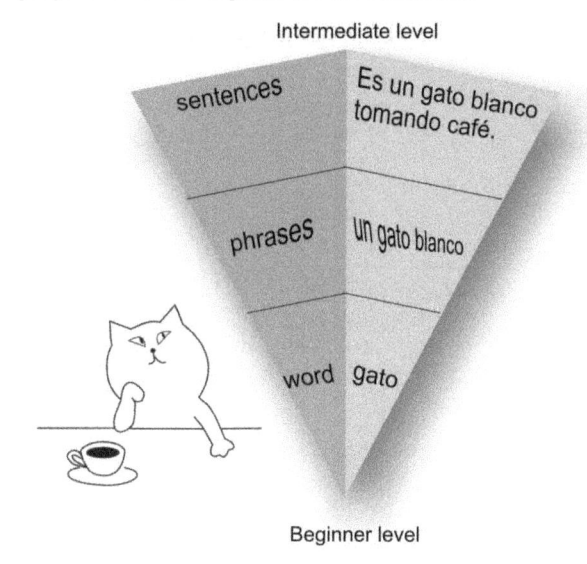

sentences — Es un gato blanco tomando café.

phrases — un gato blanco

word — gato

Beginner level

Figure 7.4 The eternal beginner: a vocabulary-based approach

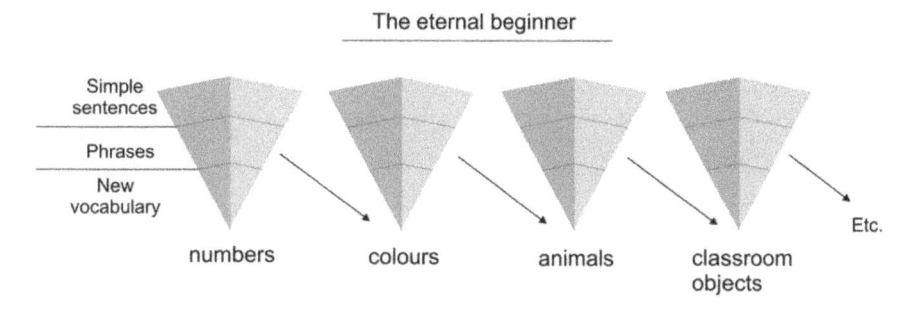

The eternal beginner

Simple sentences
Phrases
New vocabulary

numbers   colours   animals   classroom objects   Etc.

if this pattern is repeated over the course of ten or more similar 'topics' – the learner has merely acquired more vocabulary and phrases, but repeatedly finds herself at a beginner's level, moving from word to phrases and back down again.

The approach above can become disheartening after a while with the feeling that we always have to start from scratch. If, however, we organize our scheme with a slightly different approach, we can build-in progression so as to allow the learner to consolidate and extend their language skills, rather than always be confronted by what is new.

Imbedding new language into already known – as well as new – language can create a zone of proximal development for the learner, particularly when working in pairs and groups (but not exclusively). Not all new language needs to be presented with 'known' language necessarily; this is to say, the learner can be taught to cope with a large amount of unknown language because we do not have to understand every single word in order to infer meaning. This is an important lesson. For instance,

Figure 7.5 Language progression through a sentence-based approach

A sound base for progression

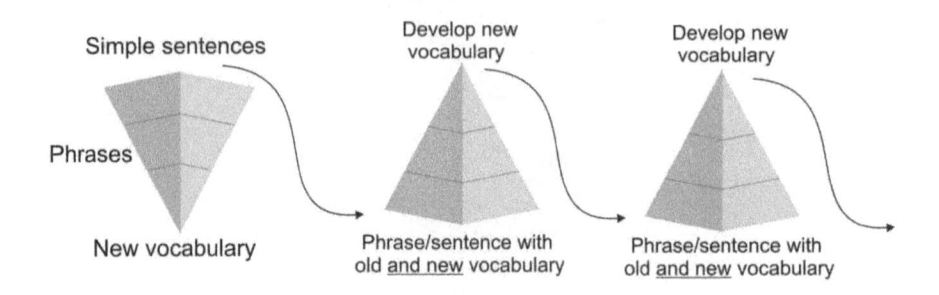

Simple sentences / Phrases / New vocabulary → Develop new vocabulary / Phrase/sentence with old <u>and new</u> vocabulary → Develop new vocabulary / Phrase/sentence with old <u>and new</u> vocabulary

identifying cognates or near-cognates (i.e. 'café' above) can help us in this process. This approach changes what we look for when we assess pupils, assessing not just their memory for Oracy and Literacy, but also their language learning strategies and their knowledge about language. We can therefore ensure that when we assess learners we focus on the right things and feel confident that we can demonstrate true progression.

> ## Pause for thought
>
> - Compare these two examples. What differences stand out for you? What might this impact on?
>
> **Sample from Scheme A**
>
> Topic 1 – Animals
> Teach some words, and put in a sentence or question–answer.
>
> Topic 2 – Parts of the body
> Teach parts of the body, and recall/recognize/say.
>
> Topic 3 – Foods
> Teach some foods, and recall/recognize/say.
>
> **Sample from Scheme B**
>
> Topic 1 – Animals
> Teach some words, put in a sentence or question–answer, focus on the use of **Es un**
>
> Topic 2 – Parts of the body
> Teach parts of the body, and recall/recognise/say, with focus on whether the noun is masculine, feminine, plural etc. es **un** gato o un**a** gata?
>
> Topic 3 – Foods
> Teach some foods, and recall/recognize/say, with the focus on providing a context, that is, *es un gato tomando café or, es una gata comiendo bananas*, etc.

While the acquisition of additional nouns and a simple context for these (as with Scheme A) may appear to be 'progress' and while it might be encouraging for learners to see how much they can recall, if we can shift away from the repeated pattern of word/noun

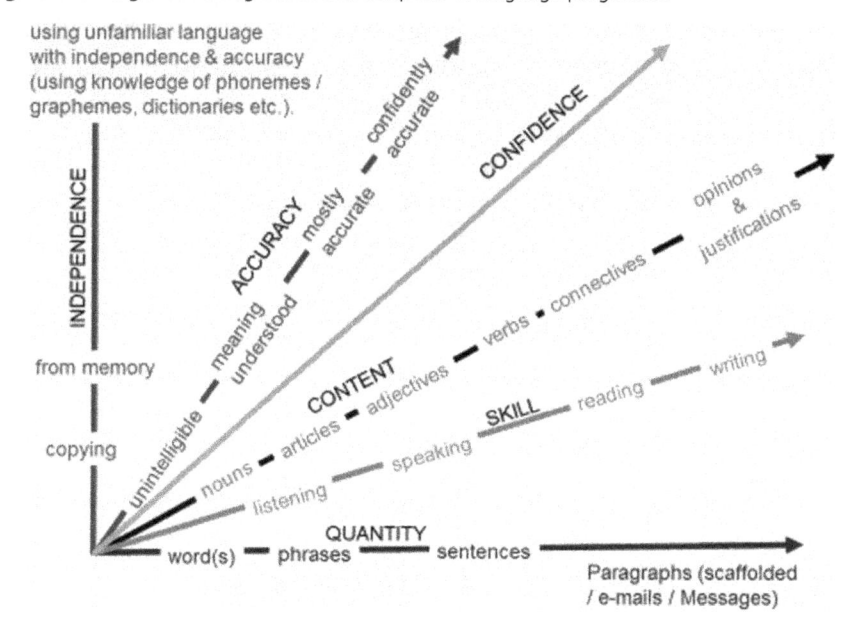

Figure 7.6 Diagram charting the different aspects of language progression

to sentence/phrase over and over again, we can focus on high-frequency or transferable skills. For example, our planning as we move through 'topics' begins to focus on *It is, There is, a/the,* opinions, use of adjectives with the nouns, connectives, etc.

As we therefore move through units, we can encourage learners to apply that new understanding to previous topics or contexts. Similarly, if we see progress as more than simply acquiring more words and phrases, we can recognize that progress is not merely seen in the volume of language, but in a variety of ways, shown in the diagram below;

> ### Pause for thought
>
> - Look at the chart shown in Figure 7.6. How would you plot yourself on this chart? Think about your own experiences of language learning. Can you identify weaknesses and strengths you may have had? Did other adults recognize them at the time?
> - Imagine you are introducing adjectives of shape and size (children already know animals and colours). How would your assessment look like for each of the areas above?
> - Is one area of progression more important than another?

If we only ever test children's ability to recall, recognize or use language (in speech, through their understanding in reading or listening, or in writing), then we may risk undervaluing those learners who are progressing in our lesson in terms of their confidence or independence, or other areas.

When we assess, therefore, we need to ensure that it is not merely through a test which can only provide us with a snapshot of where a particular individual might be at a given point on a given topic. We also need to be mindful that our approach to testing does not always focus on a particular skill, at the exclusion of those learners who may not ever be able to perform in that skill, but can in others.

For one child it may be a big leap in terms of progress for him to be able to recall ten nouns (e.g. animals) from memory with accuracy, while others in the class may recall a number of nouns from more topics and be able to write them down. However, he will always perceive himself to be weak as a linguist if is only ever assessed formally via a test or writing. Learning is also hampered if we insist that our reporting (to parents, children, senior leaders) is based around what percentage of children managed to perform well in the tests (and implicitly what percentage did not). If, however, the judgements we make and the feedback we give to learners and others does refer to other skills as well, and places a value on what learners can do, then we can legitimately recognize more progress taking place, a progress with far greater fruits.

What about bilingual children?

Many student teachers (non-TL natives) preparing to deliver languages 'fear' the bilingual child in the class because they feel they could be undermined by the child's knowledge. This could not be further from the truth. Young children are seldom aware of their language capital and expertise beyond, 'I can speak …'. Their judgement of you – if there is any – will be solely based on their limited background information (the local accent, slang or dialect they may have been brought up in). It is a good idea to assess bilingual children before your planning so that the activities are targeted appropriately. Depending on your level of TL, you might need the help of someone fluent in the TL in order to ascertain the degree of bilingualism in the child.

How bilingual is bilingual?	
Speaking	Are they completely fluent in terms of speaking and understanding the spoken language?
Reading	Can they decode their language and read it fluently?
Writing	Can they spell simple and complex words in their language accurately? Do they make any type of typical spelling mistake in the TL?*
Grammar	Do they know and understand grammatical terms like nouns, adjectives, verbs, etc.?
Cultural Understanding	How much do they know about their own culture? (music, literature, geography, etc.)

*For Spanish this means confusion around the use of s/c, v/b, ll/y, h, and accent.

> **Pause for thought**
> - What do you know about the languages spoken in your classroom?
> - Have you tried to identify who, in the school community, speaks the TL and at what level?

Finally Dan, what is your advice around assessment, to teachers willing to deliver languages in the primary classroom?

Simply to be confident in what you say about your learners and what they are demonstrating they can do, as well as to keep abreast of the latest research on assessment. For instance, a paper presented at the AERA 2014 symposium by Dylan Williams had an impact on the way I think about teaching and learning in the FLs classroom, as well as the training I do with teachers and student teachers around formative assessment and self-regulated learning. It moves your understanding forward and enriches the pupils experience by empowering them in their learning, which is ultimately what we are after.

Figure 7.7 Year 3 child's work around nouns and gender in Spanish

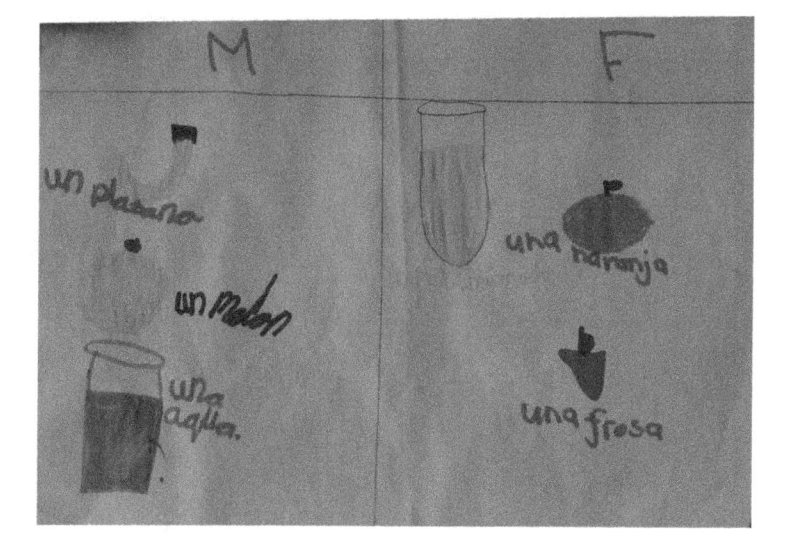

156　Mastering Primary Languages

> **Pause for thought**
>
> Look at this piece of independent work by a seven-year-old. Part of the activity (30 per cent) involved dictionary work, where children looked up words relating to their favourite things.
>
> - What do you need to know in order to assess this outcome in a valid way?
> - What can the child do and/or understand?
> - What elements do you notice that need further input?
> - How can you involve the child in this process in a reflective way?

Your answers may vary according to your level of Spanish and pedagogical approach. It is very easy to fix on the errors or misunderstandings and see them as something that needs to be addressed, however, that approach tends to leave you and the child at the word level. There are more interesting things to explore in this piece of work with the children. For instance, the word 'agua' (water) is a feminine noun (so it should be in the opposite column but that is not the main point here) which is, however, always preceded by a masculine article ('el' or 'un'), and there are a few such words in Spanish. Why might this be? Some children may be ready to explore this. The use of accents in Spanish is another avenue for discussion. What happened to all the accents in the poster? Why do Spanish words have accents? How come some children noticed this while copying?

You might for instance, present the children with word pairs (See Figure 7.8, below), and ask them to spot and discuss the difference, both in writing and in pronunciation (intonation/pitch) which means they have to see and hear the words before discussing.

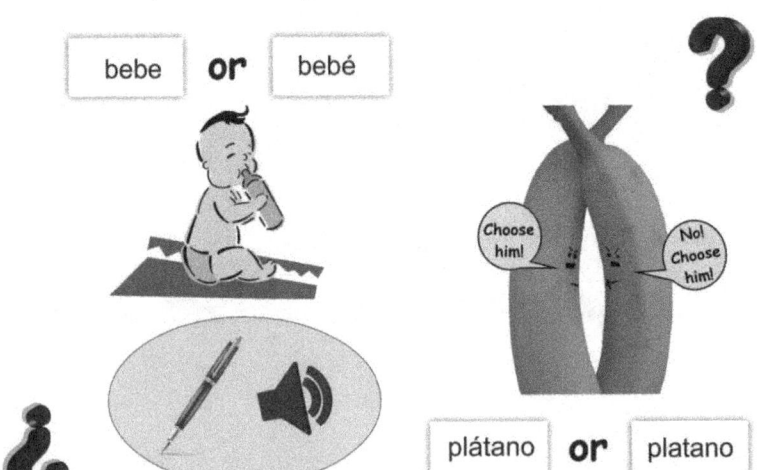

Figure 7.8 Accents in Spanish make a big difference

For the teacher's information:

bebe = (verb, imp) drink! or 3rd p.pl., he/she drinks,
bebé = (noun,m/f) baby.
plátano (n,f) = banana,
plat**a**no, with second syllable stressed, does not mean anything and sounds odd, but it's still understood.

You need to think about the whole picture in order to make a valid assessment. That is, knowing the purpose of the activity and the individual child's needs in order to give appropriate feedback. The following are possible reports/feedback you can give.

To child:
You have collected some delicious nouns in this picture. My favourite one is **plátano**. Was the gender of each word what you expected? Food for thought: Can you spot the difference between these two words? **melon** and **melón**. What can that mean? Discuss at home or with your partner.

To Head teachers and parents:
Alex has been learning about basic Spanish grammar this term. We've been working with nouns and adjectives through vocabulary relating to food. There are some posters and animation video clips of some of the work done by the children in Spanish, on the school platform. Alex has shown curiosity in particular about the way Spanish nouns are classified by gender, and he has been doing extra work with dictionaries of his own accord!

Assessment tools

There are some assessment tools presently being used in primary schools with a high degree of success. A Local Authorities (LAs) survey carried out in 2008 to find out what schools were doing to monitor and assess language learning found that 69 per cent of respondents were using European Language Portfolio (ELP). Some, particularly primary schools were using the idea of ELP to frame their own language portfolios to meet the needs of their pupils. The ELP was structured around the Common European Framework of Reference for Languages (CEFR) and its very essence of promoting and fostering autonomy in the language learner, shifting responsibility for language assessment away from the teacher towards the learner him/herself. ELP is a complex self-assessment instrument and language evaluation for young people in school right through to job interviews, applications for study grant and for mobility across European countries. It was therefore not surprising that primary teachers in the UK began to work with CILT (National Centre for Languages) to develop their own primary language portfolios (sadly, CILT no longer exists) which were much more accessible.

The European Language Portfolio

A primary language portfolio is the idea of collecting information of language learning of pupils, showcasing their achievement, progress and providing evidence of learning in one place, as the image of the ELP above indicates. This could be in a hand-kept traditional folder or it could be in a folder on the computer, or digitally kept online. Whatever the case is, the portfolio remains very much with the pupil and even travels with the pupil. In other words what a portfolio does is to paint the language learning journey of a pupil in primary school. The rationale for a language portfolio is clear. It supports learning and shows evidence of learning but what is not immediately transparent is that for a portfolio to serve its intended purpose it must be a process which engages the learner as well as shows him/her the way to build on the learning already achieved. The idea of portfolio needs to be the responsibility of both the teacher and the pupil. The teacher will be responsible for the content of the portfolio, since it is the teacher's role to plan and deliver language learning for the learner. However the pupil will also be responsible for choosing and deciding what she might want to showcase in her portfolio, it might be her 'best work', but it might simply be something that she is proud of, for example, an email message that she wrote to her penfriend abroad or tickets that she used to enter a museum while on a trip in the TL country.

Kolb (in Jones 2012) makes a clear distinction between using portfolio as a tool for assessment and an instrument to measure learning. 'Jones (2012) concludes that both dimensions are of importance and that we should consider it as a way to track learning with learners' full engagement. In Kolb's words as cited in Jones:

> A collection of pupils' work that is personal, dynamic and suitably structured, with 'footprints of learning' and the learning process, with evidence of feedback to the learner as well as learning results.
>
> (Jones, J. (2012)

Figure 7.9 The European Language Portfolio

While we agree that primary language learning should remain unshackled from the cages of testing procedures, we nevertheless strongly encourage the idea of assessment to inform learning and assessment to direct the learners on their language learning journey.

Portfolios can be a way to generate good learning habits and engage the learner and offer the pupil the opportunity to achieve whatever ability level he might be operating from. A native speaker of the TL might be able to respond orally only to many of the *'What I can do'* statements while another pupil might only be able to respond partly, and in writing, or respond only to statements related to IU. Portfolios are a way to provide differentiated learning and outcomes as it is planned alongside the programme of learning for any particular year in collaboration with the colleagues you are working with. Once the portfolio is integrated into language learning and pupils are taught how to use it, assessment for learning, self-assessment as well as an accumulated record of the learner's language experience can build a comprehensive picture of pupil's language learning which then travels with them to secondary school.

Working with 'Can Do' Statements

'Can Do' Statements stemmed from a long-term European project set by Association of Language Testers in Europe (ALTE). The aim was to establish a framework of key levels of language performance within which language can be examined objectively and collectively by members state of the European community. Hence the CEFR came into existence in 1992. The CEFR brought curriculum, pedagogy and assessment closer to one another than has been the case previously. Between 1997 and 2000, the ELP for language learners of different ages came into existence, and evolved as it was being piloted here in the UK as elsewhere in other member state countries. It is now part of the Council of Europe (CoE) official Language Education Policy. Although it is not officially part of England's Language Policy, recently, an assessment guideline written for the DFE's Expert Subject Advisory Group entitled, Modern Foreign Languages*, issued a document which clearly recommends the idea of language portfolios in both primary and secondary schools. This document suggests that documents such as CEFR and the ELP are starting points for schools and for teachers to develop and manage assessment of MFL.

The idea of a language portfolio embedding 'Can Do' statements for each child who studies MFL in primary school is designed to make the language learning process more transparent to the learner and to foster autonomy and independence in the learner. However, more to the point, the 'Can Do' Statements imply:

- a learning target
- teaching and learning activities
- assessment criteria

Figure 7.10 'Can do' Statements from the language portfolio

En français			
I can say the alphabet	I can act out or draw pictures when Mme describes	I can introduce myself and others	I can say different winter activities
I can count to 20	I can respond to instructions	I can ask and say how I am doing	I can describe what someone is wearing
I can say the days and the months	I can express my basic needs	I can ask and say my age	I can identify some French phonemes
I can say the colours	I can sing songs without help	I can say what I like and what I don't like	I can talk about some French traditions
I can say the names of farm animals	I can recite rhymes	I can ask and say where I live	I can name some shops and the items to buy in them
I can describe my family	I can play Jacques a dit game	I can describe the weather	I can ask someone to repeat
I can say parts of my body	I can name classroom items	I can use cognates to read and understand text	I can recognise question forms and negatives forms

Take a look at the table given in Figure 7.10 of 'Can Do' Statements which a teacher used with her Year 3 class. As well as displaying this grid on the wall of the classroom children also have a copy each in their portfolio folder called 'Mon Dossier' and are invited to colour in the boxes when they are able to do these things. Here assessment is not an 'add-on' but rather an integral part of the developing pedagogy of teaching and learning.

Pause for thought

Consider the benefits of language portfolios with 'Can Do' statements (Figure 7.10) within the primary classroom.

- Can you see portfolios embedded in the teaching and learning of the language lessons?
- How can you use the 'Can Do' statements of this particular language portfolio to share learning goals with pupils?
- Can pupils know and recognize the standards they are aiming for by looking at the 'Can Do' statements in this particular classroom?
- How can it involve pupils in self-assessment?
- How can feedbacks be generated which can then lead to pupils recognizing their next steps and how to take them?
- How can it serve the transition of the learner from KS2 to KS3?

Assessment and transition to secondary school

It is crucial for language learning that transition is planned carefully so that motivation remains high and progression continues to be a positive experience for the pupil. Both primary and secondary schools have improved their administrative procedures for transition but there is a further approach to transition which needs crucial attention, and that is the focus on teaching and learning and the progress that the learner has already made which needs to be systematically acknowledged and built on in the secondary classroom, as this will put pupils in a far stronger position (Jones 2010).

The Languages Review (2007), recommends that there should be informal formative classroom assessment of every child's FL development near the end of KS2 by reference to the *Languages Ladder*, so that the KS3 FL teacher is well informed about the pupil's FL achievement and needs to further his/her learning. The Languages Ladder is an assessment tool which is linked to the CEFR (Common European Framework of Reference for Languages), and the European Language Portfolio (ELP). Some schools are using these tools to devise their own assessment language ladder while others are using the Junior European Languages Portfolio in its original format. However they might be using the assessment tools, what is for certain, is that the tools provide the teacher with assessment at the level appropriate to the child in each of the four strands of learning: listening, speaking, reading and writing. Primary schools making use of these assessment tools are therefore in a very good place when passing on transition information to secondary colleagues, they are in a position to pass on summative as well as formative assessment. All the information is readily available on the Internet for you to explore.

Figure 7.11 The language ladder (have one up on your wall)

Children leaving primary schools who are well versed in AFL (most children will be) need to be challenged to articulate their learning from a secondary language learning perspective certainly, but they also need to be challenged to take more responsibility for their language learning and the portfolio approach which many secondary schools already use is a good example of how this can be achieved.

Summary

As we have already implied, we firmly believe that primary languages need to be located within a formative assessment framework which focuses on what pupils can do and which provides pupils with feedback on how they can move forward in their learning. We know that if languages are to be treated and validated as the important subject that it is, then evidence of progress will need to be shown. Even though there have been positive primary school Ofsted inspection reports around languages, pedagogically speaking as Jones (2012) asserts, 'The fundamental question is not *whether* to assess, but *how* to assess'.

Encouraging children to keep track of their progress will empower them with a sense of purpose, of beginning and end-destination. Sharing the language learning criteria at the grander scale (five strands of the framework), as well as giving them the opportunity to experience diverse areas of assessment, will allow them to see their progress in context, within a whole picture of language learning, rather than just one particular aspect.

As you see, there is no need to fear assessment because it is a natural way of learning, of moving forward. As Dan said, you need to be confident in what you say about your learners and what they are demonstrating they can do.

Recommended reading

Black and Jones (2007). Formative assessment and the learning and teaching of MFL: sharing the language learning road map with the learners. *Language Learning Journal*, 34(1). T&F group.

Chambers, G. (2014). Transition in modern languages from primary to secondary school: the challenge of change. *The Language Learning Journal*, 42(3), 242–60.

Jones, J. (2014). Student teachers developing a critical understanding of formative assessment in the modern foreign languages classroom on an initial teacher education course. *The Language Learning Journal*, 42(3), 275–88.

Morgan, C. (2006). Appropriate language assessment in content and language integrated learning. *The Language Learning Journal*, 33(1), 59–67.

Chapter 8
Practical Issues

The garden-in-bloom illusion: Success is a garden in bloom. People see the success; the roses, the flowers, the fruit and the sunshine. What people don't see are the roots; the disappointments, the dedication, the sacrifice, the hard work and the persistence.

Chapter objectives

- To provide you with examples of how to start with your own ideas or passion to plan language lessons.
- To suggest and reference resources which you might find useful for planning and for your own classroom.
- To invite you to consider resources which can support your delivery of MFL lessons and also resources which will underpin your own ongoing professional development.

This chapter considers the type of resources that best support the delivery of primary languages, for teachers, MFL coordinator's and from a whole school leadership perspective. We have implied throughout the book that the greatest resource in the classroom is you, the teacher. How resourceful you are, as well as how perceptive about what the children themselves can bring into the learning, will make all the difference. To date, there are many schools which are successfully delivering primary MFL, but we know they did not just arrive there. It takes time, trial and error, persistence and a lot of hard work, and we firmly believe that having access to the right resources is one of the key ingredients to the successful implementation of the FL curriculum for KS2.

The materials mentioned here are those commonly used in schools, university training (PGCE course) and by those teachers employed by either schools or education authorities to deliver the primary FL curriculum.

We have chosen to present the information in sections but the sections are in no way hierarchical, nor are they intended as an endorsement. Each school will have different needs for the range of resources we are presenting here and the list is not exhaustive.

Figure 8.1 Different uses of resources

Figure 8.2 represents the way in which the three main ingredients of the language classroom interact. You, the class teacher, are at the centre of interventions around teaching and learning.

This book thus far has looked in detail at the top spiral in terms of pedagogy. The Key Stage 2 Framework for Languages (see Chapter 4) has an important role to play here as it is a source of guidance and advice for teachers and curriculum managers planning to deliver primary languages. The different strands of learning (Oracy, Literacy, IU, and KAL and LLS) will not be revisited in this chapter, but we hope to guide you to unpick for yourself the multitude of ways you can draw from the framework, according to the age of the child. The framework assumes that many of its users may have little or no experience of primary language teaching, but it also caters for teachers who are coordinators and language specialist teachers.

It is worth remembering that the framework is closely aligned with the principles and ambitions contained in the 'Developing language in the primary school: Literacy and primary languages' document (National Strategies 2009). This document promotes a holistic approach to the Primary Curriculum and encourages teachers to

Figure 8.2 Looking at languages resources in context

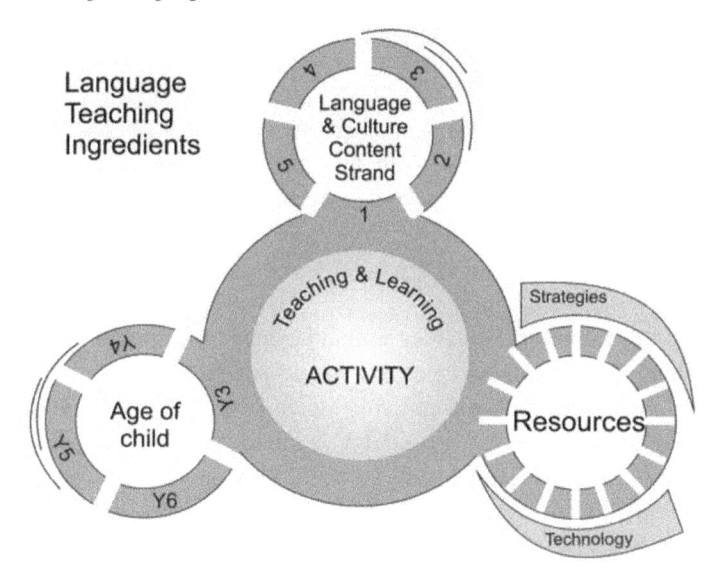

[Diagram: Language Teaching Ingredients — three interlocking rings around a central "Teaching & Learning ACTIVITY" circle: "Language & Culture Content Strand" (segments 1–5), "Age of child" (Y3, Y4, Y5, Y6), and "Resources" (Strategies, Technology)]

extend the methodology behind the full range of primary subjects, exploiting links between curriculum areas wherever possible.

> ### Pause for thought
>
> The Languages Framework is the most inclusive approach in terms of a comprehensive delivery of primary languages. If you look at the second appendix you will find a table which shows objectives from the national curriculum and the Languages Framework for beginners (or Year 3). It is worth comparing these two:
>
> - Think about which might be most useful for you, your school or staff team, in terms of developing or acquiring resources that would help you support teaching and learning (considering that the curriculum is not age specific).
> - Are there any elements of language learning missing in one and not the other?

One of the elements which is explicit in language learning but not mentioned in the national curriculum is culture. It is not surprising given the amorphous nature of culture; however, the following opening sentence from the National Curriculum for languages (2013), *Learning a foreign language is a liberation from insularity and provides an opening to other cultures,* makes it very clear that teaching languages should deepen pupils' understanding of the world as well as foster their curiosity of that world. We don't know of a better way to do both but by engaging learners with the range of cultural aspects to be found in every language, the countries where it is spoken and the people who speak that language.

The current National Curriculum for languages matches most of the strands of the Language Framework but it is on the main based on practical communication, and therefore, not as inclusive for monolingual teachers. As we have said all along in this book, your interests and ideas can be superimposed on what is introduced in the Framework. The generic nature of the learning objectives makes it possible for you to do just that.

Following from Figure 8.2, in Figure 8.3 you will see the wheel of resources in particular.

We would like to present resources around language learning in such a way as to make you think flexibly around them. We should not be in the mindset that certain resources are only suited to some particular age. One and the same resource can be used in many different ways, with different audiences. In the images of the three wheels for instance, you can see that we could pick any of the type of resources listed (i.e. song, the list is not exhaustive) and build an activity around it that supports Oracy (or Literacy or IU), for any of the year classes (3 to 6). What will change is the degree of complexity or cognitive demand required by the activity around the given resource.

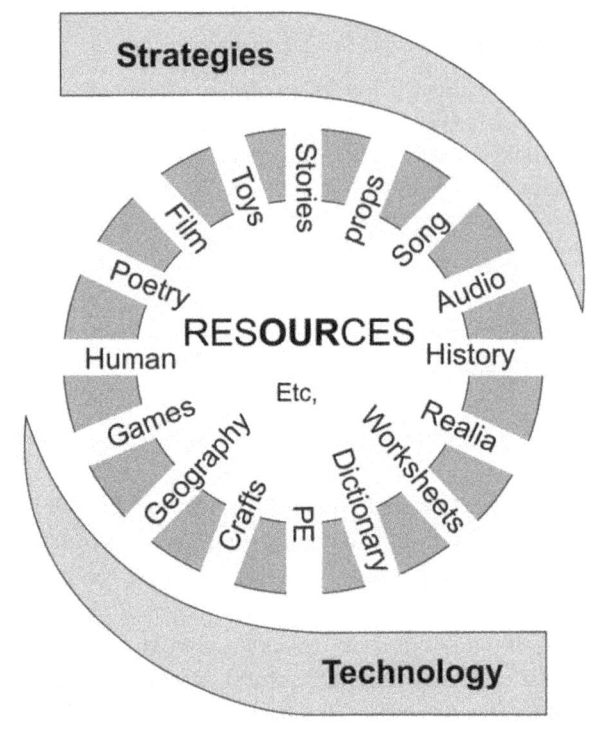

Figure 8.3 The wheel of primary languages resources

One could start the process of planning from any of the three elements suggested, but, you do need to bear all three in mind in order to encourage progression in the learner.

a   The resource. Sometimes you may come across a resource that really inspires you. This could be anything from pictures you took and experiences you had abroad, in the target country, to a book you read or movie you saw, or a child in the class whose first language is the TL (we'll come to this point later).

At this point we would like to mention Barry Jones, an inspirational teacher educator, who left us a great legacy around the use of resources, 'As a student teacher, though it's painful to have to tell you this, you'll get further searching for answers than you will by being told' (Jones 2015). This is particularly true when it comes to finding the right kind of approach or resources for your class.

b   The Year class. Older children engage differently with resources as they can critique and reflect in more depth. Some people think that using puppets, for instance, is only appropriate for the younger child, but in our experience we can all enjoy working with puppets, whatever our age. Again, the difference is in *how* we engage with them (while a seven-year-old may make the puppet say a few words, an eleven-year-old pupil can go from making a puppet, to thinking about the puppet's personality, to making a movie, etc.).

c   The language objective. This could be any or a combination of the five strands of the Languages Framework. For instance, if you are confident that your children have learnt to greet and introduce each other verbally, you may feel that they need to consolidate the literacy (reading and writing) skills which will support their learning. You might, for example, use a resource based on pictures of family members introducing themselves, and this very simple resource can allow them to make drawings of their own families introducing themselves. Older children might do this using simple software (Puppet pals for iPad), where they can write and talk, insert subtitles, etc., in first and third persons.

The strands of knowledge about language and LLS can also be done discreetly (see Chapter 4), but more often than not, they are implicit in some activities, as children need to think carefully before interpreting or saying something in the TL.

The use of technology is placed as an element that can be woven into any of the activities planned, making it another vehicle for learning rather than an end in itself. Technology does require, however, a great deal of preparation and some expertise on the teacher's part, particularly as equipment it can often be unreliable. Although the literature shows us that children engage with some forms of technology more than others, it is not necessarily educational technology children use, but rather that of social media and gaming. The current government places an emphasis on teaching children computer coding, and there is plenty of scope for the language learner in this respect (particularly around coding to make grammar games, or adding speech to characters, etc.), but this again requires some computational expertise from the teacher (i.e. creating an app game that requires the sorting of words – that may flash on the screen – by gender or number).

Applications such as Audacity (i.e. for podcasting), Stop-Motion, Puppet Pals, and video making are some of the more widely used forms of ICTs in the language classroom. We will look at one of these in detail later on.

The real 'new media' aspect of technology lies in the empowerment it can give through authorship, collaboration and distribution (Buckingham 2008). This is really important in language learning because it can give children a sense of audience impossible just over a decade ago. Being able to upload your work online (whether worldwide or just the school platform) means it has an immediate real audience, and hence, it has purpose. This can motivate children into becoming creators and authors of content rather than mere users or spectators. Indeed primary languages can provide a digital platform where pupils can secure ownership of what they are so ready and keen to do and achieve.

We will now look at some of the resources in the wheel in more detail, starting with the use of authentic resources (realia). Once again, Dan Alliot is our source of inspiration in this section.

Figure 8.4 School children shopping at a French street, and making a radio show, at the Europa Center. Top right, film about a French girl's adventures

Realia: Authentic resources

The use of 'authentic' resources within the curriculum is one such development that requires a degree of confidence and a discerning eye, to be able to select what is appropriate for the age, ability and interest of the learner, and what can provide opportunities for the learner's language development to progress effectively.

Using such resources is an opportunity not only to provide learners with exposure to resources that might give a genuine insight into the lives of those where the language is spoken, but also to trigger more authentic opportunities for the learners to use the language.

There are different ways of viewing 'authentic' resources. In terms of activities, we can have authentic contexts for learning and using the TL. Teaching specific vocabulary or phrases for the purpose of interaction can take on an entirely different slant if learners know that they will need that language to win a game, to take part in an activity effectively, to achieve an outcome, to write a message to a pen-pal in their partner school, or to meet their partners abroad (in person or virtually via a webcam). The existence of real people with names and identities and the opportunity to connect with those people abroad can provide learners with an *authentic* reason for learning and using the language, for taking an interest in their partner school's displays, timetables, menus, information, and provide a stimulus for conveying this information to their partners in the TL.

Figure 8.5 Sample of different types of resources

Then we have those 'authentic' resources which come from the country where the language is spoken, usually created for or used by native speakers of that language and not for those who are learning the language.

> ### Pause for thought
> Below are some examples of authentic resources or opportunities within a language teaching environment. Consider:
> - which of these you might already use;
> - which might fit within a module from the scheme of work you use;
> - Are there some resources that you cannot imagine using, perhaps because they appear too 'difficult' for young learners to access?

There are several things to consider when using authentic resources in our teaching, and while a ready-made resource might initially appear easy to use because it has required little work on our part in terms of making it, it can actually require more work or consideration in order to weave it into our work in a meaningful way, and to maximize the benefits of it.

Figure 8.6 Sample list of authentic resources

Shopping lists and receipts
Customs & traditions
Instructions
Indexes
Foods
Newspapers
Wildlife images
International links
Playground games
Street signs
Menus
Table games
Daily routines
Etcetera
Sport
Websites
Art reproductions
Film:
- Cartoons
- Documentaries
- Clips
- Trailers
- Travel-guide programmes
- Weather reports and forecasts
- Interviews
- Cookery programmes
- Advertisements
- Gameshows
- News
- YouTube content

Packaging

Radio broadcasts:
- Weather reports and forecasts
- Travel information
- News
- Interviews
- Music
- Games/competitions
- Ads.
- Etc.

Celebrities
Books
Historical figures
Old letters
Timetables

We might consider for example, whether the resource is actually of relevance or interest to our learners, merely because it is authentic. A train timetable might give us plenty of opportunities to access numbers, to revise times, to engage in a simple roleplay of buying a ticket (*I would like, from, to, how much is,* etc.). However, we must consider how many of our 7–11-year-olds actually spend their time accessing train timetables in their everyday lives in English, let alone in a foreign country. This is not to negate the value of the opportunities to roleplay, revisit numbers and times. If we do decide to use such a resource, then we should consider how we might make it interesting, accessible, and relevant, finding a 'hook' upon which learners' motivation can be secured.

Some learners may benefit from learning, for example, about the French underground system and how it compares to ours, or how children in their partner school travel to school in the mornings compared to us (providing opportunities for surveys, etc.). That is, creating a challenge might provide sufficient motivation. By the end of this lesson, in teams, I would like you to have found me the cheapest or fastest way to reach our partner school or the capital of the country from point x. The resource becomes meaningful, a necessary part of the activity or discussion, as opposed to an unfamiliar item that has little relevance to the sphere of interest of our learners in daily life.

We will need to consider whether the language of the authentic resource is accessible to our learners or whether we need to tailor the language shown. Sometimes high-level language need not pose a barrier to learning if our activities or objectives are not reliant upon learners understanding everything visible.

Stories as a resource for teaching and learning primary languages

Fundamentally there are two very important aspects of learning; interest and motivation of the learner. We have explored both of these in previous chapters, but here we want to connect learners' interest and motivation with stories and specifically the stories that you might go on to use in your FL classroom. In this section we deal with stories as a pedagogical tool and make a case that the effectiveness of stories will highly depend on the selection of stories and the application of methodology used with each class of learners.

Stories are essentially windows open to the world; it can be the real world or the world of imagination. Whatever the case is, stories open the door for us to view and understand people and cultural values. Stories can help learners to develop sensitivity and empathy.

> Using stories in the classroom can prepare learners for openness, awareness, tolerance and acceptance towards other ways of understanding life.
>
> (Ioannou-Georgiou, S. and Ramírez Verdugo, M.D., (2010))

Linguistically stories are opportunities to present children with grammar, vocabulary, phrases and unfamiliar sentence structures to learners in a meaningful and structured context to support understanding of the narrative world as well as the content the story is related to. Reading and listening to a story in a new language is a fun experience for children. Very often stories are dealing with interesting subjects which appeal to the listener or the reader. And so this context of listening and reading stories are often opportunities for teachers to teach, practise, consolidate or extend children's knowledge of a particular area of learning as well as the TL. *Ours Brun, Ours Brun* (Brown Bear, Brown Bear) is a very clear example of how adjectives, such as colours and animal nouns can be consolidated through a story. After listening to Brown Bear, Brown Bear in French to revise colours and animals, children were invited to write their own stories:

> Teachers also use stories to promote talk and interaction with peers. Reading and listening to stories children are provided with opportunities to react verbally and non-verbally with their teachers as well as their peers, this in turn helps them to construct ideas and knowledge of their own which they want to share with their teachers and their peers.

Stories can be a very effective tool to teach particular content but it also needs to be meaningful and most importantly it needs to feel natural to young learners.

Figure 8.7 Year 4 pupil's opening sentence of a story. Courtesy of Nadine Chadier

> Children learn and create their mother tongue not by sitting at their desks doing pencil and paper tasks in isolation from their peers ... but by interacting with and manipulating language and by engaging in meaningful use of language.
>
> (Mauro Dujmovic & Visoka uciteljska škola, Pula (2006) – Storytelling as a method of EFL Teaching)

Here we suggest a link to a website where you can be inspired to use puppets to teach and engage learners in retelling TL stories or creating their own stories in the FL. In addition to giving children opportunities to retell and to talk about an alternative ending of their choice, stories can help increase language fluency while at the same time exposure of how TL is used in an authentic context –

http://get-puppet.co/education/stories-learning-and-using-foreign-language/

The link below on the other hand is ideal for whole class shared reading using the interactive whiteboard but also for your native speakers of the TL to work independently through a range of stories which are organized into reading levels according to age. You can prepare the task prior to the lesson; choose the level learners could be further challenged without feeling out of their linguistic depth. For example, challenging learners individually or a small group to remember the plot of a TL story through collaborative task will enhance pupils' cognitive and social skills. They would probably already be familiar with the idea of identifying characters, comparing behaviours and actions of different characters in a story from their English lessons, but it would be a new challenge in the FL lessons and it would be consolidating what they already have encountered while developing thinking skills, incorporating cognitive and learning strategies in the language classroom.

http://www.childrenslibrary.org/icdl/SimpleSearchCategory?ilang=Spanish

We extend this section on stories a little further by unpicking how we can use an authentic TL resource in practical terms.

A known story in translated form, like *The Gruffalo*, is a wonderful resource to use with learners. Whether in book or cartoon form, the artwork is visually engaging, the story has a variety of characters, repetition, humour and natural settings. The original version is also written as a poem with rhyming words which make listening to the story rhythmic and intriguing. The book has also been made available in other languages, translated in a way that children abroad can read and enjoy the story, translated in a way that is sensitive to the original *and* retains the poetry and rhyme.

You may feel initially that the authentic Spanish or French versions of the story are too difficult to access for your learners, having been written for children who are native speakers of that language. An adapted version may feel more appropriate, where you tailor the language used, simplify some sections, shorten the text, and include nouns and adjectives that you want learners to recognize or to learn subsequently.

However, the authentic version could still be used in a way that benefits learners if you approach the resource with some careful thought. If learners know that they are not expected to understand every word, but to pick out words they recognize,

Figure 8.8 Twenty-seven different translations of *The Gruffalo*

Spanish (El Grúfalo),

Portuguese (O Grúfalo),
Croatian (Grubzon),
Dutch (De Gruffalo),
Estonian (Grühvel),
Finnish (Mörkyli),
French (Gruffalo),
German (Der Grüffelo),
Greek (Το Γκρούφαλο),
Hebrew (Trofoti),
Hungarian (A graffaló),
Icelandic (Greppikló),
Irish (An Garbhán),
Italian (Il Gruffalò),
Latin (Gruffalo),
Latvian (Bubulis),

Lithuanian (Grufas),
Maori (Te Tanguruhau),[1]
Polish (Gruffalo),
Romanian (Gruffalo),
Russian (Груффало),
Slovene (Zverjasec),
Swedish (Gruffalon),
Norwegian (Gruffaloen),
Turkish (Tostoraman),[8]
Welsh (Y Gryffalo),
Afrikaans (Die Goorgomgaai),
Bulgarian (Gruzulak).

the challenge can become engaging and less daunting. If they are asked to listen to the text and to indicate when they hear the rhyming words, they are developing their listening skills.

Consider, as you would with any resource that contains TL in written form, what language you want to teach learners in advance of using the resource (i.e. to enable them to access the resource effectively) and what language you deliberately don't want to teach in advance (i.e. to provide them with the opportunity to deduce meaning, to look things up, etc.).

More authentic still are books and stories written by the native speakers of the TL. There is no reason why you cannot work with classic or new literature in the same way outlined above; tailoring the language and focusing on the content that can engage your particular audience.

Figure 8.9 Using the FL classical literature to inspire and as context

Fables and other classical texts provide a world of possibilities (McLachlan 2008). Scenes from stories, for instance, can be recreated using different media. This is where the use of technology can be really effective due to the process of storyboarding and editing. The learning here takes place as children take on the roles of editors and contributors, making the process itself an authentic experience. The affordances of editing software can be seen Figure 8.10, whether this is Stop-Motion or video editing or Puppet Pals, and children get to engage with language learning and IU. They record their voices in the TL (Oracy) and obtain immediate feedback, often deleting and rerecording until satisfied. The storyboarding, credits and use of subtitles is another way of engaging with Literacy, while finding appropriate soundtrack and background can bring them into contact with authentic music and geography and imagery from the TL.

Viewing the completed work has its own, obvious rewards. This is where authorship through the power of distribution comes to the fore. Having the potential opportunity of a worldwide audience can have a significant impact on the pupils' engagement (Potter 2011). If you do this, make sure you either disable the 'add comments' feature or check/censor comments written by outside viewers before children can read them. Of course, the audience may well be just the class, the school and or the parents, but nevertheless, being recognized as the author/creator of content is often highly valued by children.

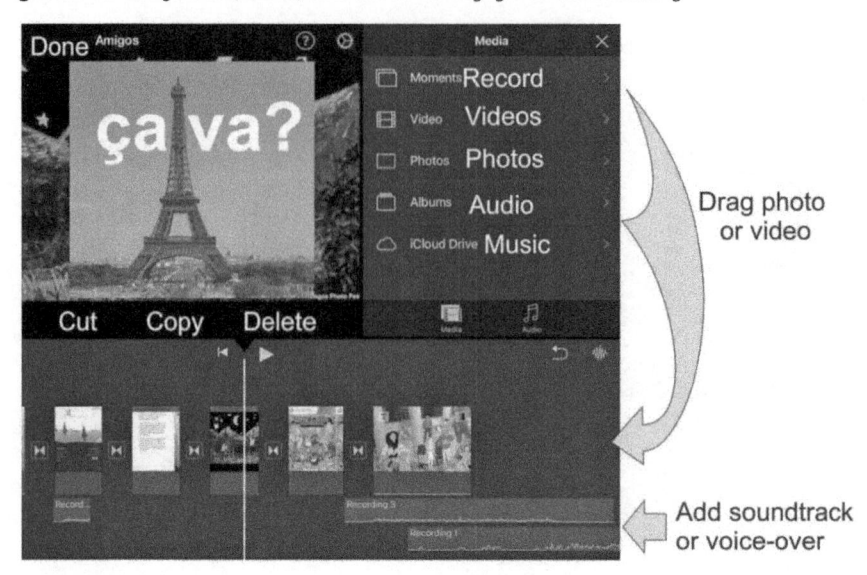

Figure 8.10 Using video (iMovie) as a vehicle for engagement and learning

It is a national curriculum requirement that learners carry out some writing in the TL, so it can become an authentic experience for them to use the French Seyès grid paper. This paper is widely used in French exercise books by their peers in France, as well as in overseas French *Départements* such as La Martinique and La Réunion. The Seyès grid paper writing shown in Figure 8.11 was generated at this website:

http://cursivecole.fr/texte1.php

There can be quite a lot to discuss with children about the French children's handwriting when a child brings a letter received from a pen-pal. Generating interest from such a letter adds to the excitement of understanding not only what the letter says in the TL written by a native speaker of the TL, but also how it is written and why numbers and letters are formed in the way that they are. This is a genuine opportunity to talk about handwriting and the French culture as it is encountered in schools. It should be said that a letter received from abroad and brought into the primary classroom can also be inspected to explore what is on the envelope carrying the letter. For example, the Indian commemorative postage stamp shown in Figure 8.12 for the 2016 International Day of Yoga typifies how much value is placed on health and spirituality in India. It is celebrating the first and twelfth steps of the Surya Namaskar (literally translated – Sun Salutation), part of a yoga position practised by millions of people around the world. To the right is a French stamp showing Marianne, who has been the face of the French Republic since 1849, she represents liberty.

Practical Issues   177

Figure 8.11 French calligraphy (Seyès grid paper)

Figure 8.12 Stamps depicting Marianne (liberty), the face of the French Republic and India's yoga's sun salutation position

> **Pause for thought**
> - Why is Marianne always on the French stamp? Why is she called Marianne?
> - Could this be a topic of conversation with your Year 5/6 class? If it could, then it would definitely be a resource which exudes authenticity because it certainly would be the preoccupation of your pupils' peers in France in their geography or history lessons.

Human resources

By human, we mean not only the class teacher (the brains behind any intervention) but also any other available adult or child in the class who speaks the TL. This can include parents, teaching or language assistants, and bilingual children.

Once you have assessed and established a good rapport with a bilingual child, making them feel valued in terms of any contribution they might offer, then – and only then – can you plan their inclusion so as to enhance the learning for everybody. While they may be able to exemplify pronunciation for the class, you can extend their own learning by providing them with opportunities to develop those areas which showed gaps in their knowledge. We need to be sensitive towards any adult or child whom we believe can support our language lessons in any way. It is important to have clear learning objectives for every child involved, as well as effective two-way discussions with support staff.

For inspiration and ideas of how to fully integrate bilingual learners of the TL in your classroom, go to the link below and see what Nadine Chadier is up to with Camenbear in St. Jérôme Church of England Bilingual School.

http://www.stjeromebilingual.org/stjerometv/

Modern language assistants in primary schools

The British Council Language Assistants Programme has been working with overseas education authorities for many years. Recently it has extended its work of facilitating language assistants into primary schools. More and more schools around the country are accessing this invaluable resource. Language assistants are usually shared between three primary schools. They make a real difference to children learning to speak European languages or Mandarin. They are also a support directly to the class teachers not only in their role as cultural ambassadors but also with their work to facilitating cross-curricular activities and projects. To find out more about this programme and how Language assistants work in primary classrooms, contact the British Council:

http://www.britishcouncil.org/language-assistants/employ/primary-schools

Online resources

Targets from the national curriculum will find their way to most of the commercial resources which are being generated. There are quite a number of commercial schemes of work available online. It is important to remember that these schemes are a resource, and as such, they should support your teaching rather than become a teacher substitute. Remember that you are at the centre of the language learning ingredients circle. It will be up to you and the school MFL coordinator to choose the best available online resources to suit your needs and the needs of the kind of curriculum your school intends to deliver.

Resources that support oracy and literacy

Music and audio

These resources will involve elements of speaking and listening. Children (particularly those new to the language) should be given as many opportunities as possible to listen and hear the TL before being asked to repeat or produce the language. They can learn to respond physically to simple classroom instructions, which you can easily find online. One possible website for this is French-resources.org. On this site you just type in 'classroom instructions' and you will see the following.

There are a number of French classroom instructions which have been put into a song. You can pause the song at any time and focus on specific language.

http://french-resources.org/level/beginners/publisher/mfl_consultant_services-896/channel/une_dizaine_de_chansons-8/worksheet/5919

In order to support the connection between the meaning and the sound of the new vocabulary, we can introduce movement or some simple sign language like Makaton.

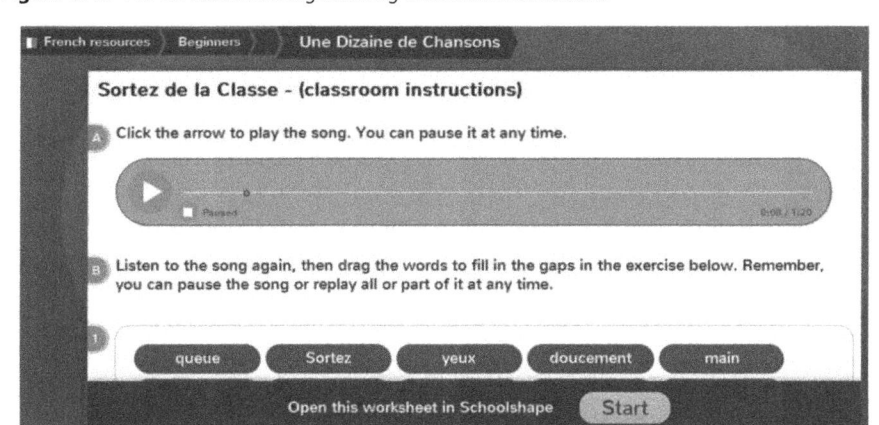

Figure 8.13 French Resources.org Learning classroom instructions

Figure 8.14 Using Makaton to enhance language learning

S'il vous plaît   Bonjour   un livre

asseyez-vous   Au Revoir

Figure 8.15 *The Guardian*'s education section for languages

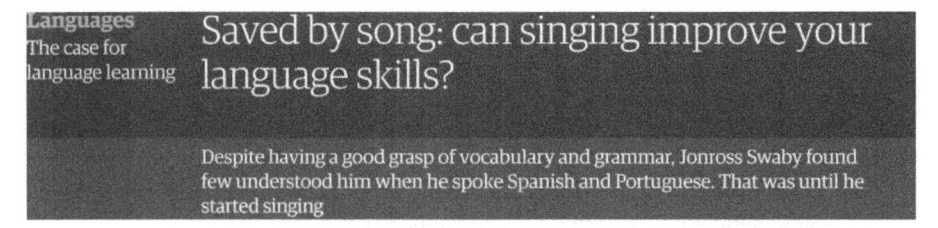

Languages
The case for language learning
Saved by song: can singing improve your language skills?

Despite having a good grasp of vocabulary and grammar, Jonross Swaby found few understood him when he spoke Spanish and Portuguese. That was until he started singing

You can also learn some 'simple Makaton signs' on YouTube which you can then use with the new vocabulary. Children also enjoy creating their own movements or signs to new words.

Children in Year 6 can use the exact same resources, but with a twist. They can, for instance, listen to the song and write down (in French or English, as the case may be) any vocabulary that they recognize or remember. They could visit the website in groups and find other resources related to speaking and listening. Alternatively, they could use the site to learn 5 new words in French and Makaton, and teach them to the rest of the class in a presentation.

Songs

http://www.theguardian.com/education/2015/feb/11/singing-improve-language-skills-spanish-portuguese

Practical Issues

It is difficult to imagine a primary classroom without songs. Equally a primary language classroom without the use of songs to either learn vocabulary or raise intercultural awareness is unheard of. There is a great deal of evidence (Richards (1969); Tierney and Hope (1998); Cheater and Farren (2001)) which supports the idea that learning a language through songs is a very positive experience for learners young and old. Songs can be a welcome change from the routine classroom activities and can provide learners with opportunities to try out new sounds without feeling exposed if they get it wrong. Songs should also be enjoyed for its own sake without due pressure on learning vocabulary or new language structures. However, songs can be used to support the teaching of the FL sentence pattern, flow or syntax as the example of *'Meunier tu dors'* below illustrates. Here the idea of direct speech being used in a sentence without the usual conventions of reported speech, children are learning the syntax as well as the rhythm. The word order can easily become fixed in the mind of learners through a song. It provides them with the opportunity to use everyday expressions and to practise pronunciation.

Meunier, tu dors
Ton moulin va trop vite
Meunier, tu dors
Ton moulin va trop fort

Comptines.TV http://comptines.tv/meunier_tu_dors

Songs can have a longer learning life depending on how they are used. We recommend that you do not use English tunes with TL lyrics, as each language has a different kind of musical phrasing, meant to fit in with their particular intonation and articulation. Find tunes that belong to the TL instead.

The advantage of allowing learners to encounter chunks of language in context cannot be underestimated. Using the lyrics of a song and substituting known vocabulary with pictures for learners to decipher as a reading comprehension once they have heard the song once or twice can be a very rewarding activity for both learners and the teacher.

The site below has songs and lyrics in French, Spanish, German, Chinese and Latin:

www.songsforteaching.com

Songs can also be a mean to consolidate and revisit vocabulary that has been learnt, keeping them fresh in learners' minds so that they can apply them in everyday conversation. The song below is easily accessible via the internet,

Lundi matin – l'empereur, sa femme et le p'tit prince
http://www.youtube.com/watch?v=noo1_wUGsIU

It is used to reinforce days of the week. There are similar songs for Spanish and other European languages.

http://www.headstartlanguages.co.uk/resources/ou-habites-tu
http://colours.headstartlanguages.co.uk/
http://www.bbc.co.uk/schools/primarylanguages/french

Figure 8.16 French poem, 'Page d'écritures' by Jacques Prévert

Page d'écritures
Jacques Prévert

Deux et deux quatre
quatre et quatre huit
huit et huit seize...
Répétez ! dit le maître
Deux et deux quatre
quatre et quatre huit
huit et huit font seize
Mais voilà l'oiseau-lyre
qui passe dans le ciel
l'enfant le voit
l'enfant l'entend
l'enfant l'appelle :
Sauve-moi
joue avec moi
oiseau !
Alors l'oiseau descend
et joue avec l'enfant
Deux et deux quatre...
Répétez ! dit le maître
et l'enfant joue
l'oiseau joue avec lui...
Quatre et quatre huit
huit et huit font seize
et seize et seize qu'est-ce qu'ils font ?
Ils ne font rien seize et seize
et surtout pas trente-deux
de toute façon
et ils s'en vont.

Et l'enfant a caché l'oiseau
dans son pupitre
et tous les enfants
entendent sa chanson
et tous les enfants
entendent la musique
et huit et huit à leur tour s'en vont
et quatre et quatre et deux et deux
à leur tour fichent le camp
et un et un ne font ni une ni deux
un à un s'en vont également.
Et l'oiseau-lyre joue
et l'enfant chante
et le professeur crie :
Quand vous aurez fini de faire le pitre !
Mais tous les autres enfants
écoutent la musique
et les murs de la classe
s'écroulent tranquillement.
Et les vitres redeviennent sable
l'encre redevient eau
les pupitres redeviennent arbres
la craie redevient falaise
le porte-plume redevient oiseau.

Song lyrics and poetry have similar affordances. For instance, using the first half of the Jacques Prévert's poem *Page d'écritures (below, up to line 27),* jumble up the lines and allow your native speakers of the TL to rebuild the poem using their previous knowledge of the poem. Then they can read their version to the whole class. This activity can also be done with the whole class by removing rhyming words of any well-known TL poem and pupils can rewrite the poem using cards with the rhyming words.

Resources around the use of drama, games and PE

Activities such as hot seating, role play or PE can be excellent ways to practice Oracy, and can be differentiated easily depending on the age and language ability of the child. You can have a simple role play with very young children, consisting of one or two exchanges (greeting); during PE sessions you can give simple instructions in

Spanish that relate to colour, size, movement, speed, direction, using PE equipment, etc. Check your local football club (premier league) as they often run FL football courses for children. For instance, Arsenal Double club run a French and a Spanish scheme, culminating with a visit to the stadium.

https://www.arsenaldoubleclub.co.uk/resources/spanish/

For a more advanced class, you can ask native speakers to pretend to be a member of the school community by giving a spontaneous description, in the first or third person singular of someone the children know well (Headteacher, teaching assistant, another child, kitchen staff, etc.). It can be live, or children can use video or audio equipment to record and then edit the footage by adding music, subtitles, etc. If live, and a brief conversation is possible, don't limit the native speakers but rather encourage the rest of the class to use phrases such as: *Répétez s'il vous plait! Pardon, excusez-moi, je ne comprends pas,* or *Qu'est-ce que ça veut dire 'concierge'?* If necessary, native speakers can use one or two words in English to respond (i.e. *ça veut dire 'school site officer'*). Native speakers can be encouraged to describe famous people such as scientists, authors, footballers, singers and so on. The section further down on King Louis XIV provides further example.

Resources that support Literacy: Crafts, posters, comics and puzzles (worksheets)

Figure 8.17 Children line up for a game involving role play

Figure 8.18 Example of an anagram jigsaw in French

Anagram Jigsaws

la direc	je	école	rou	blan
le la	le ser	la mais	la tour	les toi
les ca	le sa	la tor	le poi	la fle
la pla	la trou	le li		

l'	sse	tue	sson	vre
pin	ge	lettes	on	er
deaux	pin	pent	terelle	
che	trice	ge	m'appelle	

> le livre, le sapin, la trousse, la directrice, je m'apelle, blanche, la tortue, les toilettes, la maison, le lapin, le serpent, le poisson, la tourterelle, la fleur, les cadeaux, l'école, rouge, la plage.

Worksheets come in many forms and serve many different purposes. They do, however, carry a connotation of something that is not particularly engaging. You might want to rename your worksheets as, 'funsheets' instead. There are a multitude of on-paper activities online, and we cannot go through each one because the possibilities of use are almost endless. Their main purpose should be to consolidate understanding (reading and writing) for vocabulary or grammar. The most common forms of worksheets are matching exercises, gap-filling, word searches and anagrams. They are fairly easy to differentiate, and for older or more advanced children, crafts can play an important role, as they can create their own funsheets and get each other to complete or, 'play' them. In the example shown in Figure 8.18 (anagram jigsaw), we used words which pupils would have come across in the first half-term of their language lessons:

Setting up a graffiti *board* in your classroom can invite children from very early on to play with TL creatively and imaginatively. They can write from memory or they can bring words recognized as belonging to the TL that they encounter outside the classroom. The board is self-differentiating, and contributions from all abilities can find a space. Figure 8.19 can be a starting point.

Figure 8.19 Wall display by Spanish children celebrating the international Day of Peace

Resources around history, geography and society

Most classrooms will have a map of the world displayed somewhere. You can also find world maps in French or Spanish, which children's curiosity can explore. The world, as we refer to it in England, is just an English version, so what does the world in other languages sound like? Using real objects (realia) from the TL country is a good way of getting children's curiosity excited. You may have books, foods, clothing or any items which you obtained while on holiday on the TL country or that have been given to you from there. As suggested earlier, real objects can be used to discuss culture, to practice descriptions or as props for role play. If you have been to Paris, and visited Versailles, you will hopefully have some fantastic memories of the palace and its grandeur. This would be a great opportunity of turning experience (a human resource) into a tangible language learning resource. You can be inspired to find out more about the Sun King, Louis XIV, and use the information with the children. Did you know, for instance, that King Louis invented ballet? Ballet used to be danced by men only during his time (1643). The movements closely followed those of the planets around the solar system as well as the sport of fencing. Every movement needed to be elegant, precise and purposeful. You can watch a documentary about this on YouTube called 'The King Dances' (based on the Ballet De La Nuit, which

186   Mastering Primary Languages

Figure 8.20 The world in other languages

Figure 8.21 The Sun King, Louis IV

the king himself performed, dressed in gold), and extract the information that would suit your particular activity. For example, can we walk like Louis XIV in the ballet? What was the music like?

From this, we can give pupils speech bubbles associated with the Sun King, in the first person singular. We want children to do their own research using the internet and then to write about the Sun King in the third person singular.

http://www.youtube.com/watch?v=LDtpDlCf94g

Figure 8.22 Possible statements from the Sun King himself

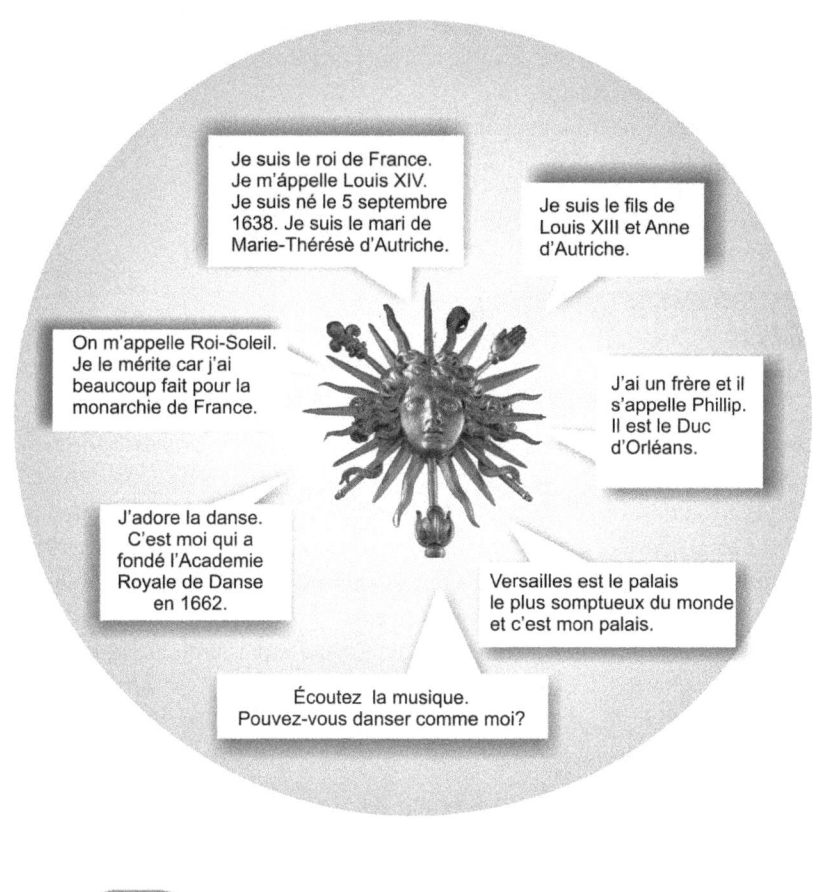

> Je suis le roi de France.
> Je m'áppelle Louis XIV.
> Je suis né le 5 septembre 1638. Je suis le mari de Marie-Thérèsè d'Autriche.

> Je suis le fils de Louis XIII et Anne d'Autriche.

> On m'appelle Roi-Soleil. Je le mérite car j'ai beaucoup fait pour la monarchie de France.

> J'ai un frère et il s'appelle Phillip. Il est le Duc d'Orléans.

> J'adore la danse. C'est moi qui a fondé l'Academie Royale de Danse en 1662.

> Versailles est le palais le plus somptueux du monde et c'est mon palais.

> Écoutez la musique. Pouvez-vous danser comme moi?

Languagenut

Languagenut is a digital language learning platform with a range of interactive and printable resources. It includes games and activities to nurture listening, speaking, reading and writing skills. There are also sentence building activities. While there is a curriculum specific to the system, there is also the option to input your own words and phrases to align it with the TL for your lessons. You can also monitor your pupils' use of the tool and completion of work you have set them from an administration area within the tool. Additionally, you can quickly find resources by searching for specific topics or activities.

We are not here to recommend or endorse commercial resources. We have argued that the choice of resources you invest in will depend on the context within which you are teaching and the children are learning. However, it would be unfortunate not to flag this up as it is organized and encourages the cross-curricular way of working that we have been promoting in this book. It has also been explored by PGCE students who found the resource to be accessible and supportive of a range of topics which are relevant for primary languages.

Please visit http://www.languagenut.com and insert the code below for free access to Languagenut for one month:

'mastprilang17'

Schemes of work

http://www.new-cilt.org.uk/Materials/TDASchemes/

The website above has the original TDA Schemes of work (Spanish, French and German) which were put together for schools to use. It is closely linked to the Key Stage 2 Framework for Languages. It can be a starting point for anyone intending to teach these languages but it also functioned as a template for many schools who have used these schemes to design their own personalized schemes of work catering for their particular school and their children's needs.

The TDA scheme is detailed and covers a range of topics with broad lesson plans which you can split into 2/3 separate lessons depending on time you have each week for language teaching. IU is already embedded within the scheme but other aspects of culture of your choice can easily be added or substituted.

http://www.lightbulblanguages.co.uk/resources-pr-fr-schemeofwork.htm

The Lightbulb website above, freely available to teachers of primary languages (Spanish, Italian and German), have their own schemes of work for Year 3 to 6. All the resources are on their website, carefully organized into languages, units and lessons.

Institut Français Culturethèque in collaboration with Catherine Cheater (an MFL practitioner, writer and adviser) has developed a Scheme of Work freely available from the link below. It is called The Primary French Project and consists of 4 different modules targeting different groups of learners: Niveau Bleu, Blanc, Rouge and Tricolore. It has PowerPoint presentations with embedded sound, cultural references, lesson plans and assessments. The resource can be used as it is or you can pick and choose how you want to add it to your own resource. **http://www.culturetheque.com/EXPLOITATION/GBR/apprendre.aspx**

http://www.accentlanguages.co.uk/

Accentlanguages is a website belonging to Nadine Chadier, a passionate FL primary practitioner. This is how she describes what she does:

'Apart from French pronunciation, I specialise in Creativity in the Curriculum, integrating music and teaching with magic tricks.'

'I love talking at conferences like the London Language Show and ALL World Language as well as running inset days for teachers.'

Figure 8.23 Nadine Chadier's alphabet pronunciation website

'If you wish to see some of my presentations, please leave your email address to receive them.'

http://www.accentlanguages.co.uk/french-is-all-around-2/

This website below will take you to the annual language show. It targets linguists, teachers and translators. It is the place to meet people looking for authentic resources and for professional development free of charge for a small fee.

http://www.languageshowlive.co.uk/

Coordinator for foreign language learning

This is an exciting opportunity for an outstanding teacher with a passion for languages to shape and develop our MFL provision. To find the right candidate, we are prepared to tailor the position and are happy to consider a part-time position teaching MFL across the school or a full-time position combining MFL and small group literacy & numeracy interventions.

(A primary school's recent advertisement for an MFL coordinator in the London area)

As an MFL teacher with primary experience, this advertisement cannot be more appealing, but what clearly comes across here is that this particular school values the learning of languages for its primary pupils. It understands that the coordinator's role is vital if the school is to be successful in implementing its MFL primary languages policy. It is willing to be flexible because it knows that the most important resource in delivering the FL curriculum is the coordinator's role to lead the MFL across the school through effective auditing, resourcing, evaluating and developing the language National Curriculum provision in the school.

Reading Ofsted Chief Inspector, Michael Wilshaw's monthly comment in May 2016, it also became clear that languages are being closely looked at in the primary school. MFL is regarded by Ofsted as a subject which can boost literacy and numeracy skills and raise standards.

So the coordinator, as we illustrate in Chapter 3, has an important role to play in supporting the school to develop and implement its FL policy. The link below will support you and keep you in touch with other MFL/FL coordinators. We understand that there is no longer a separate, direct support from the local authority to implement the statutory implementation of Foreign Languages in Primary schools, as it is now included in the whole school budget and it is the job of headteacher to allocate funds to resource FL and to ensure teachers are professionally trained and equipped to teach primary languages.

http://talkaboutprimarymfl.wikispaces.com/KS2SubjectLeader

A coordinator's activities check list may consist of the following:

- Develop the curricular framework for MFL within the framework of present school policies, both in short- and long-term planning structures.
- Promote, advise and support through exemplary MFL teacher planning appropriately to meet the needs of all pupils through differentiation.
- Monitor and evaluate teaching and learning of the development of language. Ensure curriculum continuity and progression. Monitor children's progress, keep records and evaluate children's achievements.
- Set clear targets, based on prior attainment, for pupils learning.
- Lead professional development of staff through training, support and example.
- Provide a stimulating environment, which builds confidence and promotes languages to all pupils.
- To enrich the MFL curriculum by inviting visitors into school, arranging workshops and organizing extracurricular events and visits, helping to organize MFL trips and organizing school events.
- Establish resource and staff requirements in accordance with the budget to achieve the aims of the policy.
- Support the evaluation of the effectiveness of the school's policies and developments and analyse their impact on teaching and learning of MFL.

Pause for thought

As a teacher starting out, ideally, the school who appointed you may already have the above activities visibly shaping the FL teaching and learning of the school. Imagine a scenario where this may not be so.

- Having read the previous paragraphs of this chapter what do you think would be a priority for you as a newly appointed FL curriculum leader? Considering that all of the above cannot come into existence all at once.

Further support

As a coordinator we will strongly recommend that you get your leadership team to agree to join Association for Language Learning (ALL). ALL is a national language organization. Its role is to support subject teaching in schools. It represents you as subject leader as well as provides support for the teaching of languages in Primary. It offers information, guidance, peer-to-peer support and further professional development. Its Primary members have set up a number of Primary Hubs all around the country; you can join one free, without being a member of ALL.

http://www.all-languages.org.uk/

The ALL FIPF Literature wiki is an all-French version of the established ALL Literature wiki – gathering ideas on using French literary texts.

http://fipf-litterature.wikidot.com/

The British Council provides ample support to schools in the UK; in addition to facilitating the access to Primary Language Assistants they bring a wealth of experience through teaching English around the world and therefore has links and expertise which can be useful to you and your school. The intercultural dimension to FL learning can be enhanced further by accessing their services such as the schemes:

- Schools Online
- eTwinning
- Connecting Classrooms School Partnerships
- Erasmus + for School Partnerships

The British Council Curriculum Resource area on their website is:
www.britishcouncil.org/school-resources/curriculum-resources

The British Council supports eTwinning in the UK in a very significant way. It works with Skype in the classroom to make worldwide connection even easier and to help teachers introduce students to classrooms, experts and artists in other countries – without worrying about geographical, time or cost barriers. This short video introduces Skype in the classroom. Find out how it works by going to the link below:

http://vimeo.com/44867804

Continuing professional development (CPD)

The website below provides direct access to teachers for further professional development specifically for primary language learning.

http://www.networkforlanguageslondon.org.uk/

London Schools Excellence Fund (LSEF)

The LSEF Project was led by Network for Languages London at the University of Westminster. It was an initiative partly funded by the Department for Education and was established by the mayor of London, Boris Johnson, to focus on raising the quality of teaching in primary and secondary schools and improving pupils' attainment in core subjects, including languages.

This has been very successful and greatly innovative in the approach to teaching and classroom research in the field of primary language learning. It is the first time primary FL learning has been approached in this way and we believe it is the way forward for teachers who want to pursue research in Primary MFL.

You can view the case studies here:

http://www.networkforlanguageslondon.org.uk/resource/video-case-study-the-bilingual-stream-preparing-the-children-for-the-world-of-tomorrow/

Summary

We have presented and argued for resources we believe will support and enhance motivation and progression by providing meaningful input and practice in the primary FL classroom.

Being familiar with any resource we use is essential in order to exploit it to the full, to our advantage and for the benefit of our pupils.

It is good practice to use resources which are meaningful to us and which add value to the language learning experience of the children in our class.

Recommended reading

Hawkes, R. (2009). Curriculum Now! – Published by Association for Language Learning.
Martin, C. (1995). Games & fun activities writing – Published by the Centre for Information on Language Teaching and Research (CILT).
McLachland, A. (2008). French in the Primary Classroom: Ideas and Resources for the Non-Linguist Teacher, Continuum International Publishing Group, London.
Skarbek, C. (2004). First Steps to reading and writing – Published by the Centre for Information on Language Teaching and Research (CILT).

Appendix I

Take a look at the table below to find something which appeals to you and make a start!

Integrating the geography curriculum and the Modern Language curriculum

Skills and concepts	Activities
A sense of place and space	A comparison study of the local area using pictures, maps, videos, internet and link with a school in the target country
Developing geographical and directional vocabulary	TL vocabulary and use of near, far, above, below, right, left, in the middle and so on
Developing geographical inquiry skills	In TL using pictures to locate and understand
Consolidating geographical terms	Where the place is/what it is like/how did it get to be like what it is/why is it changing?
Maps, globes and geographical skills	To describe and explain how and why places are similar to and different from other places in the same country and elsewhere in the world
Human environments, people and other lands, and natural environments	To study a locality in a country that is less economically developed
Developing familiarity with, and engaging in practical use of, maps and photographs, train and other route maps associated with the target country

Skills and concepts	Activities
	Developing an understanding of symbols and conventions in relation to maps
	A comparison study of target country:
	Language
	People and communities
	Art and culture
	Homes
	Major cities
	Work and work places
	Transport and communications
	Play and pastimes
	Climate – observations of weather
	Sport
	Tourism
	Trade and development issues
The local natural environment	Recording and displaying simple weather observations in a systematic way using graphs
	Plans of the classroom in TL
	Nature trail in TL
Physical features of Europe and the wider world	Identifying and learning the main physical features and towns of the target country in the TL
The compass points and names of towns in TL	Learning positional words, e.g. north, south, beside, above, etc., in the context of the map of Europe, the World, and the target country

Integrating the history curriculum and the Modern Language curriculum

Skills and concepts	Activities
Working as a historian	Exploration of change and continuity in the target culture/s using artefacts, paintings, and old and modern photographs
What archaeologists do?	Comparison of life in a similar era in the target country
Change and continuity Using evidence Empathy	A comparison of local festivals with feasts and festivals of the target culture – how the celebration of these festivals has changed or stayed the same A similar comparison based on games/pastimes
Early people and ancient societies	Hot seating activities in TL – to introduce Henry VIII/Wives
Life, society, work and culture in the past	Stone Age, Egyptians, Romans, Celts, Vikings and so on. The Tudors and their influence if any in relation to the target culture/s – comparison with Central and South American peoples comparison study of life, society, work and culture in the target country in a similar era, e.g. life in Louis XIV's time, life in the eighteenth or nineteenth century, and life during the Second World War A study or comparison of Henry VIII and François I
Politics, conflict and society	Revolution and change in the target country (French Revolution)
Continuity and change over time	A comparison study with the target country on themes such as Clothes Homes and urban development-Transport Food and farming Schools and education – school subjects, school life, school culture

Integrating the science curriculum and the Modern Language curriculum

Skills and concepts	Activities
Working scientifically	results of simple experiments in the TL, e.g. objects that float
	Investigating and recording information on weather patterns
	Estimating, measuring and recording weight, length, capacity, temperature, e.g. estimating and measuring how long it takes for a paper aeroplane to fall on the ground after it has been made following instructions in TL
Exploring density and buoyancy	Break the familiarity of introducing/revising vocabulary by revisiting floating and sinking using fruit. Which fruit will sink: the plum or the lemon?
Living things	Sorting and classifying objects and food using simple criteria and recording the information
	The food of the target culture comparison study – healthy and non-healthy food
	Designing nutritious meals and preparing dishes from the target culture with typical food
	Drawing and labelling the components of simple energy cycles
	Designing and recording a simple experiment to show the factors that affect growth
Plant and animal life	Food cycle
	The biological development of frog or butterfly
Changing state of materials	Water cycle
	TL – Key vocabulary – to consolidate, reintroduce or revise.
	Solid/liquid/gas – the effect heating/cooling and force has on them – dissolving/ recovery of solids – saturation points

Integrating the maths curriculum and the Modern Language curriculum

Skills and concepts	Activities
Number: Place value	TL – activities on the hundred square, e.g. what number comes before/after?
Read, write and order whole numbers and decimals	Following directions to a secret number Put your finger on … go up one box, go back two squares and so on. Addition, subtraction, multiplication and division tables and sums in the TL Multiplication Bingo in the TL Estimating answers of sums and using a calculator to check them Bingo Dice games
Measures: Length, Area, Weight, Capacity: Estimate and measure the length, area, weight and capacity of a variety of items	Activities involving measuring using various items of maths equipment e.g. ruler, metre stick, trundle wheel, weighing scales, and capacity jugs
Money	Estimate and calculate money problems Activities based on shopping Understanding and using euros and other target country currency Use of shopping catalogues in TL Creating a maths trail involving various measuring, counting and recording tasks around the classroom or school in the TL
Time	Read the 24hr clock Activities on reading the time – Time Bingo
Interpreting graphs and charts/data	Reading graphs in TL

Integrating the music curriculum and the Modern Language curriculum

Skills and concepts	Activities
Listening and responding	Listening and responding to pieces of music and songs associated with the target culture:
	Classical
	Traditional music, songs
	Film themes
	Contemporary popular music using YouTube and other listening software easily accessible in the classroom via the internet
	Learning about composers and their lives
	Comparing contemporary popular music scenes, such as R&B, Hip Hop, Rap with target country's own version
Performing: Song singing	Song singing for pleasure and performance
	using songs in the TL
	Traditional songs
	Classical pieces
	Contemporary pop songs
	Hymns and carols
	L Songs contest X-Factor style or talent show

Integrating the PE curriculum and the Modern Language curriculum

Skills and concepts	Activities
Ball games, kicking games and striking games	Comparing and Learning the vocabulary needed for playing games in the TL
Traditional games such as skipping, hop-scotch and those particular to the target culture	e.g. French *La Marelle*
Traditional playground chants and rhymes	Comparing and learning the vocabulary for cheering on and supporting a team Learning the vocabulary of traditional skipping and playground games
Dance	Learning traditional dances from the target
Exploration of traditional dance	Culture – Spanish *Flamenco*

Integrating the art curriculum and the Modern Language curriculum

Skills and concepts	Activities
Looking and responding	Looking at and responding to the work of artists from the target culture
To investigate Stone Age Paintings and sketch/paint their own in the style of cave paintings	Introduction of Lascaux cave paintings in TL Using such work as a stimulus for the children's own art work in various media Mask-making based on the theme of Carnival
Construction	Construction work related to the particular target culture, e.g. constructing a *Schultüte*, constructing crowns for *Le Jour des, Rois/Epiphanie* Constructing a town/village/landscape associated with the target culture Constructing and decorating a dream house/room Constructing an imaginary monster Constructing a model of famous target country monuments, e.g. *La Tour Eiffel, la Torre de Pizza, Templo de Debod*
Print and drawing	Designing and making posters for special events Designing and making cards for special events and festivals, Eid al-Fitr, Diwali, Easter, Mothers' Day cards
Fabric and fibre	Working in the TL Making a collage on various themes e.g. the months of the year, the seasons Designing costumes for Carnival, Mardi Gras or World Book Day Making puppets for using in the language class Designing a dream outfit and modelling it as part of a fashion show in the TL

Appendix I

Skills and concepts	Activities
Paint and colour	Exploring the colour combinations that make different colours
	Making a theme-based composition or collage using paint, crayon, charcoal, pastels, coloured pencils, markers, chalk, coloured magazines, tissue paper, etc.
	Egg painting for Easter
	Designing a theme-based calendar
Clay	Modelling characters from a favourite story in the TL modelling real or imaginary animals as part of language work on the theme of animals
	Modelling masks or monster faces

Integrating the PSHE curriculum and the Modern Language curriculum

Skills and concepts	Activities
Rights Respecting	Unicef – list in TL
Informed choices/preparation for transition to KS3	TL vocabulary and discussion – how we can choose a school that is right for us at the secondary level.
Understanding qualities and attributes of a friend	TL – what a good friend looks like

Appendix II

Comparing the Languages Framework (Year 3) to the National Curriculum for Key Stage 2

Languages Framework, Year 3	The National Curriculum for Key Stage 2
Outcomes for learning objectives at the end of the first year of language learning.	The focus of study of the National curriculum for languages is on practical communication and there are, broadly speaking, only twelve attainment targets:
INTERCULTURAL UNDERSTANDING **Appreciate** the diversity of languages spoken within their school. **Talk** about the similarities and differences of social conventions between different cultures. **Identify** the country or countries where the language is spoken. **Have** some contact with the country/countries. **Recognize** a children's song, rhyme or poem well known to native speakers. **ORACY** **Enjoy** listening to and speaking in the TL. **Listen** and respond to familiar spoken words, phrases and sentences. **Communicate** with others using simple words and phrases and short sentences. **Understand** conventions such as taking turns to speak and valuing the contribution of others. **Use** correct pronunciation in spoken work.	1. *listen attentively to spoken language and show understanding by joining in and responding.* 2. *explore the patterns and sounds of language through songs and rhymes and link the spelling, sound and meaning of words.* 3. *engage in conversations; ask and answer questions; express opinions and respond to those of others; seek clarification and help.** 4. *speak in sentences, using familiar vocabulary, phrases and basic language structures.* 5. *develop accurate pronunciation and intonation so that others understand when they are reading aloud or using familiar words and phrases.** 6. *present ideas and information orally to a range of audiences.** 7. *read carefully and show understanding of words, phrases and simple writing.* 8. *appreciate stories, songs, poems and rhymes in the language.*

Languages Framework, Year 3	The National Curriculum for Key Stage 2
LITERACY **Recognize** and understand some familiar words and phrases in written form. **Read** aloud in chorus, with confidence and enjoyment, from a known text. **Write** some familiar simple words using a model. **Write** some familiar words from memory. **KNOWLEDGE ABOUT LANGUAGE** **Recognize** that many languages are spoken in the UK. **Recognize** that many languages are spoken across the world. **Recognize** that there are different language conventions to express politeness. **Understand** that familiar things have different names in different languages, e.g. *Wasser, eau, water*.	9. *broaden their vocabulary and develop their ability to understand new words that are introduced into familiar written material, including through using a dictionary.* 10. *write phrases from memory, and adapt these to create new sentences, to express ideas clearly.* 11. *describe people, places, things and actions orally* and in writing.* 12. *understand basic grammar appropriate to the language being studied, including (where relevant) – feminine, masculine and neuter forms and the conjugation of high-frequency verbs; key features and patterns of the language; how to apply these, for instance, to build sentences; and how these differ from or are similar to English.* *The starred (*) content above will not be applicable to ancient languages.*
LANGUAGE LEARNING SKILLS **Analyse** and compare the language or languages with English. **Discuss** language learning, including the languages known by class members where appropriate. **Discuss** language learning, including the languages known by class members where appropriate. **Look** at the face of the person speaking and listen attentively. **Ask** someone to clarify or repeat.	

Bibliography

Adams, P., (2007). Exploring Social Constructivism: Theories and Practicalities. *Education 3–13*, 34 (3): 243–57.
Addison, R. and Brundrett, M. (2008). Motivation and demotivation of teachers in primary schools: the challenge of change. *Education 3-13: International Journal of Primary, Elementary and Early Years Education* 36 (1): 79–94.
Airey, J. (2004). *Can you Teach it in English? Aspects of the Language Choice Debate in Swedish Higher Education in Wilkinson, R. Integrating Content and Language: Meeting the Challenge of a Multilingual Higher Education*, Maastricht: Maastricht University Press.
Alberta Education, French Language Education Services, Canada (2014), https://education.alberta.ca/media/3115178/frimmhandbook.pdf
Alexander, R. (1990). Core subjects and Autumn Leaves: The National Curriculum and the Language of Primary Education. In Moon, B. (ed.) *New Curriculum - National Curriculum*. Milton Keynes: Hodder & Stoughton.
Alexander, R. (2012). *Improving Oracy and Classroom Talk in English Schools; Achievements and Challenges*. Cambridge: University of Cambridge.
Ambrossi, P. (2015). Language and Culture in Foreign Language Teaching. In Wyse, D., Davis, R., Jones, P. and Rogers, S. (eds) *Exploring Education and Childhood: From Current Certainties to New Visions*, 117–29. Abingdon: Taylor and Francis Inc.
Antoniou, P. and James, M. (2013). *Exploring Formative Assessment in Primary School Classrooms: Developing a Framework of Actions and Strategies*, 153–76. New York: Springer Science+Business Media.
Association for Language Learning, http://www.all-languages.org.uk/?s=CLIL
Atkinson, E. S. (2000). An Investigation into the Relationship Between Teacher Motivation and Pupil Motivation. *Educational Psychology* 20 (1): 45–57.
Bailey D. and Murray-Hall, K., (2015). 'Secondary-ready in Languages', Expert Subject Advisory Group–Modern Foreign Languages, http://expertsubjectgroups.co.uk/docs/ESAGMFLGroupAssessmentStatement.pdf
Barnes, J. (2011), Cross-curricular Policy and Practice. In *Cross-curricular Learning 3-14*, 56–69. Thousand Oaks: Sage.
Barnes, J. (2015). *Cross Curricular Learning* 3-14 (3rd edn). London: Sage.
Bellott, F. K. and Tutor, F. D. (1990). A challenge to the conventional wisdom of Herzberg and Maslow theories. Paper presented at the 19th Annual Meeting of the Mid-South Educational Research Association, New Orleans, LA.
Bilingual Immersion Education Network (BIEN): http://elac.ex.ac.uk/bien/page.php?id=5
Birdwel, J., Scott, R. and Reynolds, L. (2015). Character Nation, a Demos report with the jubilee centre for character and virtues, Demos, London (CC).
Black, and Jones (2007). Formative Assessment and the Learning and Teaching of MFL: Sharing the Language Learning Road Map with the Learners. *Language Learning Journal* 34 (1). T&F group.

Boroditsky, L. (2009). How does our language shape the way we think? EDGE Foundation online magazine, https://www.edge.org/conversation/lera_boroditsky-how-does-our-language-shape-the-way-we-think (accessed 4 October 2016).

Bourdieu, P. (1986). *Distinction: A Social, Critique of the Judgement of Taste*. London: Routledge.

Boyle, B. and Bragg, J. (2008), Making primary connections: the cross-curricular story, *The Curriculum Journal* 19 (1): 5–21.

Buckingham, D. (2008). Introducing Identity. In D. Buckingham (ed.), *Youth, Identity, and Digital Media*, 1–24. Cambridge, MA: The MIT Press.

Burnett, C. (2010). Technology and Literacy in Early Childhood Educational Settings: A Review of Research. *Journal of Early Childhood Literacy* 10(3): 247–70.

Byram, M. (1997). *Teaching and Assessing Intercultural Communicative Competence*. Clevedon: Multilingual Matters.

Byram, M. and Doyé, P. (1999). Intercultural Competence and Foreign Languages in the Primary School. In *Teaching Modern Languages in the Primary School*. Driscoll, P. and Frost, D. (eds) London: Routledge.

Byram, M. and Gribkova, B. and Starkey, H. (2002). *Developing the Intercultural Dimension in Language Teaching: A Practical Introduction for Teachers*. Language Policy Division, Directorate of School, Out-of-School and Higher Education, Strasbourg: Council of Europe.

Cable, et al. (2012). Language Learning at Key Stage 2: Findings from a Longitudinal Study. *Education 3–13: International Journal of Primary, Elementary and Early Years Education* 40 (4): 363–78.

Carney, R. and Levin, J. (2008). Conquering Mnemonophobia, with Help from the Three Practical Measures of Memory and Application. *Teaching of Psychology* 35 (176–83), Routledge.

Cézanne's virtual gallery – Aix en Province http://www.cezanne-en-provence.com/galerie/les-natures-mortes/

Cheater, C. and Farren, A. (2001). *The Literacy Link*. London: Young Pathfinder CILT

Chomsky, N. (2013). interviewed by Arianne Robichaud, Forthcoming in Radical Pedagogy, interview March 26, 2013, https://chomsky.info/20130326/

Collicott, S. L. (1986). Connections Haringey Local-National-World Links

Common European Framework of Reference for Languages (CEFR), http://www.coe.int/t/dg4/linguistic/Source/Framework_EN.pdf

Conteh J. (2003). *Succeeding in Diversity: Culture, Language and Learning in Primary Classrooms*. London: Trentham Books, 180p.

Council of Europe, European Language Portfolio:http://www.coe.int/en/web/portfolio

Coyle, D. (2007) Content and Language Integrated Learning: Towards a Connected Research Agenda for CLIL Pedagogies. *International Journal of Bilingual Education and Bilingualism*, 10 (5): 543–62.

Coyle, D. (2015). Strengthening Integrated Learning: Towards a New era for Pluriliteracies and Intercultural Learning. *Latin American Journal of Content and Language Integrated Learning* 8 (2): 84–103.

Coyle, D., Hood, H. and Marsh, D. (2010). *Content and Language Integrated Learning*. Cambridge: Cambridge University Press.

Cross, R. and Gearon, M. (2013). Research and Evaluation of the Content and Language Integrated Learning (CLIL) Approach to Teaching and Learning languages in Victorian Schools (Melbourne Graduate School of Education).

Dalton-Puffer, C. and Nikula, T. (2014). Content and Language Integrated Learning. *The Language Learning Journal* 42 (2): 117–22.

DCSF (2009). Developing language in the primary school: Literacy and primary languages.

DCSF Publications (2009). Independent Review of the Primary Curriculum: Final Report.
Dinham, S. and Scott, C. (1998). A Three Domain Model of Teacher and School Executive Satisfaction. *Journal of Educational Administration* 36(4): 362–78.
Doiz, A., Lasagabaster, D. and Juan, J. S. (2014). CLIL and motivation: the Effect of Individual and Contextual Variables. *The Language Learning Journal* 42(2): 209–24.
Dor, D. (2011). Language as a social construct http://www.ynetnews.com/articles/0,7340,L-4059809,00.html (accessed 1 November 2016).
Driscoll, P. (1999). Modern Foreign Languages in the Primary School: A Fresh Start. In: P. Driscoll and D. Frost (eds), *The Teaching of Modern Foreign Languages in the Primary School*, 9–26. London: Routledge.
Driscoll, P., Jones, J. and Macrory, G. (2004). The Provision of MFL Learning for Pupils at Key Stage 2. Research Report 572. DfES, London.
EEF (2016). Teaching and Learning Toolkit, Education Endowment Foundation, https://educationendowmentfoundation.org.uk/resources/teaching-learning-toolkit/ (accessed October 2016).
Einstein, A. (1930). 'The world as I see it' online text, https://archive.org/stream/AlbertEinsteinTheWorldAsISeeIt/The_World_as_I_See_it-AlbertEinsteinUpByTj_djvu.txt
European Language Portfolio working sample I, http://www.ncca.ie/uploadedfiles/Curriculum/inclusion/primary_elp.pdf
European Language Portfolio working sample II (CILT), http://www.agtv.vic.edu.au/files/Website%202015/8871-junior-passport.pdf
Fairclough, N. (2006). *Language and Globalization*. London: Routledge.
Feynman, R. (1973). Take the World from Another Point of View, Yorkshire television interview by British astrophysicist Fred Hoyle. https://www.youtube.com/watch?v=GN-hlNSLQAFEFig.1, © Copyright Jaggery and licensed for reuse under this Creative Commons Licence
Foucault, M. (1991). *The Foucault Reader, Practices and Knowledge*, edited byP. Rabinov, 350, Penguin, 1984 (first pub).
Freire Institute, http://www.freire.org/paulo-freire/
Freire, P. (1993). Chapter 2, Pedagogy of the Oppressed, online at, http://faculty.webster.edu/corbetre/philosophy/education/freire/freire-2.html
French Seyès grid writing, https://cursivecole.fr/texte1.php
Froiland, J. M., Mayor, P. and Herlevi, M. (2015). Motives Emanating from Personality Associated with Achievement in a Finnish Senior High School: Physical Activity, Curiosity, and Family Motives. *School Psychology International* 36(2): 207–21.
Gao, Hong. (2002). Language contact – Misunderstanding, confusion and conflicts. *Intercultural Communication Studies* 11(3): 107–14.
Gilliland, B. (2015). Reading, Writing, and Learning English in an American High School Classroom. *Reading in a Foreign Language* 27(2): 272–93.
Glenn, E. S. (1981). Man and Mankind: Conflict and Communication Between Cultures.
Goethe (lines attributed to him by creative translation of Faust), http://www.goethesociety.org/pages/quotescom.html (accessed 1 November2016).
Gokce, F. (2010). Assessment of Teacher Motivation. *School Leadership and Management* 30(5): 487–99.
Gordon, A. L. (2016). *Languages Today* (issue 24, Autumn 2016): http://rer.sagepub.com/content/63/4/489.abstract
Graham, L. J., Van Bergen, P. and Sweller, N. (2016). Caught between a rock and a hard place: disruptive boys' views on mainstream and special schools in New South Wales, Australia. *Critical Studies in Education* 57(1): 35–54.
Grand Palais : Cultural Centre for the public, http://www.jeunepublic.grandpalais.fr/JEUX-CEZANNE/jeu_cezanne2.html
Griffiths, C. (2004). *Language Learning Strategies*: *Theory and Research*.

Groh, J. (2014). *Making Space: How the Brain knows where Things are.* Cambridge, MA.: The Belknap Press of Harvard University Press.

Hall, K. (2002). Asserting 'Needs' and Claiming 'Rights': The Cultural Politics of Community Language Education in England. *Journal of Language, Identity & Education* 1(2): 97–119, p. 114.

Hamilton, E. (1959). American translator, classical scholar, writer, 1867-1963; Quoted in the *Bryn Mawr School Bulletin*, http://www.feminist.com/resources/quotes/educ.htm

Hargreaves, D. H. (1991). Coherence and Manageability: Reflections on the National Curriculum and Cross-curricular Provision. *The Curriculum Journal* 2(1): 33–41.

Harnett, P. and Beardsley, G. (2012). *Exploring Play in the Primary Classroom.* London: David Fulton Publishers, 1998, Routledge.

Hashemi, Masoud. (2011). Language Stress and Anxiety Among the English Language Learners. *Procedia-Social and Behavioral Sciences* 30: 1811–16.

Hattie, J. (2012). *Visible Learning for Teachers: Maximizing Impact on Learning*, 14. London: Routeldge.

Hayness, J. (2002). Children as Philosophers: Learning Through Enquiry and Dialogue in the Primary Classroom, Routledge Farmer.

Herger, M. (2014). 5 Types of Boredom And How to Use Them for Creativity, http://www.slideshare.net/marioherger/5-types-of-boredom-and-how-to-use-them-for-creativity

Homer, The Odyssey, parallel text translation by A.T. Murray, W. Heinmann, London, 1927. online text, http://sul-derivatives.stanford.edu/derivative?CSNID=00000519&mediaType=application/pdf

Hood, P. and Tobutt, K. (2009). Modern Languages in the Primary School.

House of Commons Library, Briefing Paper Number 07388, 12 May 2016, http://research-briefings.parliament.uk/ResearchBriefing/Summary/CBP-7388

Hoy, P. (1976). The Conditions for Success. Strasbourg. France: Council of Europe, http://all-languages.org.uk/wp-content/uploads/2016/04/Developing-languages-and-literacy.pdf

http://cultura.mit.edu/

https://www.gov.uk/government/uploads/system/uploads/attachment_data/file/524559/Foreign_languages_and_science_in_primary_schools.pdf'

http://www.ucdoer.ie/index.php/Education_Theory/Constructivism_and_Social_Constructivism_in_the_Classroom

Hunt, M. (2009). the Progression and assessment in foreign languages at Key Stage 2

Hunt, M., Barnes, A., Powell, B. and Martin, C. (2008). Moving on: The Challenges for Foreign Language Leaning on Transition from Primary to Secondary School. *Teaching and Teacher Education* 24(4): 915–26.

Hunt, S. Classics for all: championing classics in schools, http://classicsforall.org.uk/wp-content/uploads/2015/10/Steve-Hunt-Guide-full-document-1.pdf

Images from Google, Le Petit Prince, https://c1.staticflickr.com/8/7612/16272961693_245b-91462d_b.jpg

Images from Google, Quijote https://c1.staticflickr.com/1/110/303770741_ae3101b384.jpg

Images from Google, usage rights: labelled for reuse with modification. Gruffalo https://upload.wikimedia.org/wikipedia/commons/6/68/Gruffalo_Sculpture_Final.jpg

Ioannou-Georgiou, S. and Ramírez Verdugo, M. D. (2010). Stories as a tool for teaching and learning in CLIL

James, M. and Pollard, A. (2011). TLRP's Ten Principles for Effective Pedagogy: Rationale, Development, Evidence, Argument and Impact. *Research Papers in Education* 26(3): 275–328.

Jann E. Azumi and Lerman, James L., 1987. Selecting and Rewarding Master Teachers: What Teachers in One District Think. *The Elementary School Journal* 88, No2.

Johnstone, K. (2007). Impro: Improvisation and the Theatre, Bloomsbury Publishing PLC, Methuen Drama, London (a free pdf version is available online)

Jones, B. (2015), http://www.all-languages.org.uk/resources/barry-jones-archive/

Jones, J. (2010). The role of Assessment for Learning in the management of primary to secondary transition: implications for language teachers, *The Language Learning* 38 (2): 175–91.

Jones, J. (2012). Portfolios as 'Learning Companions' for Children and a Means to Support and Assess Language Learning in the Primary School. *Education* 3–13(40): 4

Jones, J. and Coffey, S. (2006). Teaching Approaches – Differentiation, Motivation and Learning Across the Curriculum. In *Modern Foreign Languages 5-11*, 68–83. London: David Fulton.

Jones, J. and McLachlan, A. (2009). Primary Languages in Practice, A guide to teaching and Learning

Kanematsu, H. and Barry, D. (2016). Theory of Creativity, Chapter 2, STEM and ICT Education in Intelligent Environments. Switzerland: Springer International Publishing.

Ketabi, Saeed and Simm, Iran Shahia (2009). Investigating Persian EFL Teachers and Learners' Attitudes Towards Humor in Class. *International Journal of Language Studies* 3(4).

Kildare Education Centre, https://www.eckildare.ie/ (last accessed on 10 October 2017).

Kirsch, C. (2008). Teaching Foreign Languages in the Primary School.

Krashen, S. (1982). *Principles and Practice in Second Language Acquisition,* 7. Oxford: Pergamon.

Kuhl, P. K. (2011). Early language learning and literacy, http://www.ncbi.nlm.nih.gov/pmc/articles/PMC3164118/

Kutnick, P., Sebba, J., Blatchford, P., Galton, M., Thorp, J., MacIntyre, H. and Berdondini, L. (2005). *The Effects of Pupil Grouping: Literature Review.* [Research report (Department for Education and Skills)] Volume/Part: 688 - Published Version.

Language Trends 2015/16: The state of language learning in primary and secondary schools in England

Languages Trends Survey 2013–14, https://www.britishcouncil.org/sites/default/files/language-trends-survey-2014.pdf

Languages Trends Survey 2014–15, https://www.britishcouncil.org/sites/default/files/language_trends_survey_2015.pdf

Languages Trends Survey 2015–16, https://www.britishcouncil.org/sites/default/files/language_trends_survey_2016_0.pdf

Lankshear, C. and Knobel, M. (2007). Chapter 1: Sampling 'The Niew' in New Literacies. In M. Knobel and C. Lankshea (eds), *A New Literacies Sampler*, 1–23. New York: Peter Lang.

Laurence Anholt: Cézanne and The Apple Boy (This is one of the collection of children's books written by Laurence Anholt. It is called the Anholt's Artists series.)

Le Guin, U. (2014). Blog entry 91, http://www.ursulakleguin.com/Blog2014.html

Le roi soleil Fichier: Ballet de la nuit 1653, https://www.google.co.uk/search?site=&tbm=isch&source=hp&biw=1190&bih=709&q=le+roi+soleil&oq=le+roi&gs_l=img.1.0.35i39k1j0l9.14233.15426.0.17786.7.7.0.0.0.0.100.502.5j1.6.0..0..1ac.1.64.img.1.6.501.0.CV92U1MXIKc#q=le+roi+soleil&tbm=isch&tbs=sur:fm&imgrc=T_kJm1TX6_z4SM.

Legg, K. (2013). An Investigation into Teachers into Teachers' Attitude Towards the Teaching of Modern Foreign Languages in the Primary School. *Education* 3–13.

Lonsdale, C. (2006). *The Third Ear*. Hong Kong: Third Ear Publishing Ltd. 2007.

Macaro, E., Graham, S. and Woore, R. (2016). Improving Foreign Language Teaching.

Mann, S. and Cadman, R. (2014). Does Being Bored Make Us More Creative? *Creativity Research Journal* 26(2): 165–173.

Martin, C. (2012). Pupils' Perceptions of Foreign Language Learning in the Primary-findings from Key Stage 2 Language Learning Pathfinder Evaluation. *Education 3-13* 40(4): 343–62.

Masgoret, A. M. and Gardner, Robert C. (2003). Attitudes, Motivations, and Second Language Learning: A Meta-Analysis of Studies Conducted by Gardner and Associates. *Language Learning* 53(1): 123–63.

Massler, U., Stotz, D. and Queisser, C. (2014). Assessment Instruments for Primary CLIL: The Conceptualisation and Evaluation of Test Tasks. *The Language Learning Journal* 42(2): 137–50.

*Mauro Dujmovi*c *&Visoka uciteljska škola, Pula* (2006). Storytelling as a method of EFL Teaching.

Maynard, S. (2012). Teaching Foreign Languages in the Primary School.

McLachlan, A. (2009). Modern Languages in the Primary Curriculum: Are we Creating Conditions for Success? *The Language Learning Journal* 37(2): 183–203.

Modern Languages in Primary Schools Initiative: MLPSI, KEC (2005), V.3

Molander, C. and Winterton, J. (1994). *Managing Human Resources*. London: Routledge

Morin, M. (2016), http://www.consider-ed.org.uk/teaching-foreign-languages-primary-schools-learned-lessons/

Muijs, D., et al. (2005). Evaluation of the key stage 2 language learning Pathfinders University of Warwick & University of Reading. Research Report no.692.

Multilingual Learning, http://www.gold.ac.uk/clcl/multilingual-learning/

NASA, http://solarsystem.nasa.gov/planets/solarsystem

National Advisory Committee on Creative and Cultural Education (1999). All Our Futures: Creativity, Culture and Education. London: DFEE.

National College for School Leadership: Leadership for personalising learning

National Library of Scotland – Innovative Learning Projects for The National Library of Scotland: The History Detectives – Teacher Resource Pack 5-14 Level C-D / A Curriculum for Excellence – Developed by Ruth Ruthven.

National Strategies, Primary (2009). Developing Language in the Primary School: Literacy and Primary Language, http://all-languages.org.uk/wp-content/uploads/2016/04/Developing-languages-and-literacy.pdf

Nelde, P. (1987). Language Contact Means Language Conflict. *Journal of Multilingual Development* 8(1–2).

Nunan, D. and Choi, J. (2010). *Language and Culture: Reflective Narratives and the Emergence of Identity*, 11. New York: Routledge.

O'Malley, J., Chamot, A., et al. (1985). Learning strategies used by beginning and intermediate ESL students. *Language Learning* 35: 21–46.

O'Neill, C. (2006), Dialogue and Drama. In Philip Taylor and Christine D. Warner (eds), *Structure and Spontaneity: The Process Drama of Cecily O'Neill*. Sterling, VA: Trentham.

Ofsted (2008). The changing landscape of languages – An evaluation of language learning 2004/2007.

Ofsted (2011). Modern Languages Achievement and Challenge 2007-2010, https://www.gov.uk/government/publications/modern-languages-achievement-and-challenge-2007-to-2010

Ofsted (2016). Foreign languages and science provision in primary schools: Foreign languages and science provision in primary schools May 2016, No. 160031.

Ofsted, School Inspection Handbook (2016), https://www.gov.uk/government/uploads/system/uploads/attachment_data/file/553942/School_inspection_handbook-section_5.pdf

Ofsted's Chief Inspector, Sir Michael Wilshaw, comments on the study of science and foreign languages in primary schools: HMCI's monthly commentary (May 2016), https://www.gov.uk/government/speeches/hmcis-monthly-commentary-may-2016

Owen, J. L. (2002). A Retrospective on Behavioural Approaches to Human Language and Some Promising New Developments. *American Communication Journal* 5(3), Spring.

Oxford, R. L. (1990). *Language Learning Strategies: What Every Teacher Should Know*. Boston: Heinle & Heinle.
Pennycook, A. (2006). *Postmodernism in Language Policy, chapter in An Introduction to Language Policy: Theory and Method*, edited by T. Ricento. Hoboken: Blackwell Publishing.
Pennycook, A. (2013). *The Cultural Politics of English as an International Language*, 7. London: Routledge.
Peterson, C. and McCabe, A. (2004). Echoing Our Parents: Parental Influences on Children's Narration. In M. W. Pratt and B. H. Fiese (eds), *Family Stories and the Life Course: Across Time and Generations*, 27–54. Mahwah, NJ: Lawrence Erlbaum Associates.
Piazzoli, E. (2012). Engage or Entertain? The Nature of Teacher/Participant Collaboration in Process Drama for Additional Language Teaching, *Scenario* 6(2), online at http://research.ucc.ie/scenario/2012/02/Piazzoli/05/en
Potter, J. (2011). New Literacies, New Practices and Learner Research: Across the Semipermeable Membrane between Home and School. In *Lifelong Learning in Europe*, Vol. XVI, ISSN: 1239-6286 issue 3/2011, 174–81. Helsinki: Kansanvalistusseura.
Primary Modern Foreign Languages Longitudinal Survey of Implementation of National Entitlement to Language Learning at Key Stage 2 Final Report (2009), https://www.nfer.ac.uk/publications/PLF01/PLF01.pdf
PSHE Association, https://www.pshe-association.org.uk/curriculum-and-resources/resources/programme-study-pshe-education-key-stages-1%E2%80%935
QCA (2004). Creativity: find it, promote it, Qualifications and Curriculum Authority, https://www.literacyshed.com/uploads/1/2/5/7/12572836/1847211003.pdf
Radnor, H. A., Parfitt, G. and Thomasson, V. (1996). A Case Study of Cross-curricular Practice through Partnership. *Mentoring & Tutoring: Partnership in Learning* 3(3): 50–8.
Richards, J. (1969). Songs in Language Learning. *TESOL Quarterly* 3(2): 161–74.
Robert, C., et al. (2001). Theoretical Issues in Language and Culture Practices. In *Language Learners as Ethnographers*, 44–63. Clevedon: Multilingual Matters.
Rogers, C. (1954). Towards a Theory of Creativity. *ETC: A Review of General Semantics* 11(4) (SUMMER 1954): 249–60.
Rogers, S. (2008). Researching Young Children's Perspectives: A Multimodal Approach. In S. Rogers and J. Evans (eds), *Inside Role-Play in Early Childhood Education, Researching Young Children's Perspectives*, 39–51. London and New York: Routledge.
Rouvin, A. (2004). Calligraphy lesson, https://www.flickr.com/photos/evdaimon/79076113
Selwyn, N. (2007). *Citizenship, Technology and Learning – A Review of Recent Literature*. Bristol: Futurelab.
Selwyn, N. (2012). Making Sense of Young People, Education and Digital Technology: The Role of Sociological Theory. *Oxford Review of Education, Taylor and Francis* 38(1).
Sercu, Lies, Bandura, Ewa and Castro, Poloma (eds) (2005). *Foreign Language Teachers and Intercultural Competence: An International Investigation*. UK: The Cromwell Press Ltd.
Sharpe, K. (2001). *Modern Foreign Languages in the Primary School: The What, Why & How of Early Foreign Languages Teaching*, 6. Hove: Psychology Press.
Sime, D. (2003). Research on Learners' Perceptions of Teachers' Non-verbal Behaviours in the Foreign Language Class.
Sinclair, C. (2008). Initial and Changing Student Teacher Motivation and Commitment to Teaching. *Asia-Pacific Journal of Teacher Education* 36(2): 79–104.
Spradley, J. and McCurdy, D. (2012). *Conformity and Conflict: Readings in Cultural Anthropology*. London: Pearson Education, Inc.
Sternberg, Robert J. (2006). The Nature of Creativity. *Creativity Research Journal* 18(1): 87–98.

Stiggins, R. J. (2007). Assessment Through the Student's Eyes, online article, *Educational Leadership* 64(8) Educating the Whole Child Pages 22–6, ASCD.http://citeseerx.ist.psu.edu/viewdoc/download?doi=10.1.1.619.5631&rep=rep1&type=pdf

Taubman (2009). Teaching By Numbers: Deconstructing the Discourse of Standards and Accountability in Education.

The Independent Review of the Primary curriculum: Final Report, http://www.educationengland.org.uk/documents/pdfs/2009-IRPC-final-report.pdf

The Key Stage 2 Framework for Languages (2005). *Department for Education and Skills*. Nottingham, UK: DfES Publications.

The Key Stage 2 Framework for Languages, http://all-languages.org.uk/wp-content/uploads/2016/04/KS2-Framework-for-Languages-part-1.pdf

The Languages Company, http://www.languagescompany.com/about-us/supporting-the-languages-strategy/supporting-primary-languages.html

The National College for Leadership of Schools and Children Services.

The National Curriculum a consultation document Department of Education and Science/Welsh Office London: 1987.

Tierney, D. and Hope, M. (1998). Young Pathfinder 7: Making the link. Relating languages to other work in the school. A CILT Series for Primary Language Teachers.

Tramonte, L. and Willms, D. (2010). Cultural Capital and its Effects on Education Outcomes. *Economics of Education Review* 29(2): 200–13.

Turner, M. (1996). Bedtime with Shahrazad, *The Literary Mind*, 5. Oxford: Oxford University Press.

Valdes, J. (ed.) (1986). *Culture Bound*. Cambridge: Cambridge University Press.

Wade, P., Marshall, H. and O'Donnell, S. (2009). Primary modern foreign languages longitudinal survey of implementation of national entitlement to language learning at key stage 2. Research Report No. RR127. London: DCSF.

Wenger, Etienne (c 2007). Communities of Practice. A Brief Introduction. *Communities of Practice*, http://wenger-trayner.com/introduction-to-communities-of-practice/ (accessed September 2016).

West-Burnham, J. (2010). Leadership for personalising learning.

What is Geography, https://www.youtube.com/watch?v=GQEJqlnnemg

Wiliam, D. (2014). Formative assessment and contingency in the regulation of learning processes, Paper presented in a Symposium entitled *Toward a Theory of Classroom Assessment as the Regulation of Learning* at the annual meeting of the American Educational Research Association, Philadelphia, PA, April 2014.

Wilson, E. (2012). *School-based Research: A Guide for Education Students*. 2nd edn. London: Sage.

Young, D. J. (2014). Affective Factors and Second Language Spanish. In *The Handbook of Spanish Second Language Acquisition*, 1st edn, edited by Kimberly L. Geeslin. New York: John Wiley & Sons, Inc.

Index

NOTE: Page numbers in *italics* refer to figures

ability-based grouping   143
Accentlanguages (website)   188–9
affective filter hypothesis   24
Alexander, Robin   50–1
ALL. *See* Association for Language Learning
Alliot, Dan   6, *145*, 146–55, 168
ALTE. *See* Association of Language Testers in Europe
anxiety, as affective factor   24
art
   artistic *vs.* creative   121
   integrated learning   56–7, 109–13, 200–1
assessment   6, 55, 141–2, 155–7
   of bilingual children   154
   head teachers' perspective   147
   learners' perspective   148–9
   notion   139–40
   parents' perspective   147–8
   teachers' perspective   146, 148
   tools   157–60
   types   142–4
Association for Language Learning (ALL)   191
Association of Language Testers in Europe (ALTE)   159
authentic resources   169–71, 185

behaviourism   20, 63
bilingual children
   assessment   154
   as resource   178
bingo, as teaching aid   65, 66
boredom   116–17
The British Council   191
   Language Assistants Programme   178
Bruner, Jerome   24
Byram, Michael   25–6, 75

Cambridge Primary Review (2009)   99
'Can Do' statements   159–60
CEDAR. *See* Centre for Education Development, Appraisal and Research
CEFR. *See* Common European Framework of Reference for Languages
Centre for Education Development, Appraisal and Research (CEDAR)   38

Chadier, Nadine   178, 188–9
   pupil's work from   *9, 19, 95, 137, 172*
Cheater, Catherine   188
choice of language   34–6
Chomsky, Noam   39, *40*, 120
class teachers   31–2
   'expert' role   10–15
   as resource   164
   role in foreign language delivery   40–1
classical literature, as learning resource   174–5
CLIL. *See* content and language integrated learning
codified knowledge   15, 16–17, 18, 20
cognitive development   23–4
commercial publishers, impact on teaching practice   20
Common European Framework of Reference for Languages (CEFR)   157, 159
community of practice   49, *50*, 72–3
   effective and sustainable   57–8
comprehensible input   85
constructivism   109
content and language integrated learning (CLIL)   23, 56–7, 101, 108–13
continuing professional development (CPD)   191
Coyle, Do   108
CPD. *See* continuing professional development
craft knowledge   15–17, 18
creativity   5, 12–13, 106, 138
   and activities   117–19
   and boredom   116–17
   and knowledge   120
   notion   115–16
   role-modelling   124–5, 127, 130
   Sternberg's theory   119–20
critical thinking   2–3, 79
cross-curricular learning   6, 94–6, 106
   notion   97–9
cultural capital   5, 24, 62
cultural knowledge   15, 16
culture
   and identity   71–2
   notion   71
   resources   185–7
   of target language   13, 53, 165–6, 176, *177*, 178

curiosity 5, 115
   and immersive approach 11–12
   and motivation 62–3
curriculum 30–3, 37

Department for Education (DFEs) 27–8, 192
'Developing language in the primary school: Literacy and primary languages' 164–5
DFEs. *See* Department for Education
dialogue 26, 60, 61, 63
digital language learning platforms 187–8

EAL. *See* English as an additional language
effective pedagogy 18, 32, 33, 143, 144
EFL. *See* English as a first language
ELP. *See* European Language Portfolio
English as an additional language (EAL) 44
English as a first language (EFL) 43
English grammar 77–80
eTwinning 191
European Language Portfolio (ELP) 157–60
expert/expertise 42–3
extrinsic motivation 58

Feynman, Richard 127
FLL. *See* foreign language learning
foreign language learning (FLL) 2–5
   'acquired' and 'learned' systems of 24
   approaches to, and personal experiences of 149–50
   attitudes towards 8, 9–10, 42–3
   for whom 43–6
   holistic approach 35
   importance 46
   need for continuum in 30
   neuroscience research 87–8
   rationale 7–8, 14–15, 40–1, 50–1
foreign language learning (FLL) in England. *See also* KS2 Framework for Languages; National Curriculum
   age criteria 43
   current scenario 29–34, 47
   provisions 5, 27–9
formative assessment 142, 143, 144, 162
Freire, Paulo 137
French 9, 34, 60–1, 86–7, 104–7, 109–13, 126–7, 179–80
funding 37–8

games, and learning motivation 63–6
geography 193–4
German 34, 126–7
graded questions 82, *83*, 102
grammar
   activities/play 65, 112, 126–33, *133*
   knowledge of 24, 76–80, 127
grammar schools 43, 61–2

Greek (ancient) 43, 61–2, 135
Griffiths, Carol 88
group work 143–4

head teachers 147
Herger, Mario 117
history 104–7, 195
Hood, Philip 101, 108
hot seating 182
human resources 178

i+1 effect 24
ICT. *See* information and communication technology
identity 71–2
immersion 11–12. *See also* content and language integrated learning
independent learning 13
Independent Review of the Primary Curriculum 28
information
   and knowledge differentiated 63
   'play' with 128–33
information and communication technology (ICT)
   and learner motivation 64, 65, 66–7, 168
   as resource 167–8
Institut Français Culturethèque 188
instrumental motivation 58–9
integrated learning 193–201
   immersion 56–7, 101, 108–13
   language and new content 101, 104–7
   language and semi-familiar content 101
   levels 101
   surface-curricular linking 101, 102
integrative motivation 58–9
intercultural communicative competence model 25–6, 75
intercultural understanding (IU) 73–6
   activities around 53, 54–5, 64, 65
   Byram's 5 savoirs model 25–6
intrinsic motivation 58
investment theory of creativity 119–20
IU. *See* intercultural understanding

James, Mary 143

KAL. *See* knowledge about language
keyword method 89
knowledge
   and creativity 120
   desire to access knowledge 62–3
   and foreign language learning 67
   and information differentiated 63
   types 15–18
knowledge about language (KAL) 24, 65, 76–80, 127
Krashen, Stephen 24, 85–6

KS2
	language provisions 28, 29–34, 47
	National Curriculum requirements 32, 91
	transition to KS3 38–9, 161–2
KS2 Framework for Languages (2005) 5, 28, 41–2, 69–71, 88–9, 91, 164, 166
	aims for children in speaking and listening 102
	compared to National Curriculum 202–3
	and value of games 64
KS3 38–9, 160–1

language acquisition theory, Krashen's 85–6
language assistants 178, 191
language capital, of existing staff 34, 46
language coordinators 38, 189–90
language learning strategies (LLS) 60–1, 88–9
Language Teaching in Schools in England 27
Languagenut (digital platform) 187–8
Languages Company 37
The Languages Framework (2005). *See* KS2 Framework for Languages
Languages Trends Survey (2015–16) 32, 34, 37, 38, 39
Latin 35, 43, 61–2, 135
Lave, Jean 72, 73
learner motivation 5, 49
	extrinsic and intrinsic 58
	and games 63–6
	and ICT 64, 65, 66–7, 168
	instrumental and integrative orientations 58–9
	multifaceted approach 59–63
	and personal experience 137
	teacher's role 13
lesson planning 94–5
	role in assessment 150–4
Lightbulb (website) 188
linguists 39–40
listening 80, 85, 172
	Framework for Languages aims for 102
literacy 42, 90–1
	games 64
	supportive resources 179–82, 183–4
LLS. *See* language learning strategies
London Schools Excellence Fund (LSEF) 192
Lord Dearing's Language Review 28
LSEF. *See* London Schools Excellence Fund

McIntire, Donald 16–17
Mandarin 34
mathematics 102–3, 197
Maynard, Sally 30
meta-cognition 61
motivation. *See* learner motivation; teacher motivation

music
	integration with language curriculum 198
	as learning resource 179–80

narrative 130
National Curriculum 32, 91, 98, 165–6
	compared to Framework for Languages 202–3
National Entitlement to Language Learning 28
National Foundation for Educational Research (NFER) 28
National Language Strategy 27–8
NFER. *See* National Foundation for Educational Research

Ofsted 145, 162, 189
	2011 survey report 29, 30–2
	criticism on 33
online resources 179, 188–9
open-mindedness 121–2, 137–8
oracy 42, 80–5
	games 64, 65
	supportive resources 179–83

paralanguage 87–8
parents
	assessment from the perspective of 147–8
	as resource 178
PE. *See* physical education
peer assessment 143–4
personal, social, health and citizenship education 201
phonics 82
phonology 82
physical education (PE) 182–3, 199
Piaget, Jean 23–4
play 19–20, 78–9, 127–33
Pollard, Andrew 143
Primary Languages Pathfinder programme 38
primary schools, challenges 36–43
professional training and development 37–8
	continuing development 191
	exchange programme 45, *73*
pronunciation 83–5, 88
	games 65

radical behaviourism 20
reading 20, 90, 172
real objects, as learning resource 169–71, 185
relational capital 62, 67–8, 122–3, 134–7
resources 6, 163, *165*, 166–8
Rogers, Carl 137
role-model, for creativity 124–5, 127, 130
role play 182–3
Rose, (Sir) Jim 28
Rose Primary Review (2009) 98
rote learning 65, 66

Sanskrit   127
schemes of work   188–9
   role in assessment   150–4
The School Inspections Handbook   145
science   196
second language acquisition (SLA)   4
   social constructivist approach   22–6
secondary schools   34, 38–9, 161–2
SEL. *See* social and emotional learning
self-confidence, as affective factor   24
self-regulation   61
Seyès grid paper   176, *177*
Sime, Daniela   87
situated learning theory   72
Skinner, Burrhus Frederic   20
SLA. *See* second language acquisition
social and emotional learning (SEL)   60–1
social constructivism   18, 22–6
social development theory   18, 19–20
songs, as learning resource   180–2
Spanish   11–12, *17*, 34, 60–1, 65, 66, 82, 84, 88, 102–3, 126–7, 132–3, *133*, 155–7
spelling games   65
spoken language   80–2, 87–8, 90
   Framework for Languages aims for   102
Sternberg, Robert J.   119–20
stories, as teaching/learning resource   171–8
summative assessment   142, 143
surface cross-curricular linking   101, 102

target language (TL)   85–7
   culture of   13, 53, 165–6, 176, *177*, 178
TDA. *See* Teacher Development Agency
teacher(s). *See also* class teachers; teacher motivation
   and assessment   146, 148

Teacher Development Agency (TDA)   45
   Schemes of work   188
teacher motivation   67
   organisational drivers   51
   personal drivers   50–8
teaching to the test   18, 55
technology. *See also* information and communication technology
   as learning resource   167–8, 175, *176*
textbooks   21–2, 142
theory
   and codified knowledge   20
   need   15–18
thought experiments   126–33
time, constraints in   37
TL. *See* target language
Tobutt, Kristina   101, 108
Tramonte, Lucia   62

vocabulary acquisition   20
   keyword method   89
   through integrated learning   104–7
Vygotsky, Lev   18, 19–20, 24, 109

Wenger, Etienne   73
Williams, Dylan   155
Willms, J. Douglas   62
Wilshaw, (Sir) Michael   32–3
worksheets   183–4
writing   20, 90–1

zone of proximal development (ZPD)   24, 109, 151
ZPD. *See* zone of proximal development